Advances in African Economic, Social and Political Development

Africa is emerging as a rapidly growing region, still facing major challenges, but with a potential for significant progress – a transformation that necessitates vigorous efforts in research and policy thinking. This book series focuses on three intricately related key aspects of modern-day Africa: economic, social and political development. Making use of recent theoretical and empirical advances, the series aims to provide fresh answers to Africa's development challenges. All the socio-political dimensions of today's Africa are incorporated as they unfold and new policy options are presented. The series aims to provide a broad and interactive forum of science at work for policymaking and to bring together African and international researchers and experts. The series welcomes monographs and contributed volumes for an academic and professional audience, as well as tightly edited conference proceedings. Relevant topics include, but are not limited to, economic policy and trade, regional integration, labor market policies, demographic development, social issues, political economy and political systems, and environmental and energy issues.

All titles in the series are peer-reviewed. The book series is indexed by Scopus.

* * *

More information about this series at https://link.springer.com/bookseries/11885

Freedom Mazwi • George Tonderai Mudimu •
Kirk Helliker
Editors

Capital Penetration and the Peasantry in Southern and Eastern Africa

Neoliberal Restructuring

Springer

Editors
Freedom Mazwi
Department of Sociology
Rhodes University
Makhanda, South Africa

George Tonderai Mudimu
Institute of Poverty, Land and Agrarian Studies (PLAAS)
University of the Western Cape
Bellville, Cape Town, South Africa

Kirk Helliker
Department of Sociology
Rhodes University
Makhanda, South Africa

ISSN 2198-7262 ISSN 2198-7270 (electronic)
Advances in African Economic, Social and Political Development
ISBN 978-3-030-89823-6 ISBN 978-3-030-89824-3 (eBook)
https://doi.org/10.1007/978-3-030-89824-3

This Springer imprint is published by the registered company Springer Nature Switzerland AG.
The registered company address is: Gewerbestrasse 11, 6330 Cham, Switzerland

Acknowledgement

This work is based on the research supported by the National Institute for the Humanities and Social Sciences (NIHSS), South Africa. As the editors of the volume we acknowledge that opinions, findings and conclusions or recommendations expressed in this publication do not reflect the views of the NIHSS- and that the NIHSS accepts no liability in this regard. This book is a joint initiative of the Unit of Zimbabwean Studies in the Department of Sociology at Rhodes University, Makhanda, South Africa and the Sam Moyo African Institute for Agrarian Studies (SMAIAS), Harare, Zimbabwe. Previous books under the auspices of the Unit of Zimbabwean Studies include Everyday Crisis-Living in Contemporary Zimbabwe (2021), Fast Track Land Occupations in Zimbabwe in the Context of the *Zvimurenga* (2021) and The Political Economy of Livelihoods in Contemporary Zimbabwe (2018). Two of the three editors for this current book are located in the Unit of Zimbabwean Studies: Dr. Freedom Mazwi is a Post-Doctoral Fellow in the Department of Sociology at Rhodes, while Professor Kirk Helliker is a Research Professor and Head of the Unit of Zimbabwean Studies. The other editor, Dr.George Mudimu, is a Post-Doctoral Fellow at the Institute for Poverty, Land and Agrarian Studies (PLAAS) at the University of Western Cape. Our most sincere gratitude goes to SMAIAS for offering support to this research project by providing research material. As well, some of the contributions here benefited immensely from scholarly debates initiated by the Institute. We are also indebted to Professor Gilton Klerck, head of the Department of Sociology at Rhodes University, for his generous support throughout the whole project. Lastly, we thank all the contributors to this volume who are drawn from various universities in Africa and beyond for sharing their research. We hope this book will be of great use to students, policymakers, academics and researchers in Africa.

Makhanda, South Africa
Western Cape, South Africa
Makhanda, South Africa

Freedom Mazwi
George Tonderai Mudimu
Kirk Helliker

Contents

Acronyms

AFC	Agricultural Finance Corporation
AIDS	Acquired Immuno Deficiency Syndrome
ANC	African National Congress
ASP	Agricultural Support Programme
BSAC	British South African Company
CBRLDP	Community Based Rural Land Development Programme
CCJP	Catholic Commission for Justice and Peace
CLA	Compulsory Land Acquisition
CLAB	Compulsory Land Acquisition Bill
DUAT	*Direito de Uso e Aproveitamento da Terra*
ESAP	Economic Structural Adjustment Programme
EU	European Union
FCP	Fertiliser Credit Programme
FDI	Foreign Direct Investment
FSP	Fertiliser Support Programme
FTLRP	Fast Track Land Reform Program
GATT	General Agreement on Tariffs and Trade
GDP	Gross Domestic Product
GMB	Grain Marketing Board
GNP	Gross National Product
GVC	Global Value Chains
HIV	Human Immuno Deficiency Virus
IFC	*International Contracting Firms*
ILO	International Labour Organisation
IMF	International Monetary Fund
KCC	Kenya Cooperative Creameries
KDDP	Komati Downstream Development Project
KMC	Kenya Meat Commission
KSA	Kenya Sugar Authority
KTDA	Kenya Tea Development Authority
LEMU	Land and Equity Movement of Uganda

LPM	Landless People's Movement
LSCF	Large-Scale Commercial Farms
LUSIP	Lower Usutu Smallholder Irrigation Project
MCP	Malawi Congress Party
MK	Malawian Kwacha
MLHUD	Ministry (of Lands, Housing and Urban Development
MPCB	Maize Produce and Control Board
NAP	National Agricultural Policy
NCPB	National Cereals and Produce Board
NCPB	National Cereals Produce Board
NDS	National Development Strategy
NGO	Non-Governmental Organisation
NSA	Namibian Statistics Agency
OECD	Organisation for Economic Cooperation and Development
PLO	Peoples Land Organisation
PSDP	Portucel Social Development Plan
RCS	Resettlement Credit Scheme
REDD+	Reducing Emissions from Deforestation and Forest Degradation
SACU	Southern African Customs Union
SAP	Structural Adjustment Programme
SDG	Sustainable Development Goals
SFCS	Small Farm Credit Scheme
SKPE	Swaziland Komati Project Enterprise
SMAIAS	Sam Moyo African Institute of Agrarian Studies
SSA	sub-Saharan Africa
SSCF	Small-Scale Commercial Farms
SWAPO	South West Africa People's Organisation
TIMB	Tobacco Marketing Board
TNC	Transnational Corporations
TRB	Tobacco Research Board
TSP	Transition Stabilisation Programme
VAAR	Vulnerability Assessment and Analysis Report
WIR	World Investment Report
WTO	World Trade Organisation
ZIMACE	Zimbabwe Agricultural Commodity Exchange
ZMOAL	Zambia Ministry of Agriculture and Livestock

Part I
Concepts and Debates

Capital Penetration and the Subordination of the Peasantry Under Neoliberalism in Africa

Freedom Mazwi, George Mudimu, and Kirk Helliker

Abstract As a dominant trajectory animating global capitalism, neoliberalism affects, in multiple ways, land and agriculture across the African continent, including the lives of the peasantry. Though its effects are uneven and differentiated, it generally tends to marginalise the peasantry further or incorporates them into the global political economy in a subordinate manner while also generating new rural inequalities. In large part, this is because neoliberalism (as a class project) facilitates and entrenches capital penetration into the agrarian economies of African nations. In focusing on the land and agricultural sector in primarily southern and eastern Africa, this chapter examines key dimensions of the neoliberal project in the land and agricultural sector in primarily southern and eastern Africa as the means for framing the following case study (or nation-based) chapters in this volume. This includes discussions around a reconfigured land reform programme, a new wave of land dispossession called 'land grabs', and restructured agricultural and marketing arrangements such as contract farming, all of which have ongoing implications for levels of food security and poverty amongst the peasantry. However, the chapter also shows that capital penetration and the subordination of the peasantry under neoliberalism in Africa is prone to crisis and resistance.

F. Mazwi (✉)
Rhodes University and Sam Moyo African Institute for Agrarian Studies, Makhanda, South Africa
e-mail: f.mazwi@ru.ac.za

G. Mudimu
Institute for Poverty Land and Agrarian Studies (PLASS), University of Western Cape, Cape Town, South Africa

K. Helliker
Rhodes University, Department of Sociology, Makhanda, South Africa
e-mail: k.helliker@ru.ac.za

F. Mazwi et al. (eds.), *Capital Penetration and the Peasantry in Southern and Eastern Africa*, Advances in African Economic, Social and Political Development, https://doi.org/10.1007/978-3-030-89824-3_1

1 Introduction

Land and agriculture continue to be central to most African economies (Moyo et al. 2019). Agriculture's contribution to the Gross Domestic Product (GDP) of African nations averages 15%, ranging from 3% in Botswana to over 50% in Chad (OECD/FAO 2016). The importance of agriculture to the continent is also underscored by the fact that it is a source of employment for over 50% of the rural labouring population and provides livelihoods to the majority of rural households, which consist of mainly peasants.

Processes of depeasantisation (and proletarianisation) occurred across the African continent during the time of colonialism and subsequently as well, leading at times to claims about the inevitable 'death of the peasantry'. However, processes of repeasantisation are also now evident (Moyo and Yeros 2005), arising in part because of the negative consequences of neoliberal restructuring. Irrespective of the extent of depeasantisation and repeasantisation as opposing trends, land and agriculture will continue to be central to any meaningful development agenda on the continent. Despite this significance and the important contribution of agriculture to national economies, Africa remains in a deep agrarian crisis characterised by poverty, malnutrition, land alienation, food insecurity and an ever-increasing food import bill (Patnaik 2011; Moyo 2014). Overall, these conditions are attributed to a broad range of factors, such as deficient state policies, unfavourable integration into the global economy, commodity price volatility, and the ongoing emphasis on exporting unprocessed primary products (Patnaik 2011).

In this context, international financial institutions (for instance, the World Bank) and neoclassical economists argue that the agrarian crisis is an outcome almost exclusively of misguided policy frameworks, market inefficiencies and distortions, and counterproductive state intervention in African economies, which undermine domestic and foreign private sector investment and productivity (World Bank 2019; FAO 2012; Kirsten and Sartorius 2002). In promoting neoliberal restructuring, they thus highlight the importance of opening up markets as well as furthering capital and technology transfers, thereby in turn presenting an opportunity for African countries to develop under the tutelage of global capital (Rodrick 2002).

In adopting an alternative argument, radical agrarian political economists attribute the crisis to the character and effects of neoliberalism as an economic and political configuration marking contemporary capitalism: this incorporates, for example, unequal exchange on global markets, large-scale land dispossessions, underfunding of the agricultural (particularly smallholder or peasant) sector, and macro-economic initiatives such as the Structural Adjustment Programmes (SAPs) of the World Bank and the International Monetary Fund (IMF). In large part, this volume of chapters on neoliberalism, capital penetration and the peasantry in Africa is consistent with the claims embedded in the perspective of radical political economy.

As a dominant trajectory animating global capitalism, neoliberalism affects, in multiple ways, land and agriculture across the African continent, including the lives of the peasantry. Though its effects are uneven and differentiated, it generally tends to marginalise the peasantry further or incorporates them into the global political economy in a subordinate manner while also generating new rural inequalities. In large part, this is because neoliberalism (as a class project) facilitates and entrenches capital penetration into the agrarian economies of African nations. In focusing on the land and agricultural sector in primarily southern and eastern Africa, this chapter examines key dimensions of the neoliberal project in the land and agricultural sector in primarily southern and eastern Africa as the means for framing the following case study (or nation-based) chapters in this volume. This includes discussions around a reconfigured land reform programme, a new wave of land dispossession called 'land grabs', and restructured agricultural and marketing arrangements such as contract farming, all of which have ongoing implications for levels of food security and poverty amongst the peasantry. However, the chapter also shows that capital penetration and the subordination of the peasantry under neoliberalism in Africa is prone to crisis and resistance.

The chapters in the volume include case studies of the following countries: South Africa, Uganda, Namibia, Malawi, Zambia, Kenya, Mozambique and Eswatini, and two on Zimbabwe. Before outlining the volume, we first provide brief notes about neoliberalism central to any analysis of neoliberalism, capital penetration and the peasantry in Africa, after which we focus more specifically on questions of land and agriculture.

2 Neoliberalism: Brief Notes

As a concept, neoliberalism has increasingly dominated the development discourse over the past half century. As well, without doubt, it has become a very slippery term (like 'development' itself), with scholarly discussions about it marked by considerable complexity and contestation (Ashman et al. 2011; Thorsen and Lie 2006). Based on a laissez-faire economic ideology (Wolford 2007; Harrison 2019), the central tenet of neoliberalism, however, is the significance of the so-called self-regulating market (as an economic institution) in supposedly facilitating and maximising economic growth and redistribution. The hallmark of the neoliberal agenda, for agrarian spaces, has been the entrenchment of landed property rights and the push for market-led land reforms, which are viewed as sine qua non to development (Moyo 2008).

Initially, neoliberalism appeared to be merely an economic project but it later expanded more explicitly into a political project as well, involving processes of state restructuring for purposes of neoliberalism's political agenda (Harrison 2005). In pursuing this agenda, the buzzword became 'good governance' which was then used to propagate and effect regime change if and when necessary (Moyo et al. 2012). As a result, various state-centred policies, programmes and agencies came about to ensure particular public sector reforms, such as output-oriented budgeting and the commercialisation-privatisation of parastatals. However, the early example of the

Chilean military junta (from the 1970s) highlights that these public sector reforms do not rest on, or require, 'good governance' as understood in terms of the principles of liberal democracy.

Despite the politics of neoliberalism, the intervention mechanisms promoted and implemented under neoliberal restructuring are presented typically as technical-scientific (or 'technocratic fixes'—Moorsom et al. 2020), camouflaging the politics intrinsic to the neoliberal project (Bond and Dor 2003), thereby tending to 'obfuscate the actually existing power relations playing out' (Moorsom et al. 2020, p. 214). Concomitant to this project is exceedingly limited social and political accountability in the relationship between states and citizens, in large part because of the marked influence of the Bretton Woods institutions in formulating and shaping the fundamentals of neoliberalism, which states then impose on the populace. Thus, with its emergence, the neoliberal project has provided limited space for state sovereignty globally (Prashad 2013; Moyo and Yeros 2005).

While some African countries have tended at times to resist the global dictates through various local initiatives (such as Zimbabwe's fast track land reform programme), destabilisation campaigns (including sanctions) are deployed by global hegemonic forces in forestalling these (Moyo et al. 2013; Moyo and Yeros 2007). Economic strangulation is thus a strategy used by monopoly capital to discipline those countries that challenge neoliberal tenets in significant ways. This raises complex questions about state autonomy vis-à-vis global capital as well as the importance of resolving the national question through pursuing relatively autonomous development paths (Moyo and Yeros 2011).

Since the 1970s, neoliberalism has been accompanied by key imperialist tendencies, taking place via the easy movement of capital throughout the global system, the prioritisation of property rights and the promotion of free trade across national boundaries while, simultaneously, crowding out the import-substitution, redistributive and heterodox economic policies prevalent prior to its emergence (Patnaik 2003; Harvey 2005). Financialisation has been increasingly central to these tendencies, which hinges on borrowing on markets often for speculative purposes, mergers and diversifications (Shivji 2011; Amanor 2019). This reflects the emergence and consolidation of fictitious capital unrelated to any form of production and which ultimately subsumes real capital (Ashman et al. 2011) or, to put it another way, it entails the subordination of the real economy to the virtual one (Ye et al. 2020). Further, the prominence of financialisation prioritises shareholder value over social value (Ashman et al. 2011). This ongoing rise and development of financialisation provide the platform for capital to penetrate new spatial and sectoral zones that provide exceedingly high rates of interest (Patnaik 2003). At the same time, '[f]inancial capital is not able (nor willing) to solve the real problems of the real world – it is only interested in further [extraction and] accumulation' (van der Ploeg 2020, p. 957).

In the end, it is possible to distil a number of—interrelated—points about neoliberalism analytically and conceptually. We bring to the fore seven points in the remainder of this section (see Klerck this volume, for an expansion of some of these points). First of all, neoliberalism is an ongoing process and not merely a condition (a 'becoming', rather than simply a 'being'); because of this, 'neoliberalisation' may be a more apt phrase. This means that it is necessary to be constantly sensitive to neoliberal reconfigurations over time. Secondly, neoliberalism is marked by variegation; in other words, it takes on different forms and trajectories, though within the broad remit of market-led growth and development (Peck and Theodore 2007; Brenner et al. 2010). For this reason, neoliberalism does not exist anywhere in a 'pure form', just as the existence of a self-regulating market is utopian. Because of this, new forms of agrarian and land restructuring are appearing in Africa, including in relation to 'land grabs' and contract farming, but not in any homogenous or blanket manner.

Thirdly, neoliberalism does not entail outright state deregulation; rather, re-regulation is taking place. States in Africa continue to provide the conditions necessary for the expanded reproduction and accumulation of capital, including facilitating capital flows and investments. Fourthly, in aligning with monopoly capital under neoliberalism (Moyo et al. 2013), the state takes on different forms: from liberal democratic to semi-autocratic ones and even military dictatorships (incorporating the notion of 'authoritarian neoliberalism'—Harrison 2019), all of which are compatible in their own way with the 'reign' of market forces (Rosset et al. 2006; Moyo et al. 2012). In this regard, the state may deploy violence and bypass democratic principles in creating enabling conditions for the market. However, as contradictory institutional arrangements, states in Africa are not at all times compliant to global forces, as they may emerge as sites of reform or outright opposition (Moorsom et al. 2020).

Fifthly, so as not to treat neoliberal restructuring as moved along by an invisible hand, it must be recognised as a social-cum-political project (specifically, a class project) with specific actors and agencies pushing it forward (Harvey 2016; Patnaik 2003, 2020; Shivji 2009, 2020). Sixthly, neoliberalisation is not a coherent project and is prone to crises; indeed, it emerged as an answer to crises in the first instance. Crises are immanent to its very existence, and it thus engenders social disorder and political instability. Certainly, wars and conflicts have been initiated by global powers for purposes of new variants of primitive accumulation (via minerals, land and natural resources) (Moyo et al. 2012; Moyo and Yeros 2005; Patnaik and Patnaik 2016). Seventhly, neoliberalism is subject to resistance and opposition, and the latter contribute to the reconfiguring of neoliberalism. Through an unstated capital-state alliance, the project of neoliberalism subordinates and marginalises the peasantry, including by means of repressive measures (Moyo et al. 2019; Nyong'o 2013; Moyo 2008), and it also reinforces social hierarchies based on class, gender, age, caste, ethnicity, and race (Ossome 2020; Andrews 2021; Moyo and Yeros 2005). This goes some way in explaining the agrarian unrest reverberating around Africa presently. Currently, numerous social movements exist which advocate for the dismantling of neoliberalism (Moyo and Yeros 2011; Moyo and Yeros 2005), including via the 'reclamation of the land' (Moyo and Yeros 2005).

3 Neoliberalism: Land and Agriculture

In this context, we consider the effects of neoliberalism on land and agriculture in Africa, and specifically on the peasantry. In speaking about the negative effects in particular on the peasantry, we are not implying an essentialised notion of the peasantry built upon romanticism, a notion which Soper (2020) has recently warned us about. More specifically, we do not claim that the peasantry is an undifferentiated whole and, further, is inherently and invariably progressive in terms of agricultural practices or politics.

Nevertheless, in various ways, neoliberalism's practices around land and agriculture in Africa (and indeed elsewhere) depend regularly on processes of extraction. This does not refer exclusively to pockets or enclaves of extraction but to a more generalised mode of production and exchange under neoliberal capitalism, or a move 'from single and dispersed activities towards a structural feature of the politico-economic system as a whole' (Ye et al. 2020, p. 156) This has become crystallised in many cases of land concentration and grabbing (by private, domestic and international capital), monopolistic control over natural resources, and new forms of production arrangements (for example, contract farming) involving agrarian capital—in which there is corporate control over flows of commodities, credit and value.

Adopted by governments throughout Africa, SAPs and later forms of neoliberal programmes have, amongst other effects, undercut petty-commodity production in agrarian economies (Shivji 2011; Moyo 2011) and, more significantly, rural food security. In addition, peasant social movements (notably La Via Campesina) link the agrarian crisis to the adoption of green revolution inputs (seeds and chemicals), which harm the soil and cause overall environmental degradation (McKeon 2015). The dominance of international agribusiness firms like Monsanto on input markets (through the supply of seeds, chemicals and fertilisers) is understood as not only detrimental to the environment but also exploitative because these agribusinesses generate super profits (Mazwi et al. 2021; McKeon 2015) through the extraction of value and unequal exchange (Shivji 2011; Sachikonye 1989).

There is no doubt that, for decades now, neoliberalism has been at the core of global capitalism and core to the crises intrinsic to its uneven development. The global neoliberal economic and political architecture has shaped (and reshaped) land and agricultural policies and practices in Africa on an ongoing basis, with serious consequences for the well-being of peasants. Since the 2007/2008 global crises (including food and energy), Africa has witnessed the penetration of capital into the land and agrarian sectors from at least 130 foreign investors drawn from approximately 30 countries (Moyo et al. 2019; Land Matrix Data 2012). These 'investments' have occurred through so-called 'large-scale land investments' in communal and 'unoccupied land', via foreign (privatised) takeovers of state-owned plantation estates by transnational corporations, and by means of the subordination of the peasantry to contract farming arrangements (Chambati et al. 2018; Hall et al. 2017).

There are contrasting views on the effects and consequences of this neoliberal restructuring (and 'investments' in land and agriculture) on the well-being of peasant farmers, as indicated earlier. While the consequences are uneven and differentiated, a general trend exists consistent with the overall arguments of radical agrarian political economists. A survey of pertinent literature demonstrates that the penetration of capital has led to increased poverty, malnutrition, hunger, growing landlessness and deepening inequalities for rural, 'working people' (Amanor 2019; Jha and Yeros 2019; Chambati et al. 2018). These interconnected challenges undermine peace, justice and stability due to the increasing number of 'working people' who are cast to the very margins of society, thus rendering them part of a growing reserve army of labour (unemployed proletariats, peasants, landless and self-employed) for which there is likely no land nor labour in the foreseeable future (Moyo and Yeros 2011). As a consequence of marginalisation and subordination, demands for an equitable distribution of resources, economic restructuring and state accountability (Patnaik and Patnaik 2016) are becoming louder, alongside diverse forms of rural mobilisation.

In recent decades, the penetration of capital has been largely driven by the desire to resolve growing food and energy deficiencies in metropolitan states (Moyo et al. 2019). Under neoliberal capitalism, two broad phases of capital penetration around land and agriculture in Africa exist. The first wave was facilitated by the SAPs (1980s and 1990s), while the second one followed the 2007/2008 food, energy and financial crises. Under the first wave, capital penetration required the freer movement of finance capital, privatisation of national assets, and trade liberalisation (Patnaik 2011, 2015; Havnevik et al. 2007; Hanson and Hentz 1999). Prior to this, and despite authoritarian tendencies, independent African nations were characterised by state-interventionist policies (including around land redistribution) and import-substitution strategies which generally supported agriculture, including peasant agriculture (Mkandawire and Soludo 1999; Moyo 2011; Yeros and Jha 2020). The second wave, which we discuss more fully below, is currently ongoing, and its effects continue to be experienced in the African countryside.

3.1 *Agricultural Restructuring Under Neoliberalism*

Capital penetration is related to ongoing primitive accumulation insofar as it facilitates the latter, leaving behind pauperised labourers and peasants. Narrow Eurocentric interpretations of primitive accumulation reduce it to corrupt activities mainly by the African ruling elite (see for example Mills et al. 2019). While such activities do exist, primitive accumulation is to be understood first and foremost in terms of the imperatives of global capitalism. Hence, according to a Marxist perspective, primitive accumulation entails:

> [T]he deployment of extra-economic force to separate peasants from the land and commodify both labour and land;...and how the capitalist system once created, continues to exploit

> labour by less transparent means, that is, by the appropriation of labour power beyond the labour time necessary for the social reproduction of the workforce (Moyo et al. 2012, p. 185).

This process is supported by Northern countries working in conjunction with multilateral development and financial agencies, and it perpetuates the historical marginalisation of peoples of Africa under neocolonialism (Nkrumah 1965). Thus, the latest wave of capital penetration under contemporary capitalism should be considered as a new round of primitive accumulation which further immiserates the peasantry (Moyo et al. 2012).

Admittedly, the neoliberal doctrine as espoused by the World Bank (in its World Development Report of 2008) and by the Food and Agricultural Organisation (FAO) rightly places primacy on rural development as a strategy for poverty alleviation in Africa (World Bank 2007; FAO 2012). However, this primacy, which in the end reinforces the global international division of labour, misses the point by suggesting that a market-driven rural development strategic framework is a panacea for agrarian underdevelopment and poverty. For over four decades now, African countries have pursued in the main a market-driven approach to rural development with minimal success (Havnevik et al. 2007). These rural policies have been advanced in the name of the fallacious mantra of 'getting prices right', which assumes that liberalisation of the agricultural sector automatically translates into an improvement in the lives of the peasantry. On the contrary, evidence from contributors to this book shows that privatising the agricultural sector and opening it up to the market mechanism tend to complicate the lives and livelihoods of the peasantry even further, with women suffering the most (for case studies of this, see Tekwa and Tekwa this volume, Lukalo this volume, and Mwando this volume).

One key outcome of the penetration of capital under neoliberalism's primitive accumulation has been the restructuring of agricultural production by reinforcing the international division of labour (Amin 2015; Jha and Yeros 2019, Moyo and Yeros 2005). Under this system, most African countries continue as major producers of commodities for metropolitan countries while producing a decreasing amount of food grains for domestic consumption (Patnaik 2011; Moyo and Yeros 2005). In India, for example, cotton production for export has increased at the expense of food security among the peasantry (Patnaik 2003). African countries became major losers under SAPs (Shivji 1992) as they resorted to the production of export crops, resulting in an oversupply of commodities on global markets and thereby triggering a fall in international prices. The far-reaching effect of this neoliberal arrangement was massive declines and losses in foreign exchange generated (Patnaik 2011).

Concomitant to rising exports have been declines in the production of food crops in Africa. This has led to increased food imports as cereal production is replaced by the production of export crops (Moyo 2011). For African states, after SAPs, there was a 33% fall in cereal production (Patnaik 2003). What then emerged under conditions of food insecurity was the rise of food aid and increased dependency on donor support. Food insecurity required African states to mobilise scarce foreign exchange for the importation of food grains from the United States, Canada, Europe, and Argentina (Patnaik 2011), thereby undercutting the growth of national economies. Even for countries that had adequate foreign exchange available, the central state was found in many cases to be simply unwilling to commit resources to import food grains for millions of people facing hunger and starvation, thus severely compromising the nutritional diets of the peasantry (Patnaik 2011). A general pattern emerging from the global food regime, for most of Africa, is that of increased incidences of poverty and malnutrition at the household level.

Another key characteristic of global agricultural production and trade during this phase has been volatile global markets, with supply and demand being key determinants (Martiniello 2016; Patnaik and Patnaik 2016). As a result of these tendencies, the possibility of capital formation for peasants becomes increasingly dependent on global market prices, and this has led to 'dependent-capitalisation' where small-scale farmers accumulate when prices are high and are reduced to paupers in periods when crops prices go down (Korovkin 1992; Mazwi et al. 2020). This global price volatility has affected farmers across the African continent (Moyo 2011).

The reconfiguration of global production systems has been accompanied by the intensification of contract farming and out-grower schemes, driven mainly by monopolistic international agribusiness corporations (Amanor 2019; Jha and Yeros 2019; Mazwi 2020). Contract farming is a mechanism used by large agribusiness firms to structure agricultural production in the peripheries by extracting value from crop commodities through capturing the input and output markets and the processing of primary commodities (Jha and Yeros 2019). These global-driven agricultural production and marketing processes reduce the autonomy and fortunes of the peasantry (see Sakata this volume, Mhlanga this volume, and Bruna this volume). As Amanor (2019) notes:

> Most international agricultural markets are characterised by concentration and monopoly and intense competition to control markets – through outsourcing, takeovers, and mergers – and the control and regulation of production through contracts. These features have considerable impact upon agricultural production (Amanor 2019, p. 31).

Through the restructuring of global finance, trade and production, international monopoly corporations use intermediaries at the local level (national and sub-national) to push forward contract farming (Amanor 2019). Additionally, they become engaged in other activities, which range from industrial manufacturing to banking and real estate (Jha and Yeros 2019). In covering wider geographical and sectoral spaces, their expansion represents a new mode of global capitalism different from colonialism (and even recent land grabs), where the metropolis directly controls land in the peripheries. Under contract farming, the control of land by monopoly capital and the metropolis is indirect (Amanor 2019), and it hence ensures a mediated form of imperial control by the metropolis over so-called developing nations (Patnaik and Patnaik 2016).

Nearly a decade ago, research showed that some countries in Africa have almost 100% of certain commodities produced under contract farming while other commodities remain underfunded (Oya 2012). The level of contract farming in African countries has no doubt increased, although there is a lack of studies showing its prevalence currently. At the same time, the scale and extent of contract farming vary from one country to another. The commodities grown under contract farming include sugar, coffee, tea, palm oil, cocoa tea, tobacco, cotton and horticultural commodities, with many of these being perishable export products (Little 2014). Production of contracted export crops (often, non-food crops) has altered land-use patterns in Africa significantly by diminishing the total land area where own consumption food grains are produced, a development which has seriously undermined food self-sufficiency (Moyo 2011; Patnaik 2011). It has also contributed to undercutting historical-cultural practices around food and agriculture, leading to, for instance, 'seek activism' (Peschard and Randeria 2020) in the face of genetic modification and related phenomena.

Available data reveal that the production of export crops grew by between 6 to 13%, while the volume of food grains produced decreased significantly in the 1990s (Patnaik 2011). More recent evidence shows that food dependency increased post the 2007/2008 global economic crisis. The FAO database indicates that cereal imports in sub-Saharan Africa rose from 24 million tons in 2007 and 2008 to about 30 million tons in 2012 and 2013. An increase in the importation of flour was also noted, from about 12 million tons in 2007 and 2008 to 17 million tons in 2012 and 2013 (Chambati et al. 2018). The declines in food grain production and subsequent rising food importations are partially explained by the shift to contract-based production.

A survey of literature on the impacts of neoliberal restructuring via contract farming not only reflects increases in poverty, malnutrition and grain imports but also growing social differentiation in the countryside (Oya 2012, 2010; Little 2014; Mazwi et al. 2020; Pérez Niño 2016; Mazwi et al. 2019). This is shown by the upward and downhill transitions of farmers. For example, some capitalist farmers and rich peasants have been accumulating through contract farming in Senegal, Mozambique and Tanzania and, in the process, displacing poor farmers, thus setting into motion acute social differentiation within communities (Oya 2012; Pérez Niño 2016; Martiniello 2015). Through this, social hierarchies have been accentuated (Martiniello 2017). Hence, 'despite contract farming schemes not involving *prima facie* the dispossession or displacement of smallholders, they lead to forms of expulsion and/or marginalisation of poor smallholders from ... agro-extractive poles through social differentiation' (de L T Oliveira et al. 2021, p. 325).

Through contract farming, commodities are produced by peasants in the peripheries for international global firms; however, no formal capital-wage relationship exists (Patnaik and Patnaik 2016). In order to reduce production costs and do away with political challenges associated with 'large-scale land investments' (in which capital-labour relations abound), contract farming is seen as a solution, with agribusiness indirectly controlling production and maximising value (Sachikonye 1989). Also fundamental in this regard is that peasants—almost by the very compulsion of circumstances under capitalism—become 'price takers' (Patnaik and Patnaik 2016, p. 50). This is because they do not have the power to set their own output prices or incomes such that, when they encounter increases in production costs, they have no option but to accept them. Thus, the peasantry subsidises capital in the production of export commodities (Shivji 1992, 2009). Indebtedness is also deployed by monopolistic agri-firms through their intermediaries to ensure that the peasantry remains subordinated to capital (McMichael 2013; Mazwi 2020). This is enforced by placing high-interest rates on inputs and by reducing farmer incomes, thereby inhibiting the independence and autonomy of the peasantry (Martiniello 2015).

The distress on the peasantry (and 'agrarian classes of labour' as a whole—Pattenden et al. 2021) has been more accentuated during the time of the Covid-19 pandemic. For instance, in the context of pandemic lockdowns, the state has imposed movement restrictions for the peasantry and informal traders (Mudimu 2020). Though perhaps less affected than large-scale farmers by pandemic-induced disruptions beyond their locality, certainly the movement-lockdowns have had severe effects on smallholders, with losses in farm produce and income taking place. More generally, the Covid-19 pandemic (and associated lockdowns) has brought to the fore fundamental problems intrinsic to the international food regime as well as challenges for the heavily indebted 'food empire' which dominates it, as the pandemic lockdowns have disrupted agricultural production and the entire food chain in which mutually-dependent nations around the world depend on some degree on global food imports (van der Ploeg 2020).

3.2 *Neoliberalism and Land Reforms*

As previously noted, neoliberalism is not only an economic programme but also a political project, as reflected in neoliberalism's reconfiguration of land reform processes in Africa, notably in relation to land distribution. The redistribution of land is particularly important in Africa because of the land inequities which arose under colonialism (Moyo 2013; Moyo et al. 2013). Land reform should address this historical dispossession and the racial and foreign domination concerning landholdings, including by the transfer of land to those without land or adequate land (Byres 2004).

Land reform gained prominence from the 1950s to the 1970s during the state-centric 'developmentalist moment' (Fraser 2008). However, the rise of neoliberalism led to a significant change in the discourse and policies around land reform. There has been a new focus on economic growth by way of market-assisted (and market-led) models of land reform, departing from broad-based and more inclusive state-led reforms. One key model promoted by the Bretton Woods institutions under the neoliberal project is the willing buyer, willing seller one.

Overall, this and related neoliberal land reform programmes focus on 'property, scale, technology and the market' as the key determinants of the character and success of land reform practices (Rosset et al. 2006, p. 6). This requires the fundamental protection of property rights in agrarian spaces as well as the ongoing (and indeed extension of) privatisation and ownership of land under freehold title (Moyo 2011). A key issue is that market-led reform entails a shift from pursuing equity and justice to efficiency and economic growth, with the efficiency discourse dominating debates on land reform over an extended period. However, for a number of reasons (including the focus on efficiency and non-cooperation on the part of rural landholders), market reform has failed to guarantee the rural poor any meaningful access to land (Moyo 1995, 2013, 2016) (see Melber this volume, Banjwa this volume).

By and large, these programmes have led to land consolidation, further privatisation of land in the name of secure land tenure, and corruption and rent seeking by political elites (Peluso and Lund 2011; Moyo 2011). But, more critically, they have failed even to address colonial land injustices (Moyo 2001). Examples of countries which have implemented market-assisted land reforms with little success include the former settler-colonial states of Kenya, Namibia, South Africa and Zimbabwe (Moyo 2008). Market land reform has often been resisted, at times via courts (for example in the Philippines) (Borras 2008). Additionally, its failures have led to variegated responses from below, including the formation and internationalisation of peasant-led movements and land expropriation by way of land occupations as in Brazil and Zimbabwe (Borras 2008; Moyo and Yeros 2005; Moyo and Yeros 2011). The state responses to these on-the-ground actions have hovered between violence and concession (Borras 2005).

Implementing land reform (specifically, land redistribution) under the guidance of international finance in the neoliberal era as a basis for addressing land injustices and rural poverty, at least under market-led reform, seems like a fraught task from the very beginning (Moyo 1995; Borras 2005), as it has no solid foundation for success as measured in terms of land justice and poverty reduction (see Mangulama and Jin this volume). Further, at least in southern Africa, for some time (in particular during the 1980s and 1990s), land reform became marginal to debates about agrarian economies because of the sustained focus on the liberalisation of agricultural markets as the basis for peasant productivity (Lahif 2003). Nevertheless, as noted, nations that sought to go beyond market-led reform and engage in state-initiated expropriation (with or without compensation) became the subject of punitive measures. This tended to discourage similar endeavours elsewhere (Moyo et al. 2013) or became a way of seeking to reverse expropriation—in the latter situation, 'reliberalisation' is seen as the only possible path, from a neoliberal perspective, to rescue the national economy and the agricultural sector specifically (Moyo and Yeros 2011).

For both settler and non-settler countries in Africa, neoliberal market land reforms were characterised by the minimal transfer of land and, importantly, processes of land commodification (Moyo 2008). The outcome of this land commodification has been land alienation of peasant households and land concentration by domestic and foreign capital (Moyo 2016). The displacement of peasants via the widespread activation of rural land markets led to their transition into a landless rural proletariat in many cases, sometimes as wage workers on the very land purchased by the nascent capitalist farmers. It has also triggered massive rural to urban migration, though such migration is taking place in the context of national economies characterised by jobless growth (Delgado Wise and Veltmeyer 2016). Former non-settler countries such Malawi and Zambia witnessed a surge of budding middle-capitalist farmers who operated alongside peasants (Kanyongolo 2008). Thus, African countries have experienced the further development and consolidation of social class differentiation within their agrarian economies, rather than a levelling process as promised by neoliberal's land redistribution agenda (Moyo 2016).

The effects of neoliberal practices around the land are most visible and dramatic in the form of what are called 'land grabs', sometimes spoken of as entailing accumulation by dispossession. The current land grabs, of which grabbing access to water is also central (de L T Oliveira et al. 2021), gained media attention in 2008 amidst the rise in global food prices and, in terms of a land grab genealogy, they mark the third phase of land alienation in Africa (Moyo et al. 2012). After the initial phrase of land dispossession during colonialism, the second wave involved the conversion of customary or communal land into private property in conjunction with market land reform, with titling supported by donors. For example, there was a clear rise in land registration and land titling in West Africa, and the growth of rural land markets increased land alienation (Moyo 2011). These localised land grabs stimulated the further formation of an aspiring African agrarian bourgeoisie through land concentration. The newest round of land dispossession (associated with private corporate investors and sovereign funds) is part of the wider project of 'globalised control of land, natural and mineral resources' (Moyo 2011, p. 62) under the impact of 'neoliberal globalisation' (Adnan 2013).

In the case of natural resources, neoliberalism has also been restructuring and ultimately politicising landscapes and local resources in significant ways (Büscher 2010). For instance, there is the rise of ecotourism as states seek to attract capital investments (Ojeda 2012). This falls broadly into 'control grabbing' (Borras et al. 2012), involving singular control over the usage of a range of resources, including wildlife. In South Africa, in relation to the Kruger National Park, conservative lobby groups and even the state regard the local communities as a problem in terms of ensuring conservation (Ramutsindela and Shabangu 2013), leading to the rise of environmental neoliberalism. Similarly, in Zanzibar, the development of ecotourism supported by 'individual titles' has led to the right of occupancy deeds being issued to foreigners and the grabbing of prime beachfront (Myers 2008). This entails a shift from protecting nature from capitalism to capitalism as the way to supposedly protect nature (Ramutsindela and Shabangu 2013). Such a shift is accompanied by the growth of privatised wildlife estates and conservancies (Moyo 2011).

4 Volume Outline

This book is divided into four broad sections. The first section (including this first introductory chapter) examines neoliberalism analytically and provides a broad overview of the forms of capital penetration under neoliberalism in the land and agricultural sector in Africa and their effects on the peasantry. In doing so, it sets the analytical stage for the following nine case study chapters.

As part of this opening section, the second chapter by Gilton Klerck analyses commercial agriculture in post-Apartheid South Africa, but it does so through an extended and illuminating examination of the constitution, character and consequences of neoliberal restructuring more broadly. In this respect, the notion of 'neoliberalism' has been widely deployed to describe the resurgence of market-orientated institutional shifts and policy realignments across the world economy since the 1980s. Following the initial analysis of these trends, much attention has been devoted to their conceptualisation. While the meaning and tractability of 'neoliberalism' continue to be topics of intense debate, recent theoretical work in the field, as shown by Klerck, has produced several important insights that have significant implications for empirical research on regulatory restructuring at all spatial scales. Against the monolithic conceptualisations that prevail in popular and academic accounts, Klerck highlights that the notion of 'variegated neoliberalisation' emphasises the uneven, hybrid, and unstable character of neoliberalising forms of regulatory transformation. By substituting an end-state view of neoliberal*ism* with emergent and tendential processes of neoliberal*isation*, the dramatic changes in South Africa's agricultural policy and practice that have unfolded since the 1980s may be cast in a new light. In particular, Klerck explores the apparent paradox between extensively liberalised product markets and highly regulated labour markets in post-apartheid commercial agriculture.

The following nine chapters focus more exclusively on national studies, with each of the three sections consisting of three chapters. The second section focuses on land, peasants and neoliberalism, including land reform, land grabs and land struggles. In the third section, attention turns to neoliberalism and agriculture, and specifically to neoliberal-configured agricultural policies and their effects on peasant production and lives. The fourth (and final) section examines the social and economic impacts of integrating the peasantry into global commodity chains, including through contract farming.

In chapter "Land for Development? Neoliberal Restructuring and the Dynamics of Land Reforms in Uganda", Adventino Banjwa examines neoliberal restructuring and the dynamics of land reform in Uganda. He notes that the idea and relevance of compulsory land acquisition is central to the claims of many modern states world over. But how should we think of this practice in a post-colonial neoliberal context? This is the question at the heart of the theoretical criticisms and debates regarding Uganda's Compulsory Land Acquisition Programme. In this debate, the government claims and affirms that a law on compulsory land acquisition is needed because the government requires 'land for development'. Banjwa intervenes in the debate by raising the question of the form of state prevailing in Uganda today and the nature of 'development' it pursues. The chapter critically reviews some past cases of compulsory land acquisition in Uganda in the post-1980 period. These cases demonstrate how in practice, the consolidation of neoliberalism requires an interventionist state, one that can, for instance, use its coercive instruments to avail land for capitalist development in agriculture. If Uganda's 'land for development' drive has resulted in a coupling of a regime of state-led forced land acquisition (more broadly, 'state-driven development') with neoliberalism, Banjwa argues that we need therefore to decouple them analytically to allow for a historically and contextually informed query on the implications of land reforms in a post-colonial neoliberal context.

In the following chapter (chapter "The Struggle Continues: Namibia's Enduring Land Question"), Henning Melber focuses on the land question in Namibia. With Independence in 1990, Namibia inherited a socio-economic structure that, in terms of land distribution, had anchored the colonial divide and rule under Apartheid: a white-owned commercial agricultural sector contrasted with communal areas based on regional-ethnic criteria. Constitutional principles accepted as the final step towards Independence and sovereignty excluded any expropriation without fair compensation and therefore contributed to limiting land restitution and redistribution. Since 1990, diversification has taken place in private land ownership in commercial agriculture. A growing number of black farm owners have benefitted from a redistributive land policy guided by state support for elite interests. In the communal areas, local traditional authorities and representatives of the central state administration abused control over land rights to further the privatisation of communal property in terms of its use. In this context, Melber argues that these land reform dimensions underlined the new pact among elites in independent Namibia in different ways and disclosed the class character of property relations and ownership related to land. But, in the absence of a coherent policy, even a neoliberal perspective and strategy is hardly visible. He concludes that government policy so far rather testifies more to the negligence of any meaningful land reform.

The last chapter on land (chapter "Land Reform or Continued Social Exclusion? Land Occupations, State Responses and Neoliberal Policies in Southern Malawi"), by Justin Alinafe Mangulama and Wu Jin, considers land reform and land occupations in Malawi. In this respect, the last five decades have witnessed an increasing number of peasants encroaching onto idle tea estate land in Thyolo district, in southern Malawi. In drawing upon a study of this district, Mangulama and Jin argue that state responses to land occupations remain contradictory. Malawi's 2002 land policy advocates for redistributive land reform. At the same time, however, the state has actively promoted the Malawi Investment Policy, which encourages land expropriation for foreign capital. Repressive measures that include policing, punitive fines and arrests of peasants stirred the land occupations further, rather than inhibiting them. The state remains in a dilemma, whether to optimise local votes from the peasants or side with white agrarian bourgeois interests for capital accumulation via a rent scheme. Thus, Mangulama and Jin point to the tension-riddled character of neoliberalism, as shown through accumulation at one pole and impoverishment of the majority at the other pole.

In turning to section three on neoliberalism, agricultural policies and the peasantry, the initial chapter (chapter "Gender, Household Food Security and Neoliberal Decimation of the Grain-Producing Peasantry in Zimbabwe") by Newman Tekwa and Happymore Tekwa focus on household food security amongst the peasantry in Zimbabwe. With over half of the Zimbabwean population now facing food hunger, this could be juxtaposed to the 1980s' dirigiste period when the state boosted peasant maize production (as a proportion of national maize output) from 3.6% in 1979/80 to 35.6% in 1984/85. Since then, though interspersed with brief periods of heavy state involvement in the 2000s, Zimbabwe has undergone three decades of economic liberalisation from a Structural Adjustment Programme (SAP) in the early 1990s to the current Transition Stabilisation Programme (TSP). The gendered effects of decades of agricultural market liberalisation on peasant households in the country remain inadequately documented and analysed. In this light, Tekwa and Tekwa first consider the extent to which the shift from dirigisme to liberalisation affected integration, efficiency and competitiveness in the agricultural sector. They then examine the distribution of benefits of market liberalisation across different scales of agricultural production in addition to interrogating how female peasants have fared in these economic restructuring processes relative to men, primarily in relation to food security. In the end, Tekwa and Tekwa argue that liberalisation negatively impacted peasant maize production and curtailed the dual role of peasant households, leading to gender-differentiated knock-on effects for household food security. This highlights the crucial role of the state in ensuring national and household food sufficiency.

In chapter "Smallholder Farmer Empowerment and Neoliberalism: Examining the Current Institutional and Policy Arrangements in Zambia" by Sam Mwando, the emphasis is on policy and institutional support for agriculture amongst the peasantry (or smallholders) in Zambia. Agriculture supports the livelihoods of up to 70% of the Zambian population. The rural population is characterised by poorly developed monetary economies and markets with inadequate infrastructure and weak institutions for supply chain development, as needed for agricultural intensification and productivity. This is despite the structural adjustment and liberalisation programmes of the early 1990s, which were hyped as the precursor to incentivising foreign direct investments and reigniting the wheels of economic growth in Zambia. Thirty years on, economic liberalisation policies, including for the agricultural sector, continue to exist, albeit in altered and haphazard form. The failure to liberalise the agricultural sector fully, with piecemeal, start-stop and frequency policy reversals, has tended to depress any possible returns and raised risks for smallholders associated with private sector investment. As well, as Mwando argues, the weak institutional support for smallholder farmers, despite some state support, has inhibited the capacity of smallholders to enhance their agricultural production and rural livelihoods. Because of this, neoliberal agricultural policies have failed to empower smallholders in Zambia. Mwando examines and highlights this agricultural trend, including through a case study in Chibombo district.

Chapter "Putting Agriculture Ahead? Some Reflections about the Early Years of Neoliberalism in Kenya" by Fibian Lukalo also examines agricultural policies and the peasantry under neoliberalism but in relation to Kenya. More specifically, it discusses the effects of the neoliberal agenda with reference to agricultural development, agricultural policies and land reform in Kenya. The centrality of the agricultural sector to rural livelihoods and to the economic development of Kenya and its linkages to land are intricately connected to the history of economic policy, politics and land reform. Lukalo examines the background and policy context surrounding the agricultural debates in Kenya across two decades (the 1980s and 1990s), including how neoliberalisation had diverse and differentiated effects on the land reform agenda, the agricultural sector and the lives of the peasantry. In bringing to the fore three policy positions (Sessional Papers) as points of reference, Lukalo presents an understanding of the historical, policy and discursive framework within which agriculture and land issues were debated and struggled over concerning the lives of rural Kenyans. Overall, it appears that neoliberalism, though not necessarily intentionally, further impoverished many Kenyans who relied on agriculture.

The last section on neoliberalism and the incorporation of the peasantry into global commodity chains start off with a chapter (chapter "Neoliberal Agrarian Policies and Terms of Incorporation in Rural Mozambique") by Natacha Bruna on Mozambique. The current scramble for resources in Africa has become a major driver of social exclusion and ensuing negative implications for rural livelihoods, albeit in differentiated ways. Pre-existing structures and inequalities that resulted from historical colonial paths and specific economic, traditional and legal contexts conditioned the heterogeneity of rural populations; and, consequently, how differently they experience and react to current processes of land grabbing. Bruna aims to understand the differentiated outcomes, implications and reactions of each segment of the rural population in the context of Mozambique specifically, building on Shivji's concept of the working people. Presently, most large-scale investments in rural areas in Mozambique involve ways of integrating the affected smallholders into the dynamics of rural development. A critical examination of such policies and approaches is presented by Bruna, by looking particularly at processes of smallholder integration, as materialised through corporate social development plans. This entails analysing the terms of incorporation of the different segments of the rural population, including wage workers, poorer peasants, women and local elites. Empirical findings show that most of the smallholders end up adversely incorporated into investment-led rural development projects, ultimately resulting in the inclusion of the few and the exclusion of the majority.

In chapter "Socio-Economic Effects of Neoliberal Transformation on Irrigated Agriculture in Eswatini: A Case of Sugarcane Farmers' Groups in the Komati Downstream Development Project", Nicollete Mhlanga-Ndlovu focuses on the incorporation of peasants (as sugarcane producers) in Eswatini into the sugar commodity chain. Since the early 2000s, the Government of the Kingdom of Eswatini has been implementing neoliberal transformations in the agricultural sector, with the aim of primarily promoting the production of cash crops (mainly sugarcane) through the conversion of subsistence farming into commercial agriculture. The main drivers behind this paradigm shift have been poverty eradication and promotion of food security as well as income generation for livelihoods improvement. Despite the intensification of irrigated agriculture since the 1990s, Mhlanga-Ndlovu shows that food security has deteriorated, with many rural communities within Eswatini remaining dependent on food aid as the local cereal production has suffered a massive decline. This has largely been caused by an increased focus on export-oriented strategies compared to food grain production. Based on interviews conducted at the Komati Downstream Development Project, the study by Mhlanga-Ndlovu shows that neoliberal reforms in Eswatini did not improve food security for the great majority of smallholder producers and that the reforms have exacerbated challenges faced in the sugar industry. The chapter concludes by recommending the strengthening of capacities of farmers' associations for an improvement in sugarcane yields.

Last but not least, chapter "Meeting Global Capital in a Village: The Expansion of Tobacco Contract Farming in Zimbabwe" by Yumi Sakata examines the expansion of the tobacco industry in Zimbabwe amongst the peasantry as contract farmers. Foreign interests in Africa's resources and markets have been rising in recent years. Various studies have described the flow as a 'new scramble' that intensified in the twenty-first century. While the continent has been depicted as being in crisis, suffering from a limited inflow of foreign investment, it is now receiving more global investment than at any time in the previous five decades. Sakata argues, however, that capital penetration often leaves farmers in precarious conditions and fosters the 'scramble' for Africa even more, without safeguarding smallholder farmers. This is demonstrated through a case study of tobacco contract farming in contemporary Zimbabwe. As shown in a series of works by the Sam Moyo African Institute of Agrarian Studies based in Harare, Fast Track Land Reform Programme (FTLRP) reconfigured the agrarian structure of Zimbabwe, including through repeasantisation as reflected in the tobacco sub-sector. Sakata presents case study based results of the socio-economic impacts of tobacco contract farming on smallholder farmers and argues that, while contract farming resuscitated the tobacco industry post-FTLRP, it also exposed smallholder farmers to the viscidities of global markets.

References

Adnan S (2013) Land grabs and primitive accumulation in deltaic Bangladesh: interactions between neoliberal globalization, state interventions, power relations and peasant resistance. J Peasant Stud 40(1):87–128. https://doi.org/10.1080/03066150.2012.753058

Amanor KS (2019) Global value chains and Agribusiness in Africa: upgrading or capturing smallholder production? Agrarian South: J Polit Econ 8(1–2):30–63

Amin S (2015) Contemporary imperialism and the Agrarian question. Agrarian South J Polit Econ 1(1):11–26

Andrews D (2021) Gendered and ecological struggles in southern Africa: land and seed. Gender Quest 9(1):1–18

Ashman S, Fine B, Newman S (2011) The crisis in South Africa: neoliberalism, financialization and uneven and combined development. Soc Reg 47:174–195

Bond P, Dor G (2003) Neoliberalism and Poverty Reduction Strategies in Africa. Discussion paper at the Regional Network for Equity in Health in Southern Africa

Borras S Jr, Kay C, Gómez S, Wilkinson J (2012) Land grabbing and global capitalist accumulation: key features in Latin America. Can J Dev Stud/Revue canadienne d'études du développement 33(4):402–416. https://doi.org/10.1080/02255189.2012.745394

Borras S Jr (2005) Can redistributive reform be achieved via market based voluntary land transfer schemes? Evidence and lessons from the Philippines. J Dev Stud 41(1):90–134. https://doi.org/10.1080/0022038042000276581

Borras SM Jr (2008) La Vı'a Campesina and its global campaign for agrarian reform. J Agrar Chang 8(2–3):258–289

Brenner N, Peck J, Theodore N (2010) Variegated neoliberalisation: geographies, modalities, pathways. Global Netw 10(2):182–222
Büscher, B. (2010) Anti-politics as political strategy: neoliberalism and transfrontier conservation in Southern Africa. Dev Chang 41(1):29–51
Byres TJ (ed) (2004) Special issue on 'redistributive land reform today'. J Agrarian Change 4 (1–2):1–225. Byres TJ 2006. Differentiation of
Chambati W, Mazwi F, Mberi S (2018) Agrarian accumulation and peasant resistance in Africa. In: Gumede V (ed) Inclusive development in Africa: transformations of global relations. CODESRIA, Pretoria
de L T Oliveira G, McKay BM, Liu J (2021) Beyond land grabs: new insights on land struggles and global agrarian change. Globalisations 18(3):321–338
Delgado Wise R, Veltmeyer H (2016) Agrarian change, migration and development. Practical Action Publishing, Rugby
FAO (Food and Agriculture Organisation). 2012. Smallholders and family farms. Sustainable pathways factsheet
Fraser A (2008) Geography and land reform. Geogr Rev 98:309–321
Hall R, Scoones I, Tsikata D (2017) Plantations, outgrowers and commercial farming in Africa: agricultural commercialization and implications for agrarian change. J Peasant Stud 44(3):515–537
Hanson M, Hentz J (1999) Neocolonialism and neoliberalism in South Africa and Zambia. Polit Sci Q 114(3):479–502
Harrison G (2005) Economic faith, social project and a misreading of African society: the travails of neoliberalism in Africa. Third World Q 26(8):1303–1320. https://doi.org/10.1080/01436590500336922
Harrison G (2019) Authoritarian neoliberalism and capitalist transformation in Africa: all pain, no gain. Globalizations 16(3):274–288. https://doi.org/10.1080/14747731.2018.1502491
Harvey D (2005) A brief history of neoliberalism. Oxford University Press, Oxford
Harvey D (2016) Neoliberalism is a political project. Jacobin 07:23
Havnevik K, Bryceson D, Birgegård L-E, Matondi P, Beyene A (2007) African agriculture and the World Bank: development or impoverishment? Nordic Africa Institute, Uppsala. urn=urn:nbn:se:nai:diva-556
Jha P, Yeros P (2019) Global agricultural value systems and the South: some critical issues at the current juncture. Agrarian South: J Polit Econ 8(1–2):14–29
Korovkin T (1992) Peasant's grapes, and corporation. The growth of contract farming in a Chilean community. J Peasant Stud 19(2)
Kirsten J, Sartorious K (2002) Linking Agribusiness and small-scale farmers in developing countries: is there a new role for contract farming? Dev South Afr 19(4):503–529
Lahif E (2003) The politics of land reform in southern Africa. Sustainable livelihoods in Southern Africa, research paper no. 19. Institute of Poverty, Land and Agrarian Studies, University of the Western Cape, Cape Town
Land Matrix (2012) The online public database on land deals. http://landmatrix.org/en/. Retrieved December 2020
Martiniello G (2015) "Don't stop the mill": South African sugar, agrarian change and outgrowers adverse incorporation in the Kilombero Valley, Tanzania. Working Paper 19. BRICS Initiative for Critical Agrarian Studies
Martiniello G (2016) "Don't stop the mill": South African capital and agrarian change in Tanzania. Third World Thematic: A TWQ J 1(5):633–652
Martiniello G (2017) Bitter sugarification: agro-extractivism, outgrower schemes and social differentiation in Busoga, Uganda. Paper presented at 5th International Conference of the BRICS Initiative for Critical Agrarian Studies. October 13–16. RANEPA. Moscow
Mazwi F (2020) Sugar production dynamics in Zimbabwe: an analysis of contract farming at Hippo Valley. Rev Afr Polit Econ 47(166):568–584

Mazwi F, Chemura A, Mudimu GT, Chambati W (2019) Political economy of command agriculture in Zimbabwe: a state-led contract farming model. Agrarian South J Polit Econ 8(1–2):232–257
Mazwi F, Chambati W, Mudimu GT (2020) Tobacco contract farming in Zimbabwe: power dynamics, accumulation trajectories, land use patterns and livelihoods. J Contemp Afr Stud 38(1):55–71
Mazwi F, Muchetu RG, Mudimu GT (2021) Revisiting the Trimodal Agrarian structure in Zimbabwe'. Agrarian South J Polit Econ https://doi.org/10.1177/2277976020973837
McKeon N (2015) Food security governance. Routledge Press, New York
McMichael P (2013) Value-chain agriculture and debt relations: contradictory outcomes. Third World Q 34(4):671–690. https://doi.org/10.1080/01436597.2013.786290
Mills G, Obasanjo O, Biti T, Herbst J (2019) Democracy works: re-writing politics to Africa's advantage. Oxford University Press, New York
Mkandawire T, Soludo C (1999) Our continent, our future: African perspectives on structural adjustment. CODESRIA, Dakar
Moorsom TL, Rao S, Gengenbach H, Huggins C (2020) Food security and the contested visions of agrarian change in Africa. Can J Dev Stud 41(2):212–223
Moyo S (1995) The land question in Zimbabwe. Institute of Development Studies, Harare
Moyo S (2001) The land occupation movement and democratization in Zimbabwe: contradictions of neoliberalism. Millennium 30(2):311–330
Moyo S (2008) African land questions, agrarian transitions and the state: contradictions of neoliberal land reforms. CODESRIA, Dakar
Moyo S (2011) Primitive accumulation and the destruction of African peasantries. In: Patnaik U, Moyo S (eds) The agrarian question in the neoliberal era: primitive accumulation and the peasantry. Pambazuka Press, Cape Town, pp 61–86
Moyo S (2013) Land reform and redistribution in Zimbabwe since 1980. In: Moyo S, Chambati W (eds) Land and agrarian reform in former settler colonial Zimbabwe. COSDERIA, Dakar, pp 29–78. Retrieved from http://www.codesria.org/IMG/pdf/2-Land_and_Agrarian_Reform_in_Zim_Moyo.pdf
Moyo S (2014) State of family farming in sub-Saharan Africa: its contribution to the rural development, food security and nutrition. Global Dialogue on Family Farming, FAO, Rome, 27–28 October
Moyo S (2016) Southern African potentials to address land-based conflicts. In: Moyo S, Yoiche M (eds) What colonialism ignored: African potentials for resolving conflicts in southern Africa. Langaa RPCIG, Bamenda, pp 37–66
Moyo S, Yeros P (eds) (2005) Reclaiming the land: the resurgence of rural movements in Africa, Asia and Latin America. Zed Books, London
Moyo S, Yeros P (2007) The radicalised state: Zimbabwe's interrupted revolution. Rev Afr Polit Econ 34(111):103–121. https://doi.org/10.1080/03056240701340431
Moyo S, Yeros P (2011) The fall and rise of the national question. In: Moyo S, Yeros P (eds) Reclaiming the nation: the return of the national question in Africa, Asia and Latin America. Pluto Press, London, pp 3–28
Moyo S, Jha P, Yeros P (2012) Imperialism and primitive accumulation: notes on the new scramble for Africa. Agrarian South: J Polit Econ 1(1):181–204
Moyo S, Jha P, Yeros P (2013) The classical agrarian question: myth, reality and relevance today. Agrarian South: J Polit Econ 2(1):93–119
Moyo S, Jha P, Yeros P (2019) The scramble for land and natural resources in Africa. In: Moyo S, Jha P, Yeros P (eds) Reclaiming Africa: scramble and resistance in 21st century. Springer, Singapore
Mudimu GT (2020) Understanding land leasing, livelihoods and capabilities in post land reform Zimbabwe. PhD Thesis. China Agricultural University
Myers GA (2008) Peri-urban land reform, political-economic reform, and urban political ecology in Zanzibar. Urban Geogr 29(3):264–288. https://doi.org/10.2747/0272-3638.29.3.264
Nkrumah K (1965) Neocolonialism: the last stage of imperialism. Thomas Nelson & Sons, London

Nyong'o AP (2013) The land question, land grabbing and agriculture in Africa. Int J Afr Renaissance Stud Multi-, Inter- Transdisciplinarity 8(2):23–31
OECD/FAO (2016) OECD-FAO Agricultural Outlook 2016–2025. OECD Publishing, Paris. https://doi.org/10.1787/agr_outlook-2016-en. Accessed 25 Jan 2021
Ojeda D (2012) Green pretexts: ecotourism, neoliberal conservation and land grabbing in Tayrona National Natural Park, Colombia. J Peasant Stud 39(2):357–375. https://doi.org/10.1080/03066150.2012.658777
Ossome L (2020) The agrarian question in gendered labour in Sam Moyo's scholarship. In: Jha P, Yeros P, Chambati W (eds) Rethinking the social sciences with Sam Moyo. New Delhi, Tulika
Oya C (2012) Contract farming in sub-Saharan Africa: a survey of approaches, debates, and issues. J Agrar Chang 12(1):1–33
Patnaik U (2003) Global capitalism, deflation, and agrarian crisis in developing countries. J Agrar Chang 3(1–2):33–66
Patnaik U (2011) The agrarian question in the neoliberal era. In: Patnaik U, Moyo S (eds) The agrarian question in the neoliberal era: primitive accumulation and the peasantry. Pambazuka Press, Cape Town, pp 8–57
Patnaik U (2015) The origins and continuation of First World import dependence on developing countries for agricultural products. J Polit Econ 4(1):1–21
Patnaik P (2020) Neoliberalism and fascism. Agrarian South: J Polit Econ 9(1)
Patnaik U, Patnaik P (2016) A theory of imperialism. Tulika Books, New Delhi
Pattenden J, Campling L, Ballivian EC, Gras C, Lerche J, O'Laughlin B, Oya C, Perez-Nino H, Sina S (2021) Introduction: Covid-19 and the conditions and struggles of agrarian classes of labour. J Agrar Chang 21:582–590
Peck J, Theodore N (2007) Variegated capitalism. Prog Hum Geogr 31(6):731–772
Peluso NL, Lund C (2011) New frontiers of land control: introduction. J Peasant Stud 38(4):667–681. https://doi.org/10.1080/03066150.2011.607692
Pérez Niño H (2016) Class dynamics in contract farming: the case of tobacco production in Mozambique. Third World Q 37(10):1787–1808
Peschard K, Randeria S (2020) 'Keeping seeds in our hands': the rise of seed activism. J Peasant Stud 47(4):613–647
Prashad V (2013) Neoliberalism with southern characteristics: the rise of the BRICS. Rosa Luxemburg Stiftung, New York
Ramutsindela M, Shabangu M (2013) Conditioned by neoliberalism: a reassessment of land claim resolutions in the Kruger National Park. J Contemp Afr Stud 31(3):441–456. https://doi.org/10.1080/02589001.2013.811791
Rodrick D (2002) After neoliberalism, What? Paper was presented at the alternatives to neoliberalism conference sponsored by the New Rules for Global Finance Coalition, May 23–24, 2002
Rosset PM, Patel R, Courville M (2006) Promised land: competing visions of agrarian reform. Food First Books, Oakland, CA
Sachikonye L (1989) The state and agribusiness in Zimbabwe: plantations and contract farming. In: Leeds southern agrarian studies 13. African Studies Unit, Leeds University
Shivji IG (1992) The roots of an agrarian crisis in Tanzania: a theoretical perspective. University of Dar es Salaam
Shivji IG (2009) Accumulation in an African periphery: a theoretical framework. Mkuki na Nyota Publishers, Dar es Salaam
Shivji IG (2011) Preface. In: Patnaik U, Moyo S (eds) The agrarian question in the neoliberal era: primitive accumulation and the peasantry. Pambazuka Press, Cape Town
Shivji IG (2020) Samir Amin on democracy and fascism. Agrarian South: J Polit Econ 9:1
Soper R (2020) From protecting peasant livelihoods to essentialising peasant agriculture: problematic trends in food sovereignty discourse. J Peasant Stud 47(2):265–285
Thorsen DE, Lie A (eds) (2006) What is neoliberalism? http://folk.uio.no/daget/What%20is%20Neo-Liberalism%20FINAL.pdf UNDP (2006)

Van der Ploeg JD (2020) From biomedical to politico-economic crisis: the food system in times of Covid-19. J Peasant Stud 47(5):944–972
Wolford W (2007) Land reform in the time of neo-liberalism: a many splendored thing. Antipode 39(3):550–570. Wright, A. and W. Wolford, 2003
World Bank (2007) World Development Report 2008, Agriculture for Development. Washington, DC. https://siteresources.worldbank.org/INTWDR2008/Resources/WDR_00_book.pdf
World Bank (2019) The World Bank Annual Report 2019: ending poverty, investing in opportunity. World Bank, Washington, DC
Ye J, Van der Ploeg JD, Schneider S, Shanin T (2020) The incursions of extractivism: moving from dispersed places to global capitalism. J Peasant Stud 47(1):155–183
Yeros P, Jha P (2020) Late neo-colonialism: monopoly capitalism in permanent crisis. Agrarian South: J Polit Econ 9:1

Neoliberalisation and Regulatory Restructuring in South Africa's Commercial Agriculture

Gilton Klerck

Abstract The notion of 'neoliberalism' has been widely deployed to describe the resurgence of market-orientated institutional shifts and policy realignments across the world economy since the 1980s. Following the initial analysis of these trends, much attention has been devoted to their conceptualisation. While the meaning and tractability of 'neoliberalism' continue to be topics of intense debate, recent theoretical work in the field has produced several important insights that have significant implications for empirical research on regulatory restructuring at all spatial scales. Against the monolithic conceptualisations that prevail in popular and academic accounts, the notion of 'variegated neoliberalisation' emphasises the uneven, hybrid, and unstable character of neoliberalising forms of regulatory transformation. By substituting an end-state view of neoliberalism with emergent and tendential processes of neoliberalisation, the dramatic changes in South Africa's agricultural policy and practice that have unfolded since the 1980s may be cast in a new light. In particular, we explore the apparent paradox between extensively liberalised product markets and highly regulated labour markets in post-apartheid commercial agriculture.

1 Introduction

As the massive wave of deregulation and liberalisation that swept global agriculture in the 1980s and 1990s receded, it deposited in its wake the market-disciplinary and beggar thy neighbour governance rationalities that have profoundly altered the global food system. Following the debt crisis of the early 1980s, neoliberal programmes of regulatory restructuring were extended globally through the efforts of the Organisation for Economic Cooperation and Development (OECD), the United States, and other G-7 states to subject states in the global South to the

G. Klerck (✉)
Department of Sociology, Rhodes University, Makhanda, South Africa
e-mail: g.klerck@ru.ac.za

F. Mazwi et al. (eds.), *Capital Penetration and the Peasantry in Southern and Eastern Africa*, Advances in African Economic, Social and Political Development, https://doi.org/10.1007/978-3-030-89824-3_2

discipline of capital markets. Bretton Woods institutions such as the General Agreement on Tariffs and Trade (GATT), the World Trade Organisation (WTO), the World Bank, and the International Monetary Fund (IMF) morphed into key vectors of transnational neoliberalism as they were mobilised to institutionalise the extension of market forces and commodification in the developing world through various structural adjustment and fiscal-austerity programmes. By the 1990s, 'neoliberalism' was widely regarded as the dominant political and ideological form of capitalist globalisation. The Uruguay Round Agreement on Agriculture, which came into force with the establishment of the WTO on 1 January 1995, tilted the field of economic policy further towards the interests of corporations, as 'trade-distorting' domestic support for agriculture was curtailed, the export competition was stimulated, tariffs barriers were subject to drastic cuts, and export subsidies were reduced in both value and volume. Twenty years later, in Nairobi in 2015, WTO members agreed that developed countries would immediately remove export subsidies on agricultural products (with some exceptions) and that developing countries would do so by 2018 (with a longer time frame in some cases).

The fundamental objective of these prescriptions is clear: governments must adopt policies that have minimal 'market-distorting' effects. Neoliberal doctrine represents states and markets as if they are diametrically opposed principles of social organisation, rather than recognising the socio-politically constructed character of all economic relations. It is also premised on a one-size-fits-all model of policy implementation, which assumes that similar results will follow the imposition of market-oriented reforms, rather than recognising the substantial variations that arise as neoliberal reform initiatives are implemented within historically specific institutional landscapes and policy environments (Brenner and Theodore 2002, p. 353). Understanding contemporary regulatory restructuring in the global food system is a necessary precursor to answering broader questions about power relations in the production, processing, distribution, and consumption of agricultural commodities. As one of the leading scholars of global value chains (GVCs) notes, there is a 'need for more dialogue between critical commodity studies and the literature on ongoing forms of neoliberalisation' (Bair 2013, p. 2546).

A useful means for conceptualising the linkages that characterise the integration of local producers into the global food system is offered by GVC analysis, which explores the transnational networks of actors that enable the production-consumption of particular commodities (Gereffi et al. 2005). This analysis highlights the fact that global trade is increasingly being organised through complex inter- and intra-firm arrangements. Horticultural GVCs, in particular, are increasingly buyer-driven and characterised by institutional innovations such as interlinked transactions, contract farming, vertical integration, E-logistics, and blockchain-based food traceability. In countries of sub-Saharan Africa (SSA), this process of 'modernisation' is most apparent in supermarket-driven supply chains and high-value agricultural export chains (Biénabe et al. 2007; Reardon and Hopkins 2006). Large, multinational retail and food companies, which are increasingly dominating global food supply chains, are also ever more involved in establishing and enforcing the quality standards of exports.

This expansion in the influence of buyers or retailers has led to changes in the structure and governance of high-value horticultural export chains (Humphrey and Schmitz 2001). There has been a move from arm's-length market relations and spot-market transactions towards 'non-market' forms of governance in value chains (Gereffi et al. 2005). Even chains with market-orientated governance structures require coordination, often assumed by lead firms that control much of the division of labour along the chain and set the terms on which other actors gain access (Bair 2009, p. 20). Food export chains now entail varying levels of vertical coordination at different nodes in the chains, which are apparent in increased hierarchical governance between developing-country producers, on the one hand, and exporters, food processors, and supermarkets, on the other (Burch and Lawrence 2007; Dolan and Humphrey 2004). Vertical coordination is mainly in the form of contract farming between agro-industrial or retail firms and local primary producers (Swinnen and Maertens 2007) or, at the extreme, primary production is vertically integrated into the ownership structure of downstream processing and retail firms (Maertens et al. 2012), thereby fostering cross-nodal concentration in GVCs.

The agricultural sector is a particularly instructive example of the evolution of neoliberal reforms. Global agrarian exports more than tripled in a period of intense restructuring: from US$220 billion in 1985 to US$720 billion in 2005, and more than tripled in value and more than doubled in volume since 1995, exceeding US $1.8 trillion in 2018 (FAOstat). While the transition from traditional exports to non-traditional, high-value exports is apparent in most developing countries, it has arguably been most dramatic in SSA, where many countries were heavily dependent on a single traditional export commodity or a few of them. In this region, high-value exports constituted 35% of total exports, but traditional exports still made up the most significant part of agri-food exports (39%) in 2008. However, the importance of conventional exports in total agri-food exports has decreased from 68% in 1985 to 39% in 2005, while the share of high-value exports more than doubled, from 14% in 1985 to 35% in 2005 (Maertens et al. 2012). Horticultural exports from SSA to high-income regions tripled from 1990 to 2005 from less than two million tons to six million tons (FAOstat). From the early 1990s onwards, the export of fruits and vegetables from SSA expanded rapidly and continuously, while the export growth of traditional agricultural commodities such as coffee, sugar, and cotton was much smaller and less constant (Maertens et al. 2012). The European Union (EU) is the primary destination market for the increased SSA horticulture exports. Several SSA countries, including Burkina Faso, Cameroon, Kenya, Uganda, Senegal, Madagascar, and South Africa (SA), have become important suppliers of fresh fruits and vegetables to northern markets.

While there is consensus that restructuring processes in GVCs have generated significant changes, the welfare implications of these changes (for example, income mobility and rural poverty reduction) are poorly understood, and empirical studies have come to diverse conclusions (Maertens et al. 2012). Despite the essential role of the production node in modern food supply chains, there are comparatively few studies of export-orientated horticulture in SSA countries. Horticultural exports are widely regarded as entailing a significant potential for raising rural incomes and reducing poverty because of the link with the rural economy, the high intrinsic value of the produce, and the labour-intensive production systems (Dolan and Humphrey 2000; Weatherspoon and Reardon 2003). Consequently, many developing countries, especially in SSA, pursue the development of horticultural export chains as a critical poverty reduction strategy. National governments, the World Bank, and other international donors have invested heavily in facilitating developing countries' integration into global horticultural markets, and many development projects have focused on enhancing the welfare benefits of increased trade in high-value horticulture (Maertens et al. 2012).

So, how do we account for the historically specific waves and patterns of both *market-disciplinary and market-constraining* regulatory restructuring that have unfolded globally, yet always in contextually specific forms, since the 1980s? Bland allusions to the 'imposition' of neoliberalism will not do. As some of the most astute scholars of neoliberalism argue, it is less of a coherently bounded '-ism' or 'end-state' than it is a *process of neoliberalisation* (Brenner et al. 2010). That is, neoliberalism only manifests as a historically specific, continuous, contested, and internally contradictory process of market-driven socio-spatial transformation rather than as a fully realised policy regime, ideological form, or regulatory framework. From this perspective, an adequate understanding of the process of neoliberalisation—itself a crisis-induced and crisis-inducing form of market-disciplinary regulatory restructuring—requires a grasp of its politico-ideological foundations as well as a systematic inquiry into its diverse institutional forms, developmental tendencies, varied socio-political effects, and multiple contradictions (Peck et al. 2012b, p. 268). Theoretically, the idea of a heterogeneous, non-linear, poly-centric, and non-sequential process of neoliberalisation underscores the contingent, contradictory, creative-destructive, and contested character of neoliberal policies and practices (Brenner et al. 2010; Harvey 2007; Jessop 2013). Substantively, it stimulates interest in 'developmental' or 'Third-Way' efforts to create flanking and supporting mechanisms to mitigate the impact of neoliberalism and boost its legitimacy while sustaining its transformative momentum (Graefe 2006; Jessop 2015).

By drawing on the notion of variegated neoliberalisation—i.e. substituting an end-state view of neoliberal*ism* with emergent and tendential processes of neoliberal*isation*—the dramatic changes in SA's agricultural policy and practice that have unfolded since the 1980s may be cast in a new light. In this view, liberalisation and deregulation should not be conceived as the elimination or absence of regulation but should instead be understood in terms of recurrent practices of re-regulation. The regulatory restructuring of agriculture in post-apartheid SA may be described, at the risk of oversimplification, as a shift from regulated product markets and deregulated labour markets under apartheid to deregulated product markets and regulated labour markets in the post-apartheid period. Regulatory restructuring in SA agriculture includes the deregulation of marketing and the liberalisation of price controls as well as the partial removal of favourable tax treatment and subsidies. In addition, the emphasis on export-orientated agriculture in the government's policies and the considerably higher prices on international food markets have fuelled the integration of specific fractions of SA agricultural capital into GVCs with divergent implications for rural labour.

The argument in this chapter will proceed as follows. First, I will sketch, in broad brushstrokes, the salient features of the critical literature on neoliberalism. Neoliberalisation, as noted above, is best interpreted as a complex synthesis of many different determinants rather than as a distinct causal entity in its own right. It is misleading to explain specific events and phenomena in terms of some general process of 'neoliberalism'. However, if re-specified along the lines suggested by critical scholars, trends towards neoliberalism can undoubtedly help to situate and interpret current changes in the spatial scale of economic (and other types of) institutions, organisations, and strategies. While the era of neoliberal globalisation has coincided with increased agricultural outputs and trade, economists tend to focus on these developments to the exclusion of the ruthless politics of this process, its flimsy underlying economics, tattered social-safety net, threadbare ideological legitimacy, rising income inequalities, and socio-economic and welfare policies that barely underwrite the basic reproduction needs of the working poor, who are trapped in dead-end, menial, and precarious jobs, and the under- and unemployed, who are seemingly permanently socially excluded.

Second, I outline the broad dynamics of neoliberal regulatory restructuring in the agricultural sector in post-apartheid SA. In particular, I explore the apparent paradox between extensively liberalised product markets and highly regulated labour markets. I show how the extant socio-political and institutional landscape has modulated and patterned the processes of deregulation and liberalisation in agricultural product markets while entrenching both farmworkers' lack of collective power in the workplace and farmers' authoritarian and paternalistic control over rural labour markets and labour processes.

2 Variegated Neoliberalisation: Mongrel Logics, Hybrid Modalities, and Striated Geographies

Neoliberalism is widely associated with the claim that 'unregulated' markets, which are 'freed' from all forms of state 'interference', constitute the optimal mechanism for economic growth and individual freedom. As such, Bourdieu (2008, p. 94) aptly depicts it as the 'utopia of unlimited exploitation'. This millennial version of free-market capitalism has metastasised into all corners of the globe. Anderson (2000, p. 17) regards it as no less than 'the most successful ideology in world history' that 'rules undivided across the globe'. At the same time, Harvey (2005, p. 2) claims that there has 'everywhere been an emphatic turn towards neoliberalism in political-economic practices and thinking'. There is, however, a growing residue of disquiet with the (varied and exacting) descriptive burden that the term 'neoliberalism' is made to carry in many contemporary analyses. Abstract, monolithic, and functionalist conceptions of neoliberalism imply an 'undifferentiated global behemoth, running on autopilot or guided by some invisible hand' (Leitner et al. 2007, p. 314). Clarke (2008, p. 137) questions whether the term has been degraded into a 'next-generation 'globalisation' concept'. Barnett (2005, p. 9) inveighs against the 'consolations" of neoliberalism and contends that 'there is no such thing as neoliberalism'! Peck (2001, pp. 449–450) highlights the 'intellectual peregrination of the slippery, hazy and contentious concept of neoliberalism'. Likewise, Brenner et al. (2010, pp. 183–184) argue that 'neoliberalism' has become 'something of a rascal concept – promiscuously pervasive, yet inconsistently defined, empirically imprecise and frequently contested'.

Some scholars use the term 'actually existing neoliberalism' to encapsulate the differences between neoliberalism in practice and the fetishistic abstractions of its advocates (Brenner and Theodore 2002). For instance, neoliberalism has not led to a 'hollowing out' of the state but to the creation of new social and economic regulations. It has reconfigured the state's role rather than diminished it (Cahill 2009). Neoliberalism, therefore, does not entail 'less state, more market'. Instead, it generates a complex reconstitution of state-economy relations in which state power and institutions are actively mobilised to secure market-based regulatory arrangements in the context of particular conjunctural challenges (Brenner and Theodore 2005, p. 102).

Whatever the differences between them, the predominant uses of the notion of 'neoliberalism' involve references to 'the tendential extension of market-based competition and commodification processes into previously relatively insulated realms of social life' (Peck et al. 2012b, p. 268). While the meaning and tractability of the notion of 'neoliberalism' continue to be topics of intense debate, recent theoretical work has produced several important insights that have significant implications for empirical research on regulatory restructuring at all spatial scales (see Brenner et al. 2010; Peck 2008, 2010; Tickell and Peck 2003; Wacquant 2012). In stark contrast to its homogenised and homogenising doctrine, the global diffusion of neoliberalism has in practice been highly uneven, both socially and geographically, and its institutional forms and socio-political ramifications have varied significantly across spatial scales. The diverse pathways of actually existing neoliberalisms provide ample evidence for this proposition.

Against the monolithic conceptualisations that prevail in popular and academic accounts, Peck et al. (2012b, p. 268) emphasise 'the constitutively uneven, institutionally hybrid, and chronically unstable character' of neoliberalising forms of regulatory transformation, which are always embedded in a context of particular assemblages of power. Brenner et al. (2010, p. 209) invoke a metaphor of successive waves of 'distinctively patterned, market-orientated' regulatory restructuring, each of which is recursively embedded in and partially transformative of prevailing institutional and normative landscapes. The resulting uneven development of neoliberalisation stems:

> On the one hand, from the continuous collision between contextually specific, constantly evolving neoliberalisation projects and inherited politico-institutional arrangements, whether at global, national, or local scales. At the same time, through this collision, neoliberalisation processes rework inherited forms of regulatory and spatial organisation,

including those of state institutions themselves, to produce new forms of geo-institutional differentiation (Brenner et al. 2010, p. 331).

A vital feature of these waves of neoliberalisation (small-n)—despite variations in timing and the effects of geo-historical specificities—is the extensive similarities in the Neoliberal (large-N) project. In essence, the challenge lies in exploring the 'hybrid' and 'messy' forms (Bair and Werner 2011; Peck and Tickell 2007) of 'actually existing neoliberalisms' (Brenner and Theodore 2002), without overlooking that there is also a 'neoliberalism-in-general' (Peck 2004). Brenner and Theodore (2005, pp. 102–103) offer a series of propositions to capture some of the key ideas developed in the literature, which may be summarised as follows: neoliberalisation is a process, which is articulated through contextually specific strategies on a contested institutional landscape, dependent on the active mobilisation of state power, generates path-dependent outcomes, is intensely contested, exacerbates regulatory failure, and continues to evolve and mutate. Analytically, we are therefore encouraged to combine the study of 'local regulatory experimentation' with an investigation of broader 'institutionalised rule regimes' (Brenner et al. 2010, p. 35).

The strategic priorities, tactics, and practices of neoliberalism are and have always been, shaped by place-specific struggles in ways that are more than merely 'contingent' (Peck and Tickell 2007, p. 29). Despite the uneven articulation of neoliberalisation processes, they have not involved a random or chaotic 'piling up' of discrete, contextually-contained regulatory experiments. Rather, according to Brenner et al. (2010), processes of neoliberalisation have generated important, distinctly patterned, and cumulative effects on the geo-institutional configuration or rule regimes of capitalism. These include the deepening of financialisation and capital mobility as well as the extension of various forms of commodification and marketisation.

Since neoliberalism and other socio-spatial projects are mutually constitutive—in the sense of its articulation and intersections with these projects through hybrid or composite structures—we should not expect to find many clean dividing lines between the neoliberal project and alternative forms of economic coordination (such as hierarchy, heterarchy, networks, and solidarity). While the various forms of neoliberalism share several generic features, each form is socially embedded in different ways as 'a multifaceted hybrid, more Hydra than Goliath' (Peck and Tickell 2007, p. 27). Since neoliberal trajectories have always been (re)produced in conditions, not of the choosing of local elites (particularly in the global South), it follows that the prevailing context is vital in the timing, form, and substance of local neoliberalisations, bestowing on each hybrid composite formation its endemic features. Likewise, shifts to neoliberalism are not clearly bounded temporal and geographical transitions but rather gain hegemonic status through 'a multisited overlapping sequence of ideological and lived confrontations that [have] deeply political origins and implications' (Martin 2007, p. 58).

Each neoliberal construction is shaped by its local context and by the struggles that gave rise to it and has its own unique propensities and liabilities, zones of over-extension and exclusion, secure citadels and undefended flanks. The process of neoliberalisation is, therefore, a socially produced, spatiotemporally specific, crisis-driven, conjunctural, unstable, and polymorphous phenomenon with uncertain, unpredictable, and path-dependent trajectories (see Duménil and Lévy 2004; Kingfisher and Maskovsky 2008; Leitner et al. 2007; Mirowski and Plehwe 2009; Saad-Filho and Johnston 2005; Springer et al. 2016).

Neoliberalism has evolved through a series of discrete 'phases' that help to explain its differential impacts and, therefore, variations across space and time. Tickell and Peck (2003) distinguish three phases of neoliberalism: 'proto-neoliberalism' associated with the pre-1980s' theoretical assault on Keynesianism and developmentalism, 'roll-back neoliberalism' of the 1980s and early 1990s focused on deregulation and structural adjustment, and 'roll-out neoliberalism' from the 1990s onwards concerned with state building. For example, the shift from the neoconservative, anti-statist neoliberalisms of Reagan and Thatcher in the 1980s to the centre-left, workfare neoliberalisms of Blair, Clinton, and Schröder during the 1990s may be understood as a path-dependent reconstitution of neoliberal strategies in response to their own contradictory, dysfunctional socio-political effects (Brenner and Theodore 2002, p. 362). In a helpful analogy, Peck and Tickell (2002, pp. 389–390) characterise these changes as a shift from 'ideological software to institutional hardware'. The roll-out phase of the neoliberal project is thus not only oriented towards the (continued) promotion of market-driven capitalist growth but also towards the establishment of flanking mechanisms and spatiotemporal fixes to shield powerful economic interests from the multiple failures of the market, the state, and governance that are recurrently generated within a neoliberal political framework (Harvey 2005; Jessop 2014). In essence, the transmutations of the 1990s onwards represent responses to market, state, and governance failures (for instance, economic stagnation, environmental degradation, under- and unemployment, and socio-spatial polarisation) that were partly or primarily initiated by neoliberalism itself.

Although roll-out neoliberalism is predicated mainly on the limitations, malfunctions, and unmanaged externalities of the deregulatory roll-back moment (including market failure, public austerity, and social abandonment), the former differs substantially from the latter. It involves (among other trends) the adoption of both market-disciplinary and market-constraining regulatory incursions, devolved or outsourced governance, and the embrace of hybrid governance in the form of public-private partnerships. Crucially, roll-out neoliberalism represents both the fragility and the extension of the neoliberal project.

To attain a deeper understanding of the path-dependent interactions between existing institutional forms and emergent neoliberal projects, Brenner and Theodore (2002, pp. 362–363) analyse actually existing neoliberalism with reference to two (dialectically-intertwined, but analytically-distinct) moments: (i) the partial destruction of existing institutional arrangements and socio-political compromises through market-oriented reform initiatives, and (ii) the tendential creation of a new structural and ideological framework for market-oriented economic growth, commodification, and the rule of capital. While both 'moments' are proliferative, neither is associated with simple convergence, but rather with the complex and variegated hybridisation of the market and non-market modes of governance and new forms of uneven socio-spatial development (Peck et al. 2012a, p. 24). This dialectical conceptualisation is particularly useful to make sense of the complex and contradictory trajectories of change that have emerged with the deployment of neoliberal political programmes at various places, territories, and scales. Brenner and Theodore (2002, p. 366) conceive this dynamic of 'creative destruction', not as a unilinear transition from one unified, context-bounded regulatory system to another, but rather as an uneven, open-ended, incomplete, contradictory, multi-scalar, multi-directional, and crisis-prone restructuring process that is characterised by (among other phenomena) institutional polymorphism, crisis tendencies, and failures and contradictions of its own.

As messy hybrids, neither of these dynamics represents a 'pure' neoliberal logic, nor do they resolve the regulatory failures and contradictions that animated their ascendency as a market-disciplinary rule regime. That is, the process of neoliberalisation, as manifested in particular political projects and policy regimes, may take many forms but can only survive through continued 'mongrelisation' (Peck et al. 2012a, p. 25). Crucially, since it can only exist in a hybrid, socially embedded form, neoliberalism can never be assigned transformative dynamics exclusively. The hybrid (re)combinations within which neoliberalism operates are 'themselves generative; it is not that neoliberalisation is active, while its socio-institutional 'hosts' are merely inert, residual' (Peck and Theodore 2012, p. 183). To be sure, the newly-developed amalgams of inherited and emergent institutional arrangements provide a political arena in and through which subsequent struggles over the regulation of accumulation and its associated contradictions can be fought out, leading, in turn, to novel, unanticipated, and often constitutively unstable layerings of political-economic space. Among other things, this conceptualisation suggests that:

> Empirical evidence underscoring the stalled, incomplete, discontinuous, or differentiated character of projects to impose market rule, or their coexistence alongside potentially antagonistic projects … does not provide a sufficient basis for questioning their neoliberalised, neoliberalising dimensions (Brenner et al. 2010, p. 332).

Methodologically, this means that studies of neoliberalisation must always be contextually embedded and, given the emergent properties of neoliberalisation as more than the sum of its local parts, have recourse to cross-case and cross-conjunctural modes of analysis (as opposed to generalisations from a particular site). While the emergent forms of neoliberalism must be understood in terms of contextual specificities, Peck and Theodore (2012, p. 180) make a convincing case for 'theorising across such armatures, in addition to within or from them'. Such forms of cross-case theorisation are essential to any adequate explanation of neoliberalisation as 'a historical process, the contradictory and uneven character of which is deeply constitutive rather than merely contingent' (Peck and Theodore 2012, p. 180). In contrast to the North-centric studies of neoliberalism, the methodological strategies developed and deployed in the literature on variegated neoliberalisation have proven helpful to scholars concerned with other regions of the world economy, such as SSA, Latin America, and Southeast Asia, where neoliberal programmes have evolved in different regulatory landscapes marked by the legacies of imperialism, import-substitution growth strategies, and, more recently, programmes of export-led industrialisation and labour market flexibility.

3 Neoliberalisation in Sub-Saharan Africa

The trajectory of neoliberalism in the North is often portrayed as the neoliberal trajectory *per se*. Yet, the spread of neoliberal developments in the 'periphery' of the global economy may be as important, if not more so, as those in the 'core'. This is nowhere more evident than in SSA, where 'neoliberalism has become not only a grand concept for researchers but also the orienting template for social and economic management for nearly 30 years' (Harrison 2010, p. 1). The successive waves of neoliberalisation in SSA countries did not break on the shores of a Keynesian-Fordism but rather battered the institutional underpinnings of various forms of 'developmental', military, authoritarian, or patrimonial states overseeing deepening socio-economic inequalities and poverty, plunder, resource exhaustion, theft, and fraud (Harrison 2010; Konings 2011; Sandbrook 2011).

The 'food regime'—i.e. a conjuncturally-specific articulation of the production, distribution, and consumption of food—that emerged globally following World War II was rooted in colonial trade and empire and typified by dependence on state institutions and support, the industrialisation and concentration of food production, and the nation-state as the dominant crucible of food policy and governance (McMichael 2009). Extensive state interventions were deemed necessary to protect farmers and consumers, ensure national food security and price stability for staple foods, encourage the adoption of new technologies, and support macro-economic stability (Ahmed et al. 2014; Talbot 1996). However, this food regime was reliant on subsidies and institutional matrices that became an unsustainable fiscal drain for many nation-states, especially in the South.

By the 1970s, it was clear that the developmentalist paradigm was failing: import-substitution policies had enabled no more than a stunted process of industrialisation, failed to reduce the reliance on the export of unprocessed primary commodities, and engendered persistent balance of payments problems, leading to increasing inequality and under- and unemployment, spiralling inflation, and a growing dependence on borrowing from northern banks. The shift to a high-interest rate regime in the North—driven in part by the monetarist strategies of the Reagan and Thatcher governments—triggered a debt crisis in the South, as a range of countries defaulted on their variable-rate loans and bolstered the leverage of creditors over debtors. Since the 1980s, Africa has been at the forefront of austerity and neoliberal policies aimed at stabilisation, deregulation, privatisation, and structural reforms of the kind witnessed in EU countries (such as Portugal, Ireland, and Greece) in the early-2010s. In the 1980s, 38 African governments accepted 244 conditional loans from the World Bank and the IMF. In the 1990s, the IMF was still operating in 36 African countries (Hilgers 2012, pp. 82–84). While the imposition of rules from the 'outside' is one of the features of neoliberalism as a contemporary form of economic imperialism, reducing it to an external imposition overlooks the historical role of Africa as a proving ground for neoliberalism (see Chalfin 2010; Harrison 2010; Konings 2011).

The global food system is undergoing rapid processes of regulatory transformation, with significant implications for developing countries (Dolan and Humphrey 2004; Freidberg 2003; Reardon et al. 2009). Significant outcomes of the wave of globalisation, liberalisation, and neoliberal statecraft from the late-1980s onwards—discussed in the section above—include the increasing integration of agri-food systems in complex GVCs, the predominance of market metrics, increasing price volatility, a marked rise in capital concentration at most nodes of agricultural GVCs, growing financialisation spurred on by speculation in agricultural derivatives markets, and the increased complexity and intensity of information flows between firms in GVCs with the growing importance of buyer requirements such as product variety, just-in-time delivery, traceability, and quality (Humphrey 2006; Isakson 2014). For many scholars, centralised procurement systems, private quality and safety standards, and the rise of contract farming are empirical manifestations of underlying changes in power relations in agricultural GVCs that bolster large retailers' market power and command over the rules that govern agricultural trade (Clapp and Fuchs 2009; Fuchs et al. 2011).

There has also been a proliferation of public and private standards in the food industry—associated with the 'whole-chain' approach—in response to public concerns about health and food safety, phytosanitary conditions, the origin of food products (traceability), animal welfare, and environmental and social impacts (Campbell 2005; Fuchs et al. 2009). Alongside these public, mandatory, process-based standards, which highlight the mounting significance of global standards, there are various collective, private standards that were developed by coalitions of private-sector companies (Bain et al. 2013; De Raymond and Bonnaud 2014). These include EUREPGAP for the horticulture sector and the International Food Standard for food processing plants. These requirements and their associated costs, combined with the need to minimise transaction costs through economies of scale, effectively exclude many small-scale farmers from global markets (Reardon et al. 2009) and induce cost-cutting by large-scale farmers. The extensive coordination and resources required by prevailing standards tend to privilege centralised producers, processors, and retailers and disadvantage small-scale farmers, who, by virtue of their numbers and geographic dispersal, are more costly to coordinate, trace, and monitor (Clapp and Fuchs 2009). The global food trade also brings together quite diverse food production systems that vary in geo-historical conditions, producer characteristics, regulatory frameworks, the configuration of labour markets, and consumer preferences. Of interest here is the capacity of powerful economic agents to move between different regulatory spaces through a process of 'regime shopping', which has valorised the quality and costs of labour at the various nodes of GVCs and served to attenuate the restraining consequences of regulatory systems that are embedded within particular geo-political jurisdictions. In short, neoliberal regulatory restructuring enables a 'race to the bottom' in labour standards as large retail monopolies scour the planet for the cheapest agricultural produce (of the required quantity and quality).

In much of SSA, direct public sector participation in agricultural markets diminished substantially following the first wave of structural adjustment and liberalisation, with the private sector playing an increasingly important role in output marketing, input supply, and service delivery (Chitundu et al. 2009). A context of extractive economies and unequal exchange relations has proven to be hostile to building developmental states but continues to sustain mutating forms of neoliberal social engineering, resulting in a 'mosaic of fractured neoliberalism' across the sub-continent (Harrison 2010, p. 2). As the state's role was recalibrated, private enterprises assumed a more significant role in food systems by becoming the primary suppliers of inputs, producers, transporters, storers, traders, processors, and retailers along value chains. The goal was to create greater market efficiency by improving market liquidity, reducing supply chain costs, generating more value-added opportunities, and facilitating producer and consumer choices. In reality, changes in the governance of horticultural value chains during the first phase of neoliberalisation created new business models that centre on consolidation, financialisation, and deregulation (Ahmed et al. 2014, pp. 11–13). The so-called Washington Consensus, widely regarded as a leitmotif of this historical conjuncture, linked loans to strict conditions relating to structural adjustment, privatisation and deregulation, public sector austerity, atrophy of the social state, and the opening of markets to international competition and foreign corporations.

Significant aspects of poverty reduction strategies in developing countries, particularly in SSA, are predicated on expanding agricultural production as well as improving the output and capabilities of small-scale farmers. However, these strategies are pursued in a context marked by the abandonment of import-substituting or state-led industrialisation schemes and by the existence of international and national policy shifts that increasingly prioritise and enable export-orientated agriculture, which tends to favour larger, integrated producers. Horticultural exports from SSA to the EU grew by 151% between 1989 and 1997, a period of intense restructuring (Temu and Marwa 2007, p. 15). Between 1988 and 2014, world agricultural exports grew from US$83.4 billion to US$1532 billion, while SSA's agricultural exports increased from US$2.7 billion to US$44.3 billion. Globally, bulk agricultural products account for a small and declining share of agricultural exports, decreasing from 25% in 1988 to 17% in 2014. By contrast, processed and semi-processed agricultural products accounted for almost 75% of global agricultural exports by 2014. The share of bulk agricultural exports also declined for Africa, but from around 60% to 42% in 2014, meaning these exports still constitute a large share of total agricultural exports. The percentage of processed and semi-processed agrarian products rose, but only to 35% by 2014 (Fukase and Martin 2018, p. 94).

Developing countries account for an increasing share of global exports and imports, which is, at least in part, an anticipated outcome of the neoliberalisation of agriculture. From 1995 to 2016, according to Glauber (2020), the share of total food imports and exports accounted for by developing countries grew from 26% to

39% and from 31% to 40%, respectively. If intra-EU trade is excluded, developing countries' imports and exports accounted for almost 60% of the global food trade in 2018. South-South trade also increased, accounting for over 24% of total trade in 2018 compared to 12% in 1995 (Glauber 2020). However, the benefits of increased trade are not only unevenly distributed to the detriment of workers and small-scale farmers but also come with (among other tendencies) the growing entanglement of local agriculture in global commodity chains dominated by large multinational corporations and mounting pressure on governments to pursue 'free' trade policies that are often weighted in favour of developed countries. Talbot's (1996) study of the global coffee trade, for instance, shows that a deregulated market inflicted severe boom-bust cycles on the millions of people in the rural periphery who depend on it for their livelihood. In addition, food production growth in SSA has failed to keep pace with demand deriving from population and income growth, resulting in rising imports for food commodities such as wheat, rice, and poultry (OECD-FAO 2020, p. 88). While there are essential differences in the timing, propulsive forces, and modalities of market-disciplinary regulatory restructuring, the changes in SA agriculture bear several striking resemblances to those in other developing countries, especially in SSA.

4 Regulatory Restructuring in South African Agriculture

Harrison (2019, p. 282) raises a simple but crucial issue: how do we make sense of cases in which economic liberalisation is not paired with social welfare retrenchment? In developing countries such as India, Brazil, and SA, neoliberalising policies were implemented alongside growth in social spending. Local movements for social and economic justice—often rooted in opposition to earlier rounds of restructuring associated with structural adjustment plans—exercise a significant and expanding influence on policy direction and implementation, and the governments in these countries have become increasingly inclined or compelled to pursue aspects of policy against prevailing neoliberal orthodoxy (Saad-Filho and Yalman 2010; Polet 2007). The diversity of neoliberal experiments in SSA, as elsewhere, must therefore be explained in large part in terms of the variety of resistances to neoliberalisation. It is mainly because of social mobilisation that neoliberal policies in SSA have not uniformly disregarded poverty or simply left its amelioration to market forces (Ferguson 2006, 2007). For instance, cash-grant programmes, land redistribution policies, and labour market regulation in SA combine neoliberal and redistributive or pro-poor features.

The regulatory restructuring of agriculture in SA since the 1990s is characterised by what may seem, at first glance, to be a paradox: deregulated product markets cohabiting with (increasingly) regulated labour markets and tenure security for farmworkers. At the risk of oversimplification, SA agriculture has witnessed a shift from regulated product markets and deregulated labour markets under the apartheid regime (1950s to early-1990s) to deregulated product markets and regulated labour markets under the post-apartheid government (1994–) (see Bernstein 1996; Marcus 1989; Mather and Greenberg 2003). The notion of 'regulated deregulation' is suggested by Aalbers (2016) to conceptualise the role of deregulation under neoliberalism, involving the process by which 'some economic agents are given greater freedom from state control, but the market framework itself is regulated' (Aalbers 2016, p. 3). The changes brought on by deregulation tend to privilege corporate and elite interests (Aalbers 2016) as the 'withdrawal' of the state is compensated by agricultural capital's increasing resort to networking and other forms of public-private partnerships to secure its reproductive requirements. In the remainder of the chapter, I briefly outline the deregulation of agricultural product markets and the re-regulation of rural labour markets in post-apartheid SA.

4.1 Restructuring Agricultural Product Markets

SA has limited agricultural potential, a semi-arid climate and produces at a relatively high cost per unit of output compared to many other countries in the world. Agriculture's contribution to SA's Gross Domestic Product (GDP) has declined from 21% in 1911 to about 2.5% in 2017. Total income for the commercial agriculture industry in 2017 was R332.8 billion, compared to R85.9 billion in 2007 (StatsSA 2020). This remarkable growth in output was accompanied by a substantial decline in employment over time. In the 1970s, agriculture employed over two million people, or about a quarter of the employed population, on farms alone. By 2018, 757,628 people were employed on farms, less than 5% of the employed (StatsSA 2020). However, the sector remains vital for employment (10%), exports (6%), and contribution to GDP (20–30%) when the value of backward and forward linkages are included (DAFF 2010, 2019). Despite its relatively small contribution to the SA economy, agriculture has been assigned an important role in employment-intensive growth strategies in terms of generating unskilled and semi-skilled jobs, providing self-employment for small-scale farmers, supporting rural livelihoods, reducing the high rates of rural unemployment, and as a vital earner of foreign exchange (Black et al. 2014).

The period from the 1940s to the early-1980s was characterised by extensive state support to white, large-scale commercial agriculture via controlled input and output prices; single-channel marketing boards; concessionary interest rates and tax relief; drought relief; guaranteed incomes; measures to stabilise prices and restrict imports; subsidies for fuel, rail transport, and fertiliser; and support for extensive irrigation and soil conservation. During the 1980s, according to Vink and Kirsten (2000, p. 31), the state granted direct financial assistance worth R1.73bn and subsidies worth R2.35bn to about 27,000 white farmers. A confluence of factors in the mid-1980s—including heightened internal and external opposition to apartheid, financial liberalisation, and a crisis *of* (rather than *in*) the extant structures of governance (Ashman et al. 2014)—rendered the high cost of continued state support to white agriculture unsustainable financially and damaging politically. Fiscal and political considerations, rather than narrowly economic ones, featured strongly in the apartheid government's first forays into the liberalisation and deregulation of the national food system.

In SA, neoliberalisation has had to engage the vestiges of its own variant of Fordism (racialised, import-substitution industrialisation) and the contested political and ideological rationalities of post-apartheid institutions. When the African National Congress (ANC) assumed political power in 1994, it was confronted by the legacy of a racially-stratified, dualistic agrarian structure: about 60,000 large-scale, commercial farmers (almost all white) owned 86% of agricultural land, whereas small-scale, 'subsistence' farmers (about two million) and 'semi-commercial' smallholders (200,000) were systematically deprived of land ownership, resources, and infrastructure and confined to 14% of agricultural land, mainly in the former Bantustans. In these so-called 'homelands', food production was embedded in (distorted and stultified) pre-colonial forms of communal land tenure. In contrast, on white commercial farms, it was premised on freehold title. In practice, white farmers were incentivised to modernise agriculture through a range of subsidies, grants, concessions, and a captive and cheap workforce. At the same time, food production for rural blacks was limited to small individual allotments administered by chiefs under the supervision of magistrates. Data from the 1997 Rural Survey show that 30% of households engaged in farming activities in the former homelands survived on monthly incomes of R400 or less, including income from remittances, pensions, employment, and other sources (cited in StatsSA and NDA 2000). Agricultural output in these areas has declined from a very low base, with only 2% of households deriving their primary form of income from agriculture and, particularly in the Eastern Cape, increasing amounts of land are underutilised, despite overcrowding, due to outmigration by able-bodied youth, the rising cost of farm inputs, an increase in rural crime and lawlessness, and changing social attitudes (Wilson, cited in Black et al. 2014).

While post-apartheid agricultural policies continued the roll-back of state involvement that commenced under apartheid and opened up market access beyond the requirements of the WTO, land redistribution policies were premised on state action, albeit in the neoliberal guise of 'willing buyer, willing seller' (Lahiff 2007). The blending of deregulatory and re-regulatory impulses is evident in the ANC's Agricultural Policy of 1994:

> The ANC broadly supports the deregulation of agricultural marketing through the removal of most of the remaining statutory powers of the control boards. A less restricted marketing environment will promote greater efficiency and work to the advantage of both commercial and developing sectors ... The removal of statutory controls does not preclude state support for market development, and the state will continue to have a role to play to ensure that broader food security objectives are achieved, and that historically disadvantaged groups are able to participate in agricultural production, processing and trade (http://www.anc.org.za/show.php?id=274).

Soon after the demise of apartheid, agricultural marketing policies were drastically reformed in ways that exposed the sector to the vagaries of international competition. Protective quotas, specific duties, and price controls were phased out and were largely abolished by 1995. The period from the late-1990s onwards was marked by continued deregulation of public controls; mounting integration into agri-food GVCs; increasing resort to labour-saving technologies and the casualisation of employment; declining government contributions to research and development and the 'privatisation' of extension services; an expansion in private regulation (such as privatised cooperatives and standards); shifts out of subsidised field crops (for example, maize) and into high-value fruit, vegetables, and flowers as well as intensive, penned livestock (for instance, poultry); and increasing concentration as struggling white commercial farmers exited the sector and farming units declined from about 60,000 in 1990 to 40,122 in 2017 (Barrientos and Kritzinger 2004; StatsSA 2020). The volume of SA's agricultural exports increased dramatically after apartheid, and the rand value of exports increased from 5% of agricultural production in 1988 to 51% in 2008 (Black et al. 2014). In short, the number of commercial farmers has declined, but the scale of production has increased (Liebenberg and Pardey 2012).

The net effect is that SA agricultural capital went from being highly protected (with a largely unprotected workforce) before 1994 to having levels of support that are currently amongst the lowest in the world (with an increasingly protected workforce). According to the OECD, producer support in SA as a share of gross farm receipts has declined from approximately 15% in 1995 to 2% in 2010 (cited in Black et al. 2014). This decline was much steeper than the average decline in OECD support levels, which remained at about 20% on average. Moreover, in 2008, the shift from low-value basic food crops to high-value export crops made SA a net importer of food in terms of volume for the first time in its history (WWF 2010, pp. 18–19). Except for Australia and New Zealand, SA farmers had the least support for the period 2008–2010, with far less support than agricultural producers in other middle-income countries such as Turkey, China, Mexico, and Russia (Black et al. 2014). Moreover, since expenditure on (redistributive) land reform is included in SA's estimates, government support for agriculture is effectively much lower than shown above.

The neoliberalisation of SA agriculture has intensified competitive pressures, deepened and partially reconfigured pre-existing divisions, and engendered a food system in which the yields from the top 25% of farms account for 75% of produce (Cousins 2012). Crucially, commercial farmers are confronted with rising levels of concentration upstream and downstream in agri-food GVCs: fertiliser production is dominated by four corporations (Sasol, Nitro, Yara, and Omnia and Foskor), four maize millers controlled 73% of the milling market in 2004, 10% of firms controlled 85% of food processing in 2005, and four retail chains controlled 66% of sales in 2006 (Bernstein 2013; Cousins 2012). Growing concentration at the retail node of value chains, in particular, means agricultural producers often have to negotiate trade deals with powerful multinational companies (Maertens et al. 2012). The concentration in retail ownership and market power has generated significant challenges to agricultural producers in the South by exerting cost-cutting and rationalisation pressures down the commodity chain.

These developments not only tilted the policy and regulatory fields decisively towards market-disciplinary regulatory reforms, leading to what Jessop (2014) aptly describes as the tendential 'ecological dominance' of neoliberalism. They also left farmers with few viable alternatives, other than reducing labour costs and intensifying work (discussed in the next section), to alleviate a constricting cost-profit squeeze.

Although there are discernible sub-sectoral dynamics, SA agriculture is increasingly integrated into world markets and the sector exports over a third of its production by volume, which is a significant increase compared to about 20% exported during the sanction years (1980–1994), but not much more than the share of production exported during 1970–1979 (Black et al. 2014). This trend is set to continue: in his 2019 State of the Nation Address, President Ramaphosa indicated that policies geared towards the development of agriculture would focus on export-oriented products. In 2018, SA's agricultural exports grew by 7% to a record level of US$10.6 billion due to increased exports of (among other products) oranges, grapes, wine, maize, apples, wool, lemons, mandarins, and pears (Farmingportal 2019). As a share of world agricultural exports, however, SA exports have been stagnant or declined—in contrast to other middle-income countries such as Brazil, Argentina, Mexico, and Thailand (Sender 2012). According to the Food and Agricultural Organisation (FAO), SA's world share of agricultural trade declined from an average of 0.53% between 1986 and 1994 to an average of 0.50% between 2006 and 2008 (cited in Sender 2016, p. 7).

Imports, by contrast, have increased sharply, partly due to broader structural shifts in the economy associated with de-industrialisation and the absence of a capital-goods sector. As a share of agricultural output, agricultural imports increased from 7% in 1975–1979 to 14% in 1990–1994 and 26% in 2006–2008 (Sandrey et al. 2011, p. 15). Imports in the latter period almost matched exports, while in 1975–1979 they were only 20% of exports (Black et al. 2014). The growing cost of imports contributed to the stagnation of farm income from the late-1980s until the early-2000s when farmers were aided by increasing economies of scale, a depreciating currency, and access to new overseas markets. Unsurprisingly, there has been a decline in investment in fixed improvements, machinery, and equipment. The real value of capital assets on commercial farms has declined nearly every year from 1980 until the early 2000s (Sandrey et al. 2011, p. 12). Neoliberalising regulatory shifts in product markets and the lack of state support to farmers have not only enabled a continuation of 'low-road' (low wages, low skills, cost-orientated, etc.) approaches to competitiveness but also constrained any meaningful shift towards 'high-road' (high wages, high skills, quality-orientated, etc.) approaches. In other words, through its capacity to impose a particular solution on an economic problem, the process of neoliberalisation in agricultural product markets has had a profound effect on the nature of work and employment in the sector, to which I now turn my attention.

4.2 Restructuring Agricultural Labour Markets

Some of the most egregious contemporary forms of social inequality, poverty, exploitation, and oppression are linked to the advent of neoliberalism. Yet, these social divisions and inequities evolve in vastly different institutional and normative landscapes. In contrast to the systematic dismantling of Keynesian-Fordist class comprises in the global North, the ANC government has not officially pursued the 'flexibilization' of labour markets, nor has it actively promoted decentralised collective bargaining, eschewed corporatist forms of interest representation, or undermined job security by diluting protections against dismissals and promoting the use of casual and precarious employment. On the contrary, SA arguably has the most militant trade unions and inclusive/protective labour legislation on the continent. However, since the statutory labour relations framework is premised on voluntarism, employers have no legal compulsion to enter into collective bargaining arrangements with their employees. In practice, this means that terms and conditions of employment in sectors with low trade union density are effectively left to the mercy and whim of employers. Voluntarism has also fuelled the development of a multitude of disparate regimes and conditions at the local level and intensified the polarisation between 'insiders' and 'outsiders' in the labour market as a whole.

By tying collective rights at the workplace to administrative requirements and a numerical threshold, most farmworkers (more than 90%) cannot access these rights in post-apartheid labour legislation because they do not belong to a registered and 'sufficiently representative' trade union. By contrast, workers in urban, formal-sector jobs who belong to majority trade unions can negotiate terms and conditions of employment and exercise various organisational rights in the workplace or sector. These divisions are deeply rooted in SA's history of colonialism, segregation, and apartheid.

The SA agrarian labour market was configured by a set of draconian laws and discriminatory institutional arrangements that offered little to no protection for farmworkers against the arbitrary and unilateral power that farmers exercised under the Master and Servant laws, which were in operation from 1841 to 1974 (Haysom and Thompson 1986; Le Roux 2002). These laws subjected capital-labour relations on the farms to the common law contract of employment, which translated to the absence of any meaningful rights for farmworkers and virtually unlimited power for farmers. The contract doctrine underpins the common law assumes that the employment relationship is characterised by a voluntary and mutually beneficial exchange between equals, which neither requires nor allows third-party intervention. This interpretation of the employment relationship reinforces a fundamental assumption underlying the contract of employment: namely, employees are consenting parties to hierarchy and subordination in the workplace.

While the post-apartheid labour market dispensation promotes fair labour practices and provides employees with numerous protections in the workplace, the voluntarist emphasis on self-regulation introduces a latent deregulation into the system of labour relations for unorganised workers that achieves much of the same outcomes as an explicit pursuit of labour market deregulation or flexibilization. For example, in the absence of trade unions and—by extension—of collective bargaining, workers in the export-orientated horticultural sub-sectors are unable to exercise any meaningful control over Taylorist work processes (built on piece-rate wage systems and close supervision) or mount any significant or lasting challenge to managers' authoritarian and paternalistic approaches to workplace relations (Bolt 2016, 2017). As the Labour Market Commission (1996, p. 16) observed, wage levels in agriculture are 'frequently determined by the power imbalance between farmers and farm workers, and not only by issues such as affordability'. Recognising the lack of bargaining power among workers in agricultural value chains, a study of farm-workers' living and working conditions, commissioned by the International Labour Organisation (ILO), recommends changes to SA's labour legislation (to allow non-unionised workers to bargain collectively and take part in protected strikes) as well as closer cooperation between the Department of Labour and ethical trade bodies (Visser and Ferrer 2015, p. 8).

An analysis of data from the 1996 Population Census reveals the following features of work and employment in SA agriculture at the dawn of the post-apartheid era:

- With 37% of employees aged between 15 and 29 years, the agricultural labour force is more youthful than that in any other sector of the economy.
- At 32%, the employed labour force in agriculture with no schooling was the highest of all the major economic sectors.
- At 19%, the proportion of women employed part-time in agriculture was the highest of all the sectors (compared with only 6% of men).
- Elementary work and skilled agricultural work dominated job opportunities in agriculture. Only in private households was the proportion of elementary workers (90%) higher than in agriculture (58%). Only 3% of those employed in the agricultural sector fell into the highest occupation category (managers and professionals), compared with 41% in the finance and 56% in the community and social services sectors.
- There were gross inequities in income distribution for people employed in agriculture than those employed in other sectors. Almost 70% of employees in agriculture had monthly incomes of R500 or less, compared with 22% among all other employees. By contrast with the agricultural sector, the proportion of employed people in the lowest income bracket (R0-R500) ranged from 8% in mining and finance to 11% in transport, 15% in manufacturing, 22% in trade, 23% in construction, and 64% in domestic work.
- There were also gross inequities in the intra-sectoral distribution of income: 79% of black Africans employed in agriculture had monthly incomes of R500 or less, while the corresponding figures were 67% for coloureds, 18% for Indians, and 10% for whites. Among whites employed in the sector, 46% had monthly incomes of R3501 or more. The annual commercial agricultural surveys show that, although the remuneration received by black Africans had increased steadily since 1994, by 1996, their wages were still only 12% of that received by white

employees. In 1996, the average monthly remuneration for whites was R4613, falling to R1608 for Indians, R676 for coloureds, and less than R535 for black Africans (cited in StatsSA and NDA 2000). Incidentally, these incomes do not include payment in kind, which was a widespread practice on commercial farms until proscribed by labour legislation in the late-1990s.

In contrast to most countries in SSA, where agriculture accounts for at least half of all employment, only 4.9% of employees in South Africa were employed in the agricultural sector in 2020 (StatsSA 2021). While estimates of aggregate employment in agriculture vary, especially with regard to small-scale agriculture, employment in the commercial farming sector is generally considered as having been on a downward trajectory for some time, primarily as a result of shifts in the structure of SA's economy and farms becoming larger and more mechanised and corporatised. The total number of farmworkers declined from 1.6 million in 1971 to 628,000 in 2005. Given the population increase over that time, agriculture's contribution to employment dropped from 8.3% to 1.3% in relative terms (WWF 2010, p. 23). Employment on commercial farms declined by 25.1% (from 1.2 million to 914,000) during the period of intense regulatory restructuring from 1988 to 1996. Nevertheless, employment in the agriculture sector in the late-1990s represented 30% of all employment for black Africans in rural SA (excluding self-employment), by far the largest single employment category for this population group (StatsSA and NDA 2000). Although agriculture formally employed 638,000 people in 2012 (StatsSA 2012), it was estimated that around 8.5-million people were directly or indirectly dependent on agriculture for their employment and income. Visser and Ferrer (2015) estimate that there are close to 600,000 households with over two million people living on farms in SA.

The decline in the number of full-time jobs was accompanied, although not matched, by the proliferation of non-standard jobs (for instance, casual, seasonal, temporary, and part-time). At 304,000, non-standard employment constituted a significant proportion of the agricultural workforce in 1996 (StatsSA and NDA 2000) and continues to account for almost half of the agricultural workforce. Since the 1990s, the division between standard (full-time, permanent) and non-standard employment has been reworked—as some farmers increasingly resort to casual and seasonal employment as well as to the use of labour brokers and undocumented migrants—and this has left the farmworkers and their households more vulnerable and precarious (Bhorat et al. 2014; Devereux 2019; Patel et al. 2020). As in most other sectors of the SA economy, the workforce in commercial agriculture is broadly characterised by a small 'core' of (mostly white) skilled and supervisory employees and a large 'periphery' of (mostly black) semi- and unskilled workers. Employees in the lower echelons of the labour market have borne the brunt of agricultural capital's efforts at 'right-sizing' the workforce through retrenchments, evictions, reduced working hours, and the casualisation or externalisation of employment. As testimony to these changes, the above-mentioned ILO study recommends adapting existing labour legislation to 'the fact that most workers are now seasonal' (Visser and Ferrer

2015, p. 8). The study also observes a shift in labour-capital relations, which it attributes to changes in the regulatory environment of the sector after 1994:

> Feudal relationships between farmers and farm workers are increasingly breaking down through movement off farms . . . and a shift away from the use of permanent workers towards the use of indirect labour and short-term employment contracts (Visser and Ferrer 2015, p. 1).

As noted above, in a reversal of trends, the liberalisation of agricultural product markets was accompanied by stronger protections in the labour market and greater tenure security for farmworkers and dwellers. In the 1990s, farmworkers were covered by a suite of labour laws—such as the Labour Relations Act, the Basic Conditions of Employment Act, the Occupational Health and Safety Act, and the Unemployment Insurance Act—for the first time in SA's history. This statutory framework governs, among others, collective bargaining, working hours, leave entitlements, dismissals, organisational rights, industrial action, workplace health and safety, and unemployment benefits. SA's commercial farmers are mostly price-takers in agri-food GVCs, compete against countries that offer greater support for their agriculture sectors, while having to comply with new tenure and labour laws that ramp up production costs. The confluence of these economic pressures has generated a cost-profit squeeze on most commercial farms. Since capital and inter-mediary costs are largely beyond farmers' control, labour costs constitute a vital target for cost-cutting rationalisation. Unsurprisingly, farmworker wages have become a politicised and contested terrain (Devereux 2019; Lekunze et al. 2016). In an explicit recognition that market forces have pushed wages in sectors like agriculture to (socially and politically) unacceptably low levels, the ANC government introduced minimum wages in various sectors of the economy, like agriculture, which were characterised by the absence of collective bargaining.

As part of establishing an agricultural minimum wage, the Department of Labour commissioned a study on employment conditions in the sector in 2000. The study underscored the historical trend of low wages in agriculture combined with considerable wage differentials across the sector. Specifically, the Department of Labour (2001a) found that the average monthly wage in the sector was only R544. Payment in kind was significant, constituting a quarter of agricultural wages. Female workers earned lower wages and had fewer benefits compared to their male counterparts. Extended working hours (often above the legal limits) without compensation was recorded among 54% of workers in the study, while 27% of workers did not receive any annual leave. In addition, farm workers recorded the lowest literacy rates in SA, and 33% of workers did not have any formal education. The Department of Labour (2001a, b) also points to the difficulties farmworkers and their families experience accessing basic resources for social reproduction—housing, water, electricity, medical care, sufficient nutritious food, etc.

In 2003, Sectoral Determination No. 8 introduced the first statutory wage for the agricultural sector, which initially followed a two-tiered system that differentiated between 'urban' areas categorised as Area A and 'rural' areas as Area B. The statutory wage shifted from a two-tier system to a single system in 2008, which lasted until 1 January 2019, when the National Minimum Wage Act came into effect, setting a wage floor of R3500 per month (DoL 2003–2020). However, since policymakers anticipated difficulties in compliance and greater proneness to job losses—relative to other categories of low-waged workers—farmworkers were initially only entitled to 90% of the national minimum wage. In 2021, they qualified for the total prescribed rate of R192.21 per working day (of nine hours).

The introduction of a national minimum wage can improve the position of workers in the low-wage sectors of the economy. Of these, agriculture and domestic work are the only sectors where more than 50% of workers earned below R3000 per month (Isaacs 2016, p. 16). Isaacs (2016) estimates that 50% of farm workers earned below the median monthly wage of R2253 per month, which made them particularly vulnerable to poverty. A minimum wage of R3000 would cover 82% of workers in the agriculture sector. Increasing it to R5000 would raise the coverage to 92%, whereas the same wage in the mining sector would only bind 35% of workers (Isaacs 2016, p. 16).

Far from being corrosive of the neoliberal project or signalling its demise, statutory wage determination is a crucial flanking mechanism designed to ameliorate some of the negative externalities associated with market-disciplinary regulatory restructuring in product markets. However, given the low rate of minimum wages and the extensive opportunities for 'fiddles' and non-compliance by employers, statutory wages on their own cannot possibly offset the numerous and destructive social consequences of neoliberalisation.

Commercial farmers' responses to the minimum wage reveal both the underlying dynamics in the workplace regime and the broader strategic selectivities (which advance particular interests while obstructing or excluding others) stemming from the ecological dominance of neoliberalisation. A key response by employers to minimum wages has been non-compliance or partial compliance with the law: Bhorat et al. (2014) estimate that upwards of 50% of farmers paid below the prevailing minimum wage rate. Yet, the dispute that led to the 2012 farmworker protests in De Doorns—which precipitated a substantial rise in the statutory minimum wage in 2013—was not due to non-compliance but rather a reaction to a legislated wage that was considered to be 'too low'. While the introduction of a minimum wage in agriculture has engendered an increase in average remuneration (especially for skilled workers), most farmworkers' wages remained very low compared to other sectors, and higher labour costs prompted a decline in employment that disproportionately affected unskilled farmworkers (Isaacs 2016; Piek and von Fintel 2020). There is a persistent dilemma in SA agriculture: on the one hand, many farmers cannot afford the minimum daily wage; on the other, most households (consisting of two adults and two children) cannot prepare meals that are of acceptable nutritional standards, even if both parents earn the minimum daily wage (Visser and Ferrer 2015, p. 7).

Farmers anticipated the minimum wage legislation and increasingly resorted to labour-saving technologies, tighter controls over productivity, labour brokers and casualisation, retrenchments, evictions, and other cost-cutting initiatives (Sihlobo 2018; Simbi and Aliber 2000; Sparrow et al. 2008). However, as Piek and von Fintel

(2020) show, minimum wages have had a differentiated impact on workers, depending on their skill level, nature of employment, and the size of the farming enterprise. Small farms are more vulnerable to employment losses due to increased wages since they do not have access to large markets and cannot afford to invest in capital equipment or hire more skilled workers. In large part, small farms struggle to absorb higher wage costs because they cannot transfer these costs to consumers. The primary response to minimum wages for small farms tends to be job shedding, while large capital-intensive farms continue to absorb unskilled workers (Piek and von Fintel 2020).

However, on both small and large farms, there has been a marked shift away from the employment of full-time, permanent labour (Patel et al. 2020; Sihlobo 2018). Non-standard workers constitute a growing (peripheral) workforce, whose chances of re-employment are tied closely to the manager's perception of their work ethic and level of subservience, and who must endure little to no job security, few prospects of promotion and training, terms and conditions of employment that fall short of the ILO's 'decent work' agenda, and arbitrary and capricious managerial decisions. In reference to the findings of a survey among semi- and unskilled farmworkers in the Eastern Cape, Naidoo et al. (2007) observe that the absence of unions and collective bargaining, combined with authoritarian management styles and an increasing bifurcation of the workforce, allowed farmers to offset some of the increases in wage costs through a process of work intensification, 'flexible' employment policies, selective compliance with labour legislation, reductions in working hours and non-wage or fringe benefits, and increased deductions for rent and amenities such as water and electricity.

5 Conclusion

Changes in the governance structures of the food system in SA, as elsewhere, are both distinctive and intimately connected to broader geo-historical regulatory transformations. The constitutively incomplete, variegated, non-linear, multi-directional, poly-centric, and contested course of actually existing neoliberalisms contrasts sharply with the notion of neoliberalism as the process of enacting a singular, grand design of market rule. Neoliberalisation has profound implications for the production of wealth, poverty, and inequality and has to be continuously (re)made. Therefore, successive rounds of market-conforming and market-constraining regulatory restructuring are shaped by the conflicts, failures, and contradictions associated with previous iterations of this 'layering' process. Aberrantly, programmes of neoliberal restructuring often 'fail forward' and typically "progress' through a roiling dynamic of experimentation, overreach, and crisis-driven adjustment' (Peck et al. 2009, pp. 105–106). The notion of variegated neoliberalisation allows us to move the debate beyond the impasse in which claims of hegemonic integrity and inexorable convergence and counterclaims of contingent frailty and unpatterned heterogeneity threaten to become mutually negating. Instead of focusing on its retreat or advance, we should explore 'concrete questions about the rise and fall of specific [neoliberal] projects in particular places' (Kingfisher and Maskovsky 2008, p. 123) and then draw cross-case comparisons.

As an open-ended, contradictory, and multi-scalar process of market-disciplinary regulatory restructuring, which must articulate in hybrid and varied ways with prevailing social forces and structures, it is misleading to characterise neoliberalism as a taxonomic state 'form', a definitive historical era, or phase of capitalism. As a set of entangled and emergent processes, neoliberalisation evolves by acting on and through state and institutional forms while articulating with geo-historical and institutional conditions and the evolution of crisis tendencies, both of accumulation and regulation (Peck et al. 2012a, p. 19). Hence, it is unlikely that neoliberalism's regulatory architecture will collapse, *in toto*, simply because neoliberalism was never a monolithic structure in the first place (Peck et al. 2009). To a greater extent than most commentators have predicted:

> Neoliberalism has demonstrated an ability to absorb or displace crisis tendencies, to ride – and capitalise upon – the very economic cycles and localised policy failures that it was complicit in creating, and to erode the foundations upon which generalised or extra-local resistance might be constructed. The transformative potential – and consequent political durability – of neoliberalism has been repeatedly underestimated, and reports of its death correspondingly exaggerated (Peck and Tickell 2002, p. 400).

The hybrid combination of market-disciplinary strategies in SA's agricultural product markets and market-constraining strategies in the labour market does not diminish the neoliberalised and neoliberalising character of regulatory restructuring that has unfolded over the last three decades. The notion of a linear, sequential transition from 'regulation' to 'deregulation' in SA agriculture—which underpins much of the literature on the topic and assumes that these are distinct, self-contained modes of economic governance that change in zero-sum ways—obscures more than it reveals (see, for example, Greyling et al. 2015; Van Zyl et al. 2001; Vink and Kirsten 2000). By contrast, an emphasis on the path-shaping and path-dependent character of neoliberal reform projects as a process of creative destruction—involving uneven waves of commodification, de-commodification, and re-commodification—provides more fertile ground for theoretical, methodological, and empirical advance. Such emphasis exposes the various complexities, contradictions, disjunctures, and unintended consequences of neoliberalism; emphasises its articulation with other modes of governance; and underscores its fault lines and problems of legitimation. The conception of neoliberalisation as a geographically-differentiated and historically-evolving, patterned and patterning process (Brenner et al. 2010) also highlights the non-attainability of the neoliberal utopia of absolute (individual) freedoms, which not only means that the neoliberal project is 'always incomplete, always frustrated, always impure' but also that—irrespective of the extent of its ideational, ideological, or institutional dominance—neoliberalism 'always exists amongst its others, usually antagonistically' (Peck 2013, p. 139). Since it always exists in such (uneasy and messy) hybrid formations, neoliberalism's work is never complete and cannot ever be completed.

References

Aalbers MB (2016) Regulated deregulation. In: Springer S, Birch K, MacLeavy J (eds) Handbook of neoliberalism. Routledge, New York, pp 563–573
Ahmed G, Hamrick D, Gereffi G (2014) Shifting governance structures in the wheat value chain: implications for food security in the Middle East and North Africa. Duke University, Center on Globalization, Governance and Competitiveness, Durham, NC
Anderson P (2000) Renewals. New Left Rev 2(1):5–24
Ashman S, Fine B, Padayachee V, Sender J (2014) The political economy of restructuring in South Africa. In: Bhorat H, Hirsch A, Kanbur R, Ncube M (eds) The Oxford companion to the economics of South Africa. Oxford University Press, Oxford, pp 67–74
Bain C, Ransom E, Higgins V (2013) Private agri-food standards: contestation, hybridity and the politics of standards. Int J Sociol Agric Food 20(1):1–10
Bair J (2009) Global commodity chains. In: Bair J (ed) Frontiers of commodity chain research. Stanford University Press, Stanford, pp 1–34
Bair J (2013) Dis/articulating producers, markets, and regions: new directions in critical studies of commodity chains. Environ Plan A 45:2544–2552
Bair J, Werner M (2011) Commodity chains and the uneven geographies of global capitalism: a disarticulations perspective. Environ Plan A 43:988–997
Barnett C (2005) The consolations of "neoliberalism". Geoforum 36(1):7–12
Barrientos S, Kritzinger A (2004) Squaring the circle – global production and the informalisation of work in South African fruit exports. J Int Dev 16(1):81–92
Bernstein H (1996) How white agriculture (re)positioned itself for a 'new' South Africa. Crit Sociol 22(3):9–36
Bernstein H (2013) Commercial agriculture in South Africa since 1994: "Natural, simply capitalism". J Agrar Chang 13(1):23–46
Bhorat H, Kanbur R, Stanwix B (2014) Estimating the impact of minimum wages on employment, wages, and non-wage benefits: the case of agriculture in South Africa. Am J Agric Econ 96(5):1402–1419
Biénabe E, Boselie D, Collion M, Fox T, Rondot P, van de Kop P, Vorley B (2007) The internationalization of food retailing: Opportunities and threats for small-scale producers. In: Vorley B, Fearne A, Ray D (eds) Regoverning markets: a place for small-scale producers in modern agrifood chains? Gower Publishing, Aldershot, pp 3–18
Black A, Conradie B, Gerwel H (2014) Should agriculture receive greater support as part of an inclusive growth strategy?, 26 November, Econ 3x3, Available at: http://www.econ3x3.org/article/should-agriculture-receive-greater-support-part-inclusive-growth-strategy
Bolt M (2016) Accidental neoliberalism and the performance of management: hierarchies in export agriculture on the Zimbabwean-South African border. J Dev Stud 52(4):561–575
Bolt M (2017) Becoming and unbecoming farm workers in Southern Africa. Anthropol South Afr 40(4):241–247
Bourdieu P (2008) Acts of resistance: against the tyranny of the market. Free Press, New York
Brenner N, Theodore N (2002) Cities and the geographies of "actually existing neoliberalism". Antipode 34(3):349–379
Brenner N, Theodore N (2005) Neoliberalism and the urban condition. City 9(1):101–107
Brenner N, Peck J, Theodore N (2010) Variegated neoliberalization: geographies, modalities, pathways. Glob Netw 10(2):182–222
Burch D, Lawrence G (eds) (2007) Supermarkets and agri-food supply chains: transformations in the production and consumption of foods. Edward Elgar, Cheltenham
Cahill D (2009) Is neoliberalism history? Soc Altern 28(1):12–16
Campbell H (2005) The rise and rise of EurepGAP: European (re)invention of colonial food relations? Int J Sociol Agric Food 13:1–19
Chalfin B (2010) Neoliberal frontiers: an ethnography of sovereignty in West Africa. University of Chicago Press, Chicago

Chitundu M, Droppelmann K, Haggblade S (2009) Intervening in value chains: lessons from Zambia's task force on acceleration of Cassava utilisation. J Dev Stud 45(4):593–620
Clapp J, Fuchs D (eds) (2009) Corporate power in global agrifood governance. The MIT Press, Cambridge
Clarke J (2008) Living with/in and without neo-liberalism. Eur J Anthropol 51:135–147
Cousins B (2012) Agricultural policy and the right to food in South Africa. Available at: https://serfindex.uconn.edu/wp-content/uploads/sites/1843/2016/08/Cousins-Agricultural-policy-and-the-right_-to-food-in-SA-UCT-May-2012-1.pdf
De Raymond AB, Bonnaud L (2014) Beyond the public–private divide: GlobalGAP as a regulation repository for farmers. Int J Sociol Agric Food 21(2):227–246
Department of Agriculture, Forestry and Fisheries (DAFF) (2010) Estimate of the contribution of the agriculture sector to employment in the South African economy. DAFF, Pretoria
Department of Agriculture, Forestry and Fisheries (DAFF) (2019) Economic review of South African agriculture: 2018/9. DAFF, Pretoria
Department of Labour (DoL) (2001a) Investigation into minimum wages and working conditions for the agricultural sector: briefing notes:13th September 2001. DoL, Pretoria
Department of Labour (DoL) (2001b) Recommendations of employment conditions commission on a determination for the agricultural sector. DoL, Pretoria
Department of Labour (DoL) (2003–2020) Annual sectoral determination. DoL, Pretoria
Devereux S (2019) Violations of farm workers' labour rights in post-apartheid South Africa. Development Southern Africa, Available at: https://repository.uwc.ac.za/bitstream/handle/10566/5177/Violations-of-farm-workers-labour-rights-in-postapartheid-South-Africa2019Development-Southern-Africa.pdf?sequence=1&isAllowed=y
Dolan C, Humphrey J (2000) Governance and trade in fresh vegetables: the impact of UK supermarkets on the African horticultural industry. J Dev Stud 37(2):147–176
Dolan C, Humphrey J (2004) Changing governance patterns in the trade in fresh vegetables between Africa and the United Kingdom. Environ Plan A 36(3):491–509
Duménil G, Lévy D (2004) Capital resurgent: roots of the neoliberal revolution. Harvard University Press, Cambridge, MA
Farmingportal (2019) South Africa's agricultural exports grew by 7% y/y in 2018. Available at: https://www.farmingportal.co.za/index.php/all-agri-news/news-of-the-day/1571-south-africa-s-agricultural-exports-grew-by-7-y-y-in-2018#:~:text=In%20more%20detail,%20Africa%20remained%20South%20Africa's%20largest,exports,%20demanding%20a%2025%%20export%20share%20in%202018
Ferguson J (2006) Global shadows: Africa in the neoliberal world order. Duke University Press, Durham & London
Ferguson J (2007) Formalities of poverty: THINKING about social assistance in neoliberal South Africa. Afr Stud Rev 50(2):71–86
Food and Agriculture Organisation Statistics (FAOstat). Available at: www.fao.org/faostat
Freidberg S (2003) Cleaning up down South: supermarkets, ethical trade and African horticulture. Soc Cult Geogr 4(1):27–43
Fuchs D, Kalfagianni A, Arentsen M (2009) Retail power, private standards, and sustainability in the global food system. In: Clapp J, Fuchs D (eds) Corporate power in global agrifood governance. The MIT Press, Cambridge, pp 29–59
Fuchs D, Kalfagianni A, Clapp J, Busch L (2011) Introduction to symposium on private agrifood governance: values, shortcomings and strategies. Agric Hum Values 28:335–344
Fukase E, Martin W (2018) Agro-processing and horticultural exports from Africa. In: Newfarmer RS, Page J, Tarp F (eds) Industries without smokestacks: industrialization in Africa reconsidered. Oxford University Press, Oxford, pp 90–112
Gereffi G, Humphrey J, Sturgeon T (2005) The governance of global value chains. Rev Int Econ 12(1):78–104
Glauber JW (2020) *The current state of agricultural trade and the World Trade Organization*. Statement of Senior Research Fellow, International Food Policy Research Institute before the

Senate Finance Committee, 29 July. Available at: https://www.ifpri.org/news-release/current-state-agricultural-trade-and-world-trade-organization
Graefe P (2006) Social economy policies as flanking for neoliberalism: transnational policy solutions, emergent contradictions, local alternatives. Polic Soc 25(3):69–86
Greyling JC, Vink N, Mabaya E (2015) South Africa's agricultural sector twenty years after democracy (1994 to 2013). Prof Agric Work J 3(1):1–14
Harrison G (2010) Neoliberal Africa: the impact of global social engineering. Zed Books, London
Harrison G (2019) Authoritarian neoliberalism and capitalist transformation in Africa: all pain, no gain. Globalizations 16(3):274–288
Harvey D (2005) A brief history of neoliberalism. Oxford University Press, Oxford
Harvey D (2007) Neo-liberalism as creative destruction. Ann Am Acad Polit Soc Sci 610(1):21–44
Haysom N, Thompson C (1986) Labouring under the law: South Africa's farmworkers. Ind Law J 7(2):218–240
Hilgers M (2012) The historicity of the neoliberal state. Soc Anthropol 20(1):80–94
Humphrey J (2006) Policy implications of trends in agribusiness value chains. Eur J Dev Res 18(4):572–592
Humphrey J, Schmitz H (2001) Governance in global value chains. IDS Bull 32(3):1–16
Isaacs G (2016) A national minimum wage for South Africa. National Minimum Wage Research Initiative, Summary Report No. 1. University of the Witwatersrand, Johannesburg
Isakson SR (2014) Food and finance: the financial transformation of agro-food supply chains. J Peasant Stud 41(5):749–775
Jessop B (2013) Putting neoliberalism in its time and place: a response to the debate. Soc Anthropol 21(1):65–74
Jessop B (2014) Capitalist diversity and variety: variegation, the world market, compossibility and ecological dominance. Capital Class 38(1):45–58
Jessop B (2015) The course, contradictions, and consequences of extending competition as a mode of (meta-)governance: towards a sociology of competition and its limits. Distinktion J Soc Theory 16(2):167–185

Kingfisher C, Maskovsky J (2008) The limits of neo-liberalism. Crit Anthropol 28(2):115–126
Konings P (2011) The politics of neoliberal reforms in Africa: state and civil society in Cameroon. Langaa and African Studies Centre, Bamenda and Leiden
Labour Market Commission (1996) Restructuring the South African labour market. Department of Labour, Pretoria
Lahiff E (2007) Willing buyer, willing seller: South Africa's failed experiment in market-led agrarian reform. Third World Q 28(8):1577–1597
Le Roux R (2002) Agricultural workers: a historical and contemporary perspective. Development and Labour Monograph 1/2002. Institute of Development and Labour Law, University of Cape Town, Cape Town
Leitner H, Peck J, Sheppard ES (2007) Squaring up to neoliberalism. In: Leitner H, Peck J, Sheppard ES (eds) Contesting neoliberalism: Urban frontiers. The Guildford Press, New York, pp 311–328
Lekunze JN, Luvhengo U, Shoko RR (2016) Structural analysis of minimum wage rates, unemployment and food prices of farm workers in South Africa: Co-integration approach. J Agribus Rural Dev 4(42):577–590
Liebenberg F, Pardey PG (2012) A long-run view of South African agricultural production and productivity. Afr J Agric Resour Econ 7(1):14–38
Loïc W (2012) Three steps to a historical anthropology of actually existing neoliberalism. Soc Anthropol 20(1):66–79. https://doi.org/10.1111/j.1469-8676.2011.00189.x
Maertens M, Minten B, Swinnen J (2012) Modern food supply chains and development: evidence from horticulture export sectors in Sub-Saharan Africa. Dev Policy Rev 30(4):473–497
Marcus T (1989) Modernizing super-exploitation: restructuring South African agriculture. Zed Books, London

Martin P (2007) Mexico's neoliberal transition: authoritarian shadows in an era of neoliberalism. In: Leitner H, Peck J, Sheppard ES (eds) Contesting neoliberalism: urban frontiers. The Guilford Press, New York & London, pp 51–70
Mather C, Greenberg S (2003) 'Market liberalisation in post-apartheid South Africa: the restructuring of citrus exports after "deregulation". J South Afr Stud 29(2):393–412
McMichael P (2009) A food regime genealogy. J Peasant Stud 36(1):139–169
Mirowski P, Plehwe D (eds) (2009) The road from Mont Pèlerin: the making of the neoliberal thought collective. Harvard University Press, Cambridge
Naidoo L, Klerck G, Manganeng L (2007) The 'bite' of minimum wages: Enforcement of and compliance with the sectoral determination for farm workers. South Afr J Labour Relat 31(1):25–46
OECD-FAO (2020) Agricultural Outlook: 2020–2029. Available at: https://www.oecd-ilibrary.org/agriculture-and-food/oecd-fao-agricultural-outlook-2016_agr_outlook-2016-en
Patel L, Mthembu S, Graham L (2020) The national minimum wage in the agriculture and domestic work sectors: report of a qualitative study of stakeholder responses to the national minimum wage. Centre for Social Development in Africa, University of Johannesburg, Johannesburg
Peck J (2001) Neoliberalizing states: thin policies/hard outcomes. Prog Hum Geogr 25(3):445–455
Peck J (2008) Remaking laissez-faire. Prog Hum Geogr 32(1):3–43
Peck J (2010) Constructions of neoliberal reasoning. Oxford University Press, Oxford
Peck J, Tickell A (2002) Neoliberalizing space. Antipode 34(3):380–404
Peck J (2004) Geography and public policy: constructions of neoliberalism. Prog Hum Geogr 28 (3):392–405. https://doi.org/10.1191/0309132504ph492pr
Peck J, Tickell A (2007) Conceptualizing neoliberalism, thinking Thatcherism. In: Leitner H, Peck J, Sheppard E (eds) Contesting neoliberalism: urban frontiers. Guildford Press, pp 26–50
Peck J, Theodore N (2012) Reanimating neoliberalism: process geographies of neoliberalisation. Soc Anthropol 20(2):177–185. https://doi.org/10.1111/j.1469-8676.2012.00194.x
Peck J (2013) Explaining (with) neoliberalism. Territory Polit Gov 1(2):132–157. https://doi.org/10.1080/21622671.2013.785365
Peck J, Theodore N, Brenner N (2009) Postneoliberalism and its malcontents. Antipode 41(1):94–116
Peck J, Theodore N, Brenner N (2012a) Neoliberalism, interrupted. In: Cahill D, Edwards L, Stilwell F (eds) Neoliberalism: beyond the free market. Edward Elgar, Cheltenham, pp 15–30
Peck J, Theodore N, Brenner N (2012b) Neoliberalism resurgent? Market rule after the great recession. South Atlantic Q 111(2):265–288
Piek M, von Fintel D (2020) Sectoral minimum wages in South Africa: disemployment by firm size and trade exposure. Dev South Afr 37(3):462–482
Polet F (ed) (2007) The state of resistance: popular struggles in the global south. Zed Books, London
Reardon T, Hopkins R (2006) The supermarket revolution in developing countries: policies to address emerging tensions among supermarkets, suppliers and traditional retailers. Eur J Dev Res 18(4):522–545
Reardon T, Barrett CB, Berdegué JA, Swinnen JFM (2009) Agrifood industry transformation and small farmers in developing countries. World Dev 37(11):1717–1727
Saad-Filho A, Johnston D (eds) (2005) Neoliberalism: a critical reader. Pluto Press, London
Saad-Filho A, Yalman GL (eds) (2010) Economic transitions to neoliberalism in middle-income countries: policy dilemmas, economic crises, forms of resistance. Routledge, London
Sandbrook R (2011) Polanyi and post-neoliberalism in the global South: Dilemmas of re-embedding the economy. New Polit Econ 16(4):415–443
Sandrey J, Punt C, Grinsted H, Vink N (2011) Agricultural Trade and Employment in South Africa. OECD Trade Policy Working Paper 130. OECD, Paris. Available at: https://www.oecd-ilibrary.org/trade/agricultural-trade-and-employment-in-south-africa_5kg3nh58nvq1-en
Sender J (2012) Fictions and elephants in the rondawel: a response to a brief chapter in South Africa's national development plan. Transf Crit Persp South Afr 78:98–114
Sender J (2016) Backward capitalism in rural South Africa: prospects for accelerating accumulation in the Eastern Cape. J Agrar Chang 16(1):3–31

Sihlobo W (2018) Growth and jobs in South Africa's agricultural sector. Agricultural Business Chamber, Paarl. Available at: https://agbiz.co.za/uploads/AgbizNews18/181116_WC%20info%20session%20Wandile%20Sihlobo.pdf

Simbi T, Aliber M (2000) Agricultural employment crisis in South Africa. TIPS Working Paper 13_2000. Trade and Industrial Policy Secretariat, Pretoria. Available: http://www.tips.org.za/files/415.pdf

Sparrow G, Ortmann GF, Lyne MC, Darroch MA (2008) Determinants of the demand for regular farm labour in South Africa, 1960–2002. Agrekon 47(1):52–75

Springer S, MacLeavy J, Birch K (eds) (2016) Handbook of neoliberalism. Routledge, London

Statistics South Africa (StatsSA) (2012) Quarterly labour force survey: 2012. StatsSA, Pretoria

Statistics South Africa (StatsSA) (2020) Census of commercial agriculture, 2017: financial and production statistics. StatsSA, Pretoria

Statistics South Africa (StatsSA) (2021) Quarterly labour force survey: quarter 4: 2020. StatsSA, Pretoria

Statistics South Africa (StatsSA) & National Department of Agriculture (NDA) (2000) Employment trends in agriculture in South Africa. StatsSA & NDA, Pretoria

Swinnen JFM, Maertens M (2007) Globalization, privatization, and vertical coordination in food value chains in developing and transition countries. Agric Econ 37(1):89–102

Talbot JM (1996) Regulating the coffee commodity chain: internationalization and the coffee cartel. Berkeley J Sociol 40:113–149

Temu AE, Marwa NW (2007) Changes in the governance of global value chains of fresh fruits and vegetables: opportunities and challenges for producers in Sub-Saharan Africa. South Centre, Geneva. Available at: http://www.southcentre.int/research-paper-12-june-2007/

Tickell A, Peck J (2003) Making global rules: globalisation or neoliberalisation. In: Peck J, Yeung H (eds) Remaking the global economy. SAGE Publications, pp 163–182

Van Zyl J, Vink N, Kirsten J, Poonyth D (2001) South African agriculture in transition: the 1990s. J Int Dev 13:725–739

Vink N, Kirsten J (2000) Deregulation of agricultural marketing in South Africa: lessons learned. FMF Monograph No. 25. The Free Market Foundation, Sandton

Visser M, Ferrer S (2015) Farm workers' living and working conditions in South Africa: key trends, emergent issues, and underlying and structural problems. International Labour Organisation, Pretoria. Available at: https://www.ilo.org/wcmsp5/groups/public/%2D%2D-africa/documents/publication/wcms_ 385959.pdf

Weatherspoon DD, Reardon T (2003) The rise of supermarkets in Africa: implications for agri-food systems and the rural poor. Dev Policy Rev 21(3):333–355

World Wildlife Fund (WWF) (2010) Agriculture: Facts & Trends: South Africa. Available at: http://awsassets.wwf.org.za/downloads/facts_brochure_mockup_04_b.pdf

Part II
Land Reform Struggles in a Neoliberal Era

Land for Development? Neoliberal Restructuring and the Dynamics of Land Reforms in Uganda

Adventino Banjwa

Abstract The idea and relevance of Compulsory Land Acquisition are central to the claims of many modern states world over. But how should we think of this practice in a post-colonial neoliberal context? This is the question at the heart of the theoretical criticisms and debates regarding Uganda's Compulsory Land Acquisition Programme. In this debate, the government claims, and affirms, that a law on Compulsory Land Acquisition is needed because the government requires 'land for development'. This chapter intervenes in the debate by raising the question of the form of state prevailing in Uganda today and the nature of 'development' it pursues. The chapter critically reviews some past cases of Compulsory Land Acquisition in Uganda in the post-1980 period. These cases demonstrate how in practice, the consolidation of neoliberalism requires an interventionist state, one that can, for instance, use its coercive instruments to avail land for capitalist development in agriculture. If Uganda's 'land for development' drive has resulted in a coupling of a regime of state-led forced land acquisition (more broadly, 'state-driven development') with neoliberalism, I argue that we need therefore to decouple them analytically to allow for a historically and contextually informed query on the implications of land reforms in a post-colonial neoliberal context.

1 Introduction

In the early 1960s, Frantz Fanon argued that '[f]or a colonised people, the most essential value, because the most concrete, is first and foremost the land: land which will bring them bread and, above all, dignity' (Fanon et al. 1963, p. 44). These words have never lost credence in Africa, a continent that is still dominated by people whose existence is premised on subsistence activities based on land. Reflecting on peasants' anti-colonial struggles, Fanon insisted that the peasants' approach to the colonial question, of giving primacy to land and food questions, 'may seem

A. Banjwa (✉)
Makerere Institute for Social Research (MISR), Makerere University, Kampala, Uganda

F. Mazwi et al. (eds.), *Capital Penetration and the Peasantry in Southern and Eastern Africa*, Advances in African Economic, Social and Political Development, https://doi.org/10.1007/978-3-030-89824-3_3

shrunken and limited, [but it] is, in the end, the most worthwhile and the most efficient mode of procedure' (1963: 50). No late colonial context can disprove Fanon's cogent observations, for late colonial political modernity was first and foremost a project propelled not just plainly by flagrant land dispossession but, most importantly, by the redefinition of social relations based on land (Mamdani 2017).

Fanon wrote in the early 1960s. But the issues he articulated are as relevant today as they were for the generation of the 1960s. In Uganda today, the catalogue of cases relating to what critics of these call 'land grabbing' are hard to exhaust (see for example Zeemeijer 2011; Grainger and Geary 2011; Martiniello 2013, 2015; Carmody and Taylor 2016; Ahikire et al. 2017; LASPNET 2019). In many of these cases, state bodies, private companies and organisations, foreign countries, finance capital and individual actors are involved in what one may call a 'land grabbing enterprise'. Any serious critical scholarly engagement with these practices in Uganda automatically takes one to the debate generated by the government's attempts to make a law on Compulsory Land Acquisition.

Thus, this chapter aims at a preliminary theoretical critique of discourses on Compulsory Land Acquisition in Uganda. I critically analyse the centrality of 'development' in the proposed Compulsory Land Acquisition programme in the context of the changing form of the state and state-society relations as a result of neoliberalism. I argue that to fully grasp the rationality behind Uganda's proposed Compulsory Land Acquisition programme, it is necessary to come to terms with the present conjuncture of neoliberalism, and the implications of this conjuncture for the state and its activities, including attempts to engineer top-down legalistic reforms on land.

Discourses on Compulsory Land Acquisition in Uganda are silent on the question of the form of the current state. There is an overwhelming acceptance of the 'developmental'[1] claims of the current state as embedded in the official talk of needing 'land for development'. Current critical discourse on the Compulsory Land Acquisition programme in Uganda merely concentrates on the details of the programme, especially the process of compensation. However, I argue in this chapter that not only does the present conjuncture suggest a shift in the form of the state, as the kind of 'development' the Ugandan state is pursuing has also changed. As previous cases of Compulsory Land Acquisition in Uganda (explored later in the chapter) will demonstrate, neoliberalism, despite its outspoken assault on the state, actually requires, for its formation and consolidation, a particular kind of

[1] I here draw a distinction between what Issa Shivji (1989) calls the *ideology of development*, or *developmentalism*, and the notion of the 'developmental state'. The independent, post-colonial state relied on the ideology of development to legitimise its operations but, at the same time, this state was 'developmental' in the sense of its investments in productive activities, social services and so on. In this sense, the 'developmental state' has not survived the onslaught of neoliberalism, but what Shivji called the *ideology of development*, or *developmentalism*, has—for up to now, as we shall see, the Ugandan state still finds it important to rationalise its activities in the name of 'development'.

state interventionism, one in favour of neoliberal developmentalism. The implications of the proposed Compulsory Land Acquisition programme, thus, cannot be understood outside these shifts—shifts in the form of the state and the nature of 'development' it is pursuing.

2 Land Reforms, Land Grabbing, and the Law: A Review of Literature

It has been argued that the development process has been undergirded by the discourse and practice of law (Manji 2006). However, in contexts like Uganda, the centrality of the law in land reforms is a quite recent development. It comes to life only with the advent of colonial rule in the last quarter of the nineteenth century. With colonial political modernity, the law, as Manji (2006) rightly observes, *inter alia* served the development of capitalism. Before colonial political modernity, land reforms took different forms for different purposes. Archie Mafeje, for example, writes that nineteenth century *Kabakas* (kings) of the Buganda Kingdom in present-day Uganda enforced reforms on land to centralise power, particularly by replacing *Bataka* (clan heads) with *Batongole* (centrally appointed chiefs) (Mafeje 1973). This historical insight speaks to the qualitative difference between pre-colonial and colonial (and post-colonial) land reforms. The nineteenth century *Kabakas* of Buganda Kingdom did not introduce *Batongole* in order to commodify land and human beings. Commodification is the milestone achieved by the colonial land reforms of 1900 in Uganda, thus aiding both colonial state formation and the development of capitalism in the country. It is thus arguable that the crowning moment for the law as the guiding rationality in Uganda's land reforms was 1900, with the signing of the Buganda Agreement. Over time, land reforms became increasingly depoliticised, as a pervasive legalism gradually took the place of politics. This legalism presents land reforms in a technical mould, as an *apolitical* process, which only requires the intervention of supposedly neutral legal experts.

2.1 *Land Grabbing and Land Reforms*

Practices in which the state, in conjunction with other actors (private companies, foreign states, individual players, finance capital and so on), take over lands on which people live for multiple purposes (setting up large-scale agricultural enterprises, gazetting parks, carbon farming, construct infrastructures, etc.) have been theorised differently. Some writers cautiously use the term 'land grabbing', while others critique the notion for conceptual inadequacy (see for instance, Borras et al. 2010; Amanor 2012; Martiniello 2013; Mamdani 2013; Sachs 2010, 2015; Hall et al. 2015; Carmody and Taylor 2016). While emphasising the need to take into consideration changes in land-use and property relations in communities subjected to these processes, Borras and Franco (2012, p. 35) write that much as land grabbing was originally a politically loaded term, it has been depoliticised in the hands of international finance circles through the notion of 'large-scale land investment' (see also Borras et al. 2010). Writing in the context of Northern Uganda, Martiniello (2013) prefers the term 'new enclosures', insisting that land grabbing should 'be understood as a persistent process of capitalist primitive accumulation driven by power interests of (inter)national agribusiness' (2013, p. 1). He generally draws on David Harvey's conception of *accumulation by dispossession* as a continuous condition of late modern capitalism noting that, in the case of Africa, this is driven by an ideology that portrays the continent as endowed with abundant free land (2013, p. 15). For Martiniello (2013, p. 14), land grabbing is preceded by 'a set of legal and political mechanisms as well as new economic disposition and social configurations'. In the case of Uganda, he observes that contemporary land grabbing is driven by neoliberal policies in agriculture (see also Mamdani 2013).

Literature on land reforms is wide-ranging (for instance, De Janvry 1981; Borras 2001; Bernstein 2002; Walker 2005; Moyo and Yeros 2005; Manji 2006; Moyo 2006, 2011). Moyo and Yeros (2005, p. 52) classify land reforms into three broad categories: *state-led*, *market-led*, and *popular*. At different times and places, these models may be combined differently depending on the forces and interests involved. Overall, there is a degree of consensus around a distinction between 'redistributive land reform' and 'tenurial/legalistic land reform' (Borras 2001; Manji 2006; Moyo 2006). In this formulation, Structural Adjustment Programmes in Africa, and the subsequent advent of neoliberalism, led to the displacement of 'redistributive land reforms' in favour of the law as a *modus operandi* for land reform. This pervasive legalism is said to be contrary to observed historical experiences in countries like Zimbabwe and the Philippines where social mobilisation in combination with elements of state reformism led to a generally successful land reform programme (Moyo 2006; Borras 2001[2]).

In instances where they are used in this chapter, *land grabbing* and *land dispossession*[3] are used interchangeably. I totally agree with Hall (2011) and others on the fact that not only is what is *grabbed* beyond land—to incorporate water, minerals, genetic resources, 'cheap labour' and the like (see also Carmody and Taylor 2016). Additionally, the 'grabbers' are not only foreign but also local,[4] not just individuals

[2]Borras analyses the Comprehensive Agrarian Reform Programme (CARP) of the Philippines, where he dismisses the usual binary of state-centred/society-centred approaches to land reforms. The success of the CARP programme, for Borras, was premised on the interaction between reformist elements from the state and social mobilisation from society (i.e. from below).

[3]This entails thinking of 'dispossession' in the broader sense articulated by Butler and Athanasiou (2013, p. 3), as 'what happens when people lose their land, their citizenship, their means of livelihood and become subject to military and legal violence'.

[4]In the case of Uganda, Kafureeka's (1992, pp. 79–80) work in Mbarara district of Uganda notes the following about local land grabbers: '[they] tend to survey and fence semi-communal lands which they refer to as individually owned land, but to which the rest of people still have some use rights.

but also states, private companies, finance capital, to mention a few. If we take seriously what many scholars have observed as the post-1980 perversity of legalism in land reforms, we can think of the proposed Compulsory Land Acquisition programme in Uganda as a legalistic land reform programme—for it seeks to legally alter power relations on land between the state and citizens. To the extent that this legalistic land reform programme seeks to usher in a kind of 'redistribution', that is, from the majority to the few, from the poor to the rich, I argue that these 'reforms' have much in common with previous forms of dispossession since the dawn of colonial political modernity. Yet still, to the extent that, through these reforms, the state (armed with the legitimising language of *eminent domain, development*, etc.) confiscates land from citizens only to offer it to private profiteers, it must be emphasised that this process brings in something new, one that cannot be understood without coming to grips with the nature and function of the post-colonial state under neoliberalism.

3 'Compulsory Land Acquisition' and the Politics of Naming

Within Uganda's official circles, 'Compulsory Land Acquisition' is used to denote the ensemble of state practices involving forced takeover of privately and/or communally/customarily owned lands and properties with the claim that these will be used for the 'public good'. These processes go back to colonial times. For instance, the colonial state required more land to expand Makerere College (now Makerere University) and to set up an experimental cotton station for the Empire Cotton Growing Corporation, so it moved swiftly to use Article 15 of the 1900 Buganda Agreement, which gave the state powers to compulsorily acquire any land in the colony for 'public works'. However, because the language of 'public works' could not fit into the purposes for which this land was required, the colonial state moved to amend the language of Article 15 from 'public works' to 'public purposes', which was also resisted (LASPNET 2019, p. 49). Such tactics have continued into the post-colonial period. The independent state's many 'development projects' since the 1960s were all rationalised in the name of 'development' and the 'public good', even when 'a tragedy in the commons' (Toulmin 2005, p. 4731) ensued due to their implementation (see for example Mafeje 1973; Kafureeka 1992; Muhereza 2001). The contemporary debate on Compulsory Land Acquisition in Uganda simply adds another layer to this historical development.

They avoid areas where there are permanent developments for fear of stiff resistance. Fencing land, which is being used as semi-communal land increases pressure on the rest of the community. This results in conditional sales due to lack of grazing areas or firewood. This is at times followed by punishing anybody caught trespassing fenced land. This itself is in disregard of the fact that they fence off paths and do not allow even goats to graze, under the pretext of disease control'.

Colonial acts involving state acquisition of large chunks of land and displacement of villages for whatever purpose (whether to 'control tsetse flies', set up 'experimental schemes' to mention a few—see Bonneuil 2000) are today rightly conceptualised as *forced removals* (see especially Mamdani 2017). This is because there was a complete disregard for the people concerned who were, in the colonial political order of things, *subjects* as opposed to *citizens* (Mamdani 2017). Post-colonial equivalents, from the ranching schemes of the 1960s to the present-day sugarcane plantations and carbon forests, are ironically called 'development projects'. The reason for the distinction is because a *qualitative* difference is generally assumed between the colonial and post-colonial practice of 'development'. The latter is assumed to be a pro-people development, unlike the former, which, as Mamdani cogently observes, was propelled by a regime of compulsions: of forced labour, forced crops, forced sales, forced removals and forced contributions, all undergirded by a regime of containerised Native Authorities (Mamdani 2017).[5] The distinction, between colonial and post-colonial practices of development, obfuscates significantly, particularly when it comes to projects in our neoliberal age. Many of these projects share key characteristics with colonial *forced removals.* To maintain a distinction between colonial *forced removals* and post-colonial *development projects* is to overestimate the discontinuity between colonial and post-colonial development practices, and hence foreclose the possibility of colonial elements in the postcolony, as well as missing the point *apropos* of shifts in the form of the state as a result of neoliberalism (for an elaborated critique, see in particular Moyo and Yeros 2005; Shivji 2008).

4 Background to Uganda's Compulsory Land Acquisition Programme

The most recent top-down legalistic intervention in Uganda's land matters is the proposed law on Compulsory Land Acquisition, through the 'Compulsory Land Acquisition Bill 2019' (henceforth, CLAB 2019). The aim of the proposed law is to repeal the Land Acquisition Act of 1965.[6] The Government insists that this new law is in the interest of the country's 'development'.[7] The immediate context to this law is the failed Constitutional Amendment Bill (2017), which had sought to amend Article 26 (2) of the Uganda Constitution (1995). The point of amending Article

[5] For Mahmood Mamdani (2017), force, which sums up the regime of compulsions, was constitutive of the colonial notion of 'development', and in his view 'development' continued to be backed up by force even after independence, particularly in 'radical' post-colonial states like Tanzania.

[6] See *Daily Monitor*, March 21, 2019, 'Government softens on compulsory land acquisition', available: https://www.monitor.co.ug/News/National/Govt-softens-compulsory-land-acquisition/688334-5034818-3ax317/index.html.

[7] On this point, see next section below.

26 (2) of the Constitution was to remove the constitutional requirement for the government to adequately compensate land and property owners *prior* to taking possession of their properties. The larger context is the ruling by the Constitutional Court in 2013[8] and its affirmation by the Supreme Court in 2014[9] on the unconstitutionality of Section 7(1) of the 1965 Land Acquisition Act,[10] which had empowered the line minister to acquire any land and possess it in the 'public interest' before adequate compensation to property owners (MLHUD 2017; Muhindo 2017; Parliament of Uganda 2018; LASPNET 2019).

The court ruling in 2013, reaffirmed in 2014, was significant at least in one important sense: it created a disjuncture between the current regime and all previous regimes since colonial times on matters concerning land. All previous regimes had legal provisions enabling them to confiscate people's land and properties in the name of 'public good/interest/purposes' and 'development'. The colonial government used Article 15[11] of its 1900 Buganda Agreement; the first post-colonial government enacted the 1965 Land Acquisition Act[12], while the Amin regime enacted the 1975 Land Reform Decree—all to serve similar ends. The current regime, despite making a new constitution in 1995 and a Land Act in 1998, continued to invoke the 1965 Land Acquisition Act to effect compulsory land acquisition before adequate compensation until this was declared unconstitutional.

The suspension of these powers by the Supreme Court in 2014 forced the government to find ways to reinstate the same powers. The first move was to disguise the importation of provisions of the 1965 Land Acquisition Act into the prevailing constitution in the form of a 'constitutional amendment'. This move backfired, and

[8] For the details of the case, see: 'Advocates for Natural Resources Governance and Development; Irumba Asumani; Peter Magelah versus Attorney General; Uganda National Roads Authority', Constitutional Petition number 40 of 2013. Available: https://ulii.org/ug/judgment/supreme-court-uganda/2013/10.

[9] For the details of the case, see: 'Uganda National Road Authority Versus Irumba Asumani; Peter Magelah', Constitutional Appeal No. 02 of 2014. Available: https://ulii.org/ug/judgment/supreme-court/2015/22.

[10] For details of the Act, see: https://ulii.org/ug/legislation/consolidated-act/226.

[11] The key (last) paragraph of article 15 of the agreement states: 'Her Majesty's Government, however, reserves to itself the right to carry through or construct roads, railways, canals, telegraphs, or other useful public works, or to build military forts or works of defense on any property, public or private, with the condition that not more than 10 per centum of the property in question shall be taken up for these purposes without compensation, and that compensation shall be given for the disturbance of growing crops or of buildings'. Available: http://www.kituochakatiba.org/sites/default/files/legal-resources/The%20Buganda%20Agreement%201900.pdf.

[12] The controversial article 7(1) of this act, through which the line minister could take possession of any land/property in the 'public interest' before compensation, states thus: 'Where a declaration has been published in respect of any land, the assessment officer shall take possession of the land as soon as he or she has made his or her award under section 6; except that he or she may take possession at any time after the publication of the declaration if the Minister certifies that it is in the public interest for him or her to do so'. Available: https://ulii.org/ug/legislation/consolidated-act/226.

the government withdrew the constitutional amendment bill.[13] In the meantime, the government moved to prepare a bill on Compulsory Land Acquisition. This move culminated in an officially sanctioned, NGO-led, 'National Dialogue on Compulsory Land Acquisition in Uganda', with the first one held in Kampala on March 21, 2019.[14] Co-funded by the government of Uganda and the Embassy of Germany, the 'dialogue' saw a curious convergence of actors and interests: the state, (land) NGOs, the academia, the 'donor community', to mention a few.

Attending this dialogue, one could not help asking: why was LANDnet, a local 'Land NGO', leading the organising of a state-sanctioned dialogue on land issues? What more could a land NGO bring on board that the state could not? Obviously, it could not be financial resources, given the fact that the dialogue was already co-funded by the government of Uganda and the Germans. However, considering the fact that the government failed twice on the issue,[15] the shift from imposing the state's legal solutions to 'dialogue' before legal reforms necessarily meant that a 'neutral' actor had to be sought after, even if for no other reason than public relations. Yet allusions to 'neutrality' became immediately questionable when the same organisers began expressing worries for investors.[16] Moreover, the option for a city-based 'dialogue' held in English, as opposed to a countrywide debate in people's languages, made the neutrality of the organisers even more questionable.

[13] See Parliament of Uganda, 2018, 'Government withdraws constitutional amendment bill 2017', available: https://www.parliament.go.ug/news/2182/government-withdraws-constitution-amendment-bill-2017 see also: *Daily Monitor* September 5, 2018, 'Government withdraws land amendment bill', available: http://www.monitor.co.ug/News/National/Government-withdraws-Land-Amendment-Bill/688334-4743898-e8jcv7/.

[14] See: https://www.landnet.ug/national-dialogue-compulsory-land-acquisition-uganda.

[15] First in the Supreme Court appeal case against the annulment of section 7(1) of the 1965 Land Acquisition Act, and then in the Constitutional Amendment Bill 2017.

[16] The Ambassador of Germany, in his speech to the National Dialogue on Compulsory Land Acquisition held in Kampala on March 21 2019, gave a brief background to Uganda government's search for a 'neutral' actor to organise a national dialogue on land reforms: 'Over a year ago, in a discussion with *State House representatives who were worried – like myself – about the reluctance of German investors to propose new projects for Uganda*, I was asked whether the German Embassy could assist the Government of Uganda to facilitate a national dialogue on compulsory land acquisition. *I was made to understand that in view of the complicated and often heated discussions in the local media ever since the first attempts to ease compulsory land acquisition had been made, State House seemed adamant to find a neutral broker to facilitate a technical exchange at national level between experts and key stakeholders from Government, Academia, Civil Society and the Private Sector.* (...) Together with GIZ [Deutsche Gesellschaft für Internationale Zusammenarbeit – a German Development Agency], very experienced in the related sector, my Embassy has taken the initiative for organising this National Dialogue. With the full buy-in of the Government of Uganda and LANDnet as our partner, we established a steering committee, bringing together for a free-wheeling dialogue government agencies, development partners, CSOs [Civil Society Organisations], and the private sector' (see Embassy of the Federal Republic of Germany 2019, emphasis added).

5 The Case for Compulsory Land Acquisition in Uganda

The official theme for Uganda's Compulsory Land Acquisition programme is that the government needs 'land for development'. From this perspective, the state is portrayed as the harbinger of the 'development process'. Here I go through some of the arguments related to this, from both the official and non-official points of view.

In 2017, during the first attempt to amend Article 26 (2) of the 1995 Uganda Constitution, the lead Ministry (of Lands, Housing and Urban Development—henceforth MLHUD) argued that 'compulsory acquisition is a critical development tool for Governments, and for ensuring that land is available when needed for essential infrastructure—a contingency that land markets are not always able to meet' (MLHUD 2017, p. 2). This initial proposition depicts Compulsory Land Acquisition as a tool with which the state outsmarts market forces.

In this era of the 'second internationalised development agenda' (see Banjwa 2017), governments and other entities in the global South feel obliged to align their activities to the blueprint of Sustainable Development Goals (SDGs), even if mechanically. The SDGs provide an easy legitimation for all sorts of programmes. Thus, the Ministry of Lands insists that Compulsory Land Acquisition is necessary because 'sustainable development requires governments to provide public facilities and infrastructure...' (MLHUD 2017, p. 2). For this reason, the Ministry argues that 'it is critical [to] expedite the process of land acquisition for strategic and development activities...' (MLHUD 2017, p. 7).

According to the MLHUD, the then proposed amendment was to enable the government to obtain '*land for development* purposes without depriving the property owners the right to prompt, fair and adequate compensation, prior to taking possession of the property' (MLHUD 2017, p. 11, emphasis added). This statement itself is a contradiction in terms, considering the fact that the government was introducing the amendment to do away with Article 26 (2) of the 1995 Uganda Constitution, which emphasises prior and prompt compensation before the government's possession of private/communal property. The Ministry deeply detested this requirement because, once the amount proposed by the government valuer is 'rejected by the property owner or persons having an interest in property, Government cannot proceed with payment as per the Constitutional requirement and thus Government cannot take possession to proceed with the development projects' (MLHUD 2017, p. 25).

In their rejection of the above amendment, members of parliament on the Committee of Legal and Parliamentary Affairs (see Parliament of Uganda 2018) did not object to the official position on compulsory land acquisition but only suggested that it was better to address the issues within the framework of the Land Acquisition Act, instead of amending the constitution. Hence, in replicating the language of the Ministry of Lands (see above), the committee emphasised that 'Compulsory acquisition is a critical development tool for governments, and for ensuring that land is available when needed for essential infrastructure, a contingency that land markets are not always able to meet' (Parliament of Uganda 2018, p. 5).

In her ministerial statement to the first 'National Dialogue on Compulsory Land Acquisition in Uganda', the then Minister of Lands, Housing and Urban Development, Betty Amongi Ongom, revealed that '[the Compulsory Land Acquisition Bill 2019] has been drafted [...] to bring it into conformity with Article 26 of the Constitution of Uganda' (Amongi Ongom 2019). The new bill 'is expected to facilitate expeditious compulsory acquisition of land by Government or Local Government to avoid delaying Government or Local Government infrastructure and investment projects, while at the same time, allowing for persons dissatisfied with the compensation amount awarded to resolve the disputes in court...' (Amongi Ongom 2019). The idea that matters can be resolved in courts, as the government puts the acquired land to use as per its proposed purposes, is key to the proposed law: it creates the *façade* of prior and prompt payment before acquisition of private/communal properties as required by the prevailing (1995) Constitution.

In the same forum, the German Ambassador to Uganda, whose embassy co-organised the event, reiterated the Ugandan government's need for 'infrastructural development' and overall 'further development' of the country. In his speech, the Ambassador revealed why Uganda's 'German [development] partners' and investors were not proposing new development projects, an issue that worried the Ugandan government dearly. The problem was land. In particular, it was decried that investor acquisition of land in Uganda is a very cumbersome process, which alienated development partners and investors like those from Germany (Embassy of the Federal Republic of Germany 2019).

5.1 Critical Responses to Uganda's Compulsory Land Acquisition Programme

The discourse of (especially Land) NGOs provides the initial critical response to Uganda's Compulsory Land Acquisition programme. Yet still, these NGOs have no quarrels with the official claim that government needs 'land for development'. They rightly critique the failure of the government to guarantee the rights of the poor and the vulnerable (especially women and children) without interrogating the claim that needed lands are for 'development' purposes. Hence the Land and Equity Movement of Uganda (LEMU) talks of the need to find a middle ground, where 'Government can implement its development plans, communities can enjoy the infrastructure and services which they need and people can also be secure that their Government is protecting their rights' (LEMU 2009a, b. *cf.* LANDnet 2019; LASPNET 2019; Muhindo 2017; ANARDE 2017).

Yet, even amidst this rather stark image of acquiescence with the official claim of needing 'land for development', there are some voices that went beyond it. In an open letter to the parliament of Uganda over the proposed Constitutional

Amendment Bill 2017, Oxfam Uganda reminded the members of parliament: '[Y]ou must not sacrifice your people at the altar of development...' (see Oxfam Uganda 2018). The then head of the Uganda Human Rights Commission, Med Kaggwa, asked searching questions of the 'development' said to be driving the government's push for Compulsory Land Acquisition: 'Development for whom and for what? Closing playing fields and building shopping malls for the public which doesn't have purchasing power'?[17] In his keynote speech to the first 'National Dialogue on Compulsory Acquisition in Uganda', Mamdani (2019) cautioned attendants to be vigilant when it comes to official development discourse. 'Developmental talk' argued Mamdani, 'needs to be put to public scrutiny: how aligned is it to the public good? Does the half-billion-dollar hospital...[serve] the public good? Does every infrastructural project serve the public good'? (Mamdani 2019).

As I argue in this chapter, the form of the state is key to understanding the rationale behind the proposed Compulsory Land Acquisition Programme. Since the form of the state is taken for granted in many discussions on Compulsory Land Acquisition in Uganda, the version of development pursued by a particular form of state is also taken for granted. Yet any hope for 'benefits' from the 'land for development' agenda being aggressively pushed must first of all seek to understand what kind of 'development' it is. I argue that both the form of the state and the kind of 'development' it is pursuing cannot be understood unless one understands fully the implications to both of the present conjuncture of neoliberalism in vogue since the 1980s. Scrutinising both the form of the current state and the developmentalism that accompanies its discourse on land reform is vital if we are to fully grasp, as Bernstein (2004) would put it, what is *changing before our very eyes*.

6 Beyond the Official Narrative

Is the current Ugandan state 'developmental' as official talk on Compulsory Land Acquisition would have us believe? Are there differences between Uganda's post-independence state of the 1960s and the current (post-1980) state? These are important questions to ask before buying into the 'land for development' talk. The assumption of continuity when it comes to the nature of the state since the 1960s, an assumption that is at the heart of official talk on Compulsory Land Acquisition in Uganda, is one that should be challenged. For much has changed since the 1960s, and, if in this sense only, new dynamics and conjunctures (Young 2004) have to be taken seriously. For our present moment, the 1980s' decade marks an important dynamic, the rise of neoliberalism, and this has had a definitive impact on the form of the state and its role in society.

[17] See *New Vision*, September 17, 2016. 'Hold referendum on compulsory land acquisition'. Available: https://www.newvision.co.ug/new_vision/news/1435535/hold-referendum-compulsory-land-acquisition.

Perhaps it is high time we discarded a widely shared certitude according to which twenty-first century states, especially those in the global South, can be inserted into the category of 'developmental states', similar to their twentieth century counterparts in South East Asia and elsewhere. Bagchi (2000, p. 398), for instance, suggests that under capitalism, the state remains 'developmental' but it 'puts economic development as the top priority of governmental policy and is able to design effective instruments to promote such a goal'. Along similar lines, a recent volume on the subject edited by Michelle Williams suggests that what is different between twentieth and twenty-first century 'developmental states' are the conditions that these states must face. In the case of twenty-first century states, the authors suggest that 'economic restructuring' (moving from industry to knowledge and service production), 'domestic politics' (democratisation), epistemic shifts (from development as growth to more inclusive social and human development) as well as ecological limits (care for the natural environment) constitute the magic wand for the success of twenty-first century developmental states (Williams 2014a, p. xiii, 2014b, p. 8). Evans, drawing on Amartya Sen, calls such states 'capability-expanding developmental states' (Evans 2014, p. 235).

The idea that 'development' continues to be an important language of states in the twenty-first century is quite incontestable. That does not mean the category 'developmental' should follow automatically when it comes to twenty-firs century states, especially, in our case, post-colonial states. In an important sense, it seems helpful to draw a distinction between 'developmentalism' and the 'developmental state'. *Developmentalism* as a legitimation ideology, what Issa Shivji (1989) has called 'the ideology of development', is different from the 'developmental state'. One can say that all post-colonial states in Africa have relied on developmentalism, but all have not necessarily been 'developmental', if by a 'developmental state' we refer specifically to that active state which not only engaged in investment and production (for instance, in Africa, through state-controlled parastatals) but also vigorously engaged in provisioning for public goods and services (such as roads, educational and health facilities among others).[18] The year 1980 becomes critical in the life of the 'developmental state' seen in this sense.

It seems to me that the common ground for developmental states is to be found not in the reliance on developmentalism as an ideology, which, as I have indicated, is a terrain shared with the state after 1980, but in the direct interventionism of these states in production and investment through state-controlled entities, and in state provisioning for public goods and services. The neoliberal turn since the 1980s

[18] Shivji (2007) has observed that this 'developmental' move was rendered possible by the earlier colonial suppression of the development of an African middle class which would have been at the forefront of production and investment in the period after independence. The independent state had to do it on its own. He writes: '[T]he colonial state had deliberately suppressed and undermined the development of a middle class, which would have become an agency for development. So, it fell to the state. Regardless of the variety of the ideology, whether capitalist or nominally socialist, the state became a site of private and public accumulation. The public sector played the dominant role in all African countries, from socialist Tanzania to capitalist Malawi' (Shivji 2007, p. 14).

marked the end of that kind of developmental state. As Shivji (2007, p. 25) cogently observes, with neoliberalism, 'the developmental role of the state is declared dead and buried'. 'Instead', Shivji argues, 'it is assigned the role of 'chief' to supervise the globalisation project under the tutelage of imperial – now called development partners or 'true friends'' (Shivji 2007, p. 25; see also Fine 1999). This 'chief supervisor of the globalisation project', or what Frantz Fanon foresaw as 'the general president of a company of profiteers' (Fanon et al. 1963, p. 166), is what we can call the post-colonial neoliberal state.

7 Previous Cases of Compulsory Land Acquisition in Uganda

Official discourse on Compulsory Land Acquisition in Uganda gives primacy to the so-called 'public infrastructural projects', as components in the official account of 'development', for which, it is said, much of the land is needed. There is no need to rehearse these cases here. One can find plenty of them in official and NGO writings. I would go as far as to argue that even these so-called 'public infrastructure projects' cannot be fully understood outside the new function of the state under neoliberalism. Below I only highlight cases involving the Ugandan state and other actors, particularly big finance capital. These cases are indeed numerous, and here I only mention a few.

The first of these came up at the beginning of this century, in 2001, when a German Coffee Company, Neumann Kaffe Gruppe (henceforth Neumann Kaffe), moved to establish coffee plantations in Uganda through its local subsidiary, Kaweri Coffee Plantation Ltd. Over 2500 ha of land are involved, covering up to four villages of about 4000 people in Mubende district of central Uganda. When the government and Neumann Kaffe reached an agreement on the latter's land lease, the narrative was that the land was empty, uninhabited. The over 4000 residents living on this land were branded 'illegals', and were not compensated, which forced many of them to file lawsuit after lawsuit (see FIAN 2016, p. 3;[19] Ahikire et al. 2017, p. 17). Interestingly, after successfully grabbing land from over 4000 occupants through state support, Neumann Kaffe went on to secure funding from the German

---

[19] On this, FIAN's research report notes the following: 'The eviction was described by the evictees as particularly cruel. The inhabitants were threatened and forced to leave at gunpoint and several of those being evicted were beaten in the process. The soldiers set houses on fire and demolished them, including the fully equipped private clinic of the community and six churches. Movable properties were looted and crops were cut down and uprooted. The Kitemba primary school (a formal school of the villages) has since then been used as the headquarters of Kaweri/NKG Coffee plantation and this situation has created negative consequences on the education of the children at primary and secondary school levels. Following the eviction there was an increase of illnesses and deaths as most of the evictees were cut off from their access to food, shelter, clean water and health care' (FIAN 2016, p. 3).

'development agency' GIZ/GTZ and from the African Development Bank (AfDB) (for more on this, see Doss et al. 2014; Borras et al. 2016; FIAN 2016; Ahikire et al. 2017; Vertin 2019).

Another case involves a local sugar corporation, Kakira Sugar Works (owned by a local conglomerate, Madhvani group), moving to establish another sugar estate (Amuru Sugar Works) in the Amuru district of Northern Uganda. The contestation was on ownership of the land in question. The District Land Board (DLB) claimed the land belonged to it, while the communities concerned maintained that this was land owned customarily and that the 1998 Land Act safely protects their rights. Like in the case of Neumann Kaffe, the government and officials from the Madhvani group maintained that the land in question was empty! The unspoken reality was that by the time the land was surveyed, people were still being forcefully interned in Internally Displaced Peoples' Camps as a result of the fighting between government forces and the Lord's Resistance Army rebels. Madhvani had hoped for 40,000 ha with the government owning 40% shares in the company. However, the initial lease granted in 2008 by the DLB was for 20,000 ha (see Martiniello 2013, p. 10; Doss et al. 2014; Ahikire et al. 2017; Madhvani 2012). In this case, the whole government apparatus, including the head of state,[20] was deployed to corner residents into accepting to sacrifice their land in the name of 'development'.

As contestation over the land in question continued, Mayur Madhvani (see Madhvani 2012), a Managing Director at Kakira Sugar Works, opined in 2012 that the 'Amuru Sugar Project *will bring development to Northern Uganda*' (emphasis added).[21] Despite reports to the contrary, Madhvani maintained the claim that the land in question was isolated and 'totally free of inhabitants', and that it had 'no infrastructure such as electricity, water or proper roads'. He compares Northern Uganda (Amuru) with Busoga region, where Kakira Sugar Works is located: while the latter is now 'developed', thanks to his Sugar Works, the former is not. It is for this reason, he argues, that his Sugar Company is taking 'development to Northern Uganda' through the establishment of a new sugar plant. However, on the company's out-grower scheme in the Busoga region (celebrated by Madhvani), a study by Martiniello concludes that in areas where the scheme operates, there is a clear 'trajectory of agrarian change characterised by social differentiation, dispossession and expulsion of poor or less competitive peasants from sugar agro-extractive poles to make space for capitalist entrepreneurs and more commercially-oriented farmers' (Martiniello 2020, p. 13; 2017, p. 15).

Besides Mubende and Amuru cases, there are numerous other cases involving government and big agricultural finance capital. Oxfam International analyses the case of New Forests Company (NFC) in which the government undertook forced eviction of over 22,000 people branded 'illegal encroachers' in order to clear land for

[20] See *Observer*, August 18, 2017: 'Museveni intervenes in Amuru land saga'. Available: https://observer.ug/news/headlines/54460-museveni-intervenes-in-amuru-land-saga.

[21] See *Daily Monitor*, February 9, 2012. Available: https://mobile.monitor.co.ug/Oped/691272-1322852-format-xhtml-ds78ymz/index.html.

NFC in Kiboga, Mubende and Bugiri districts (Grainger and Geary 2011). In Mayuge and Dokolo districts, Lyons and Westoby (2014) have written about the 'dark side of green', which they have described as 'carbon colonialism', in which between 8000 and 40,000 residents have been forcefully evicted by the government since 1996 to pave the way for carbon trading forests of a Norwegian plantation forestry company, Green Resources.[22] In the case of Apaa in Northern Uganda, the government demarcated over 20,000 ha of land for 'conservation' and tourist purposes, fuelling a conflict that is still ongoing (Martiniello 2013, p. 13). There is also a case in which the District Land Board awarded highly-placed political personalities[23] huge chunks of land belonging to internally displaced people (Martiniello 2013, p. 13).

A longer version of these cases since 2007 is listed by Zeemeijer (2011, p. 99). Zeemeijer lists 24 cases in the period of four years, between 2007 and 2011 (some of the cases he lists, such as Amuru Sugar Works and Neumann Kaffe have an earlier presence as above-mentioned). What is striking about this list is that an overwhelming number of cases (18 of the 24) are private companies, local and foreign.[24] Others are collaborations between government bodies and other companies or states (3 cases), investments in Uganda by other states (2 cases) and one case by a government body (Uganda Wildlife Authority). Yet many as they are within such a short period of time, these cases are just a tip of the iceberg. Martiniello (2013, p. 2), citing Friis and Reenberg (2010, p. 12), notes that 14% of the national agricultural land in Uganda is covered by land deals involving foreign corporations and states.

Among other negative implications, critics of these cases have given primacy to the human rights abuses on these projects, the gendered nature of these projects (for instance, Ahikire et al. 2017), and exploitation of the locals (including grabbing their land without adequate and prior compensation). In the end, the 'solutions' they advance do not escape the legalism decried by writers like Manji (2006). And as Harvey (2007, p. 70) observes, legalism fits well into the neoliberal framework, which despises any democratic exercise.

---

[22] Available at: https://www.oaklandinstitute.org/sites/oaklandinstitute.org/files/Report_DarkerSideofGreen_hirez.pdf.

[23] Specifically, General Julius Oketa and Harriet Aber, wife of General Salim Saleh, the president's brother.

[24] These include: BIDCO in Kalangala which is already possessing 10,000 hectares and plans for 40,000 ha; Neumann Kaffe (2512 ha, Mubende district); New Forest Company (9300 ha, Mubende, Kiboga and Bugiri); Hebei company (40,500 ha in 8–10 years, Masindi district); Mukwano Group (2833 ha, Masindi district); Zziwa ranches (15,378 ha in Masindi); Nexus Biodiesel Ltd. (400 ha in Masindi) among others.

8 Learning from Past Experience

First of all, the cases above are key to understanding the changing form of the state and the reconfiguration of the state-society relations in the 'age of globalisation [/neoliberalism]' (Shivji 2008). These cases are key to understanding what is meant by 'development' in the official rhetoric of 'land for development'. From these cases, we see clearly that debating the Compulsory Land Acquisition programme with allusions to the developmental form of the current state is a very questionable assumption. It is to underestimate the transformative nature of the era of structural adjustment and more recent neoliberal restructuring. These and many other cases thus demonstrate that the contemporary post-colonial state, like its immediate post-independence counterpart, deploys *developmentalism* as a legitimation ideology (hence the talk of 'land for development'). But it is not the active, interventionist state of the 1960s, 'doing development' itself through state-controlled parastatals and the like.

If the current post-colonial state in Uganda is interventionist, it is only so to the extent that is necessary to pave way for the march of private capital. This is a particularly important point, considering the conventional view of neoliberalism as an essentially anti-state ideology. Considering these cases, one unavoidable conclusion is that in practice, against the commonplace assumption, the consolidation and reproduction of neoliberalism actually requires an interventionist state, one that can use its coercive instruments to avail land for capitalist development in agriculture. As we have seen in the few cases highlighted above, this state will deploy all tools at its disposal (legal, police, military, and the like) to ensure that nothing stands in the way of private capital. I suggest that the proposed legal fix in the name of Compulsory Land Acquisition has to be placed in this context. Ashis Nandy (2010, p. 295) writes that 'the state [in third world societies] often looks like some kind of specialised coercive apparatus or private business venture'. To the extent that this is true, such speciality in coercion cannot be delinked from the grand task of safeguarding the neoliberal order.

Secondly, and related to the above, these and other cases demonstrate clearly that by 'land for development', it is not meant that the state exclusively, or even primarily, requires land to establish so-called 'public infrastructures'. By 'land for development', what is meant, at least from the above cases, is that the state needs land to facilitate the development of capitalism, particularly the development of capitalism in the countryside. As Mamdani has observed in his contribution to Uganda's Compulsory Land Acquisition debate (Mamdani 2019), the guiding ideology in this move is that the panacea to "rural [capitalist] development" is the penetration of capital in these areas. This is the spirit in which a person of Madhvani's (2012) stature can mockingly write that his Sugar Corporation is 'bring[ing] development to Northern Uganda'!

It seems to me that in trying to resolve the agrarian question of transition (to capitalism), Uganda's post-colonial neoliberal state resorts to force not in the classical Preobrazhensky-ian sense (of 'socialist primitive accumulation'—see

Akram-Lodhi and Kay 2010), but to root for and protect private companies in these areas. Toulmin (2005) has called this development the 'new tragedy in the commons', a phenomenon peculiar to the age of neoliberalism. Lin Chun (2015, p. 137) observed similar developments in India and China, where 'enclosures' since the 1990s are defended 'in the name of modernisation'. Like in the Ugandan case, Chun notes that in both China and India, "the deprivation of variously land-dependent communities is the work of big capital-developers, investors, agro-businessmen, financiers, and the like – much as the state' (Chun 2015, p. 137).

Thirdly, the above cases are also illuminating on the question of 'land reform' in the context of Uganda's proposed Compulsory Land Acquisition Programme. Within literature on land reforms, a distinction is drawn between 'tenurial/legal' land reforms and 'redistributive' land reforms. Manji (2006), for instance, emphasises that under neoliberalism, 'tenurial[/legalistic] land reform' has displaced 'redistributive land reform', with the effect that the question of land reform under neoliberalism has been completely depoliticised. For Martiniello (2015, p. 5), 'neoliberal land (tenure) reforms switched focus from land redistribution to land reforms, from politics to law, with the effect of depoliticising the debate and neutralising alternative paths of reforms'. The point is to assign 'tenurial/legal land reforms' to the post-1980 neoliberal era, and 'redistributive land reforms' to an earlier period. In an important sense, the Ugandan cases above reveal a trajectory beyond the 'tenurial' vs. 'redistributive' land reforms binary. A kind of land 'redistribution' can be observed which takes a 'consolidative' form, in which the state forcefully dispossesses the majority to offer such lands to the few, from the 'poor' to the 'rich'—and the law is used to facilitate this process. This is precisely what happens when the government, using the state apparatus (police, army, lawyers, and the like), evicts thousands and tens of thousands of people off their land in order to lease it to a single 'investor'.

9 Conclusion

This chapter has aimed at a preliminary theoretical critique of discourse on Compulsory Land Acquisition in Uganda. In a discursive environment where official 'developmental' claims that accompany the push for Compulsory Land Acquisition are generally taken for granted, this chapter has raised the question of the form of the state prevailing in Uganda today. The chapter has also raised questions on the nature of development being pursued by this particular state form on lands acquired by force from citizens. If the idea of 'land for development', central to the official narrative on Compulsory Land Acquisition in Uganda, has resulted in a coupling of a regime of state-led forced land acquisition with the notion of 'state-driven development', I have argued that today we need to decouple these in order to allow for a historically and contextually informed query on the implications of top-down legalistic land reforms in a post-colonial neoliberal context. For a country like Uganda that faithfully implemented the post-1980s World Bank/IMF-dictated Structural

Adjustment Programmes (SAPs), the 'developmental' assumption regarding the current state is untenable—particularly if one takes seriously the neoliberal turn SAPs ushered into the country and its effect on the form of the state and state-society relations. With the change in the form of the state and its role in society as a result of neoliberalism, the kind of 'development' being pursued ultimately changed. This is what inter alia the cases above indicate, in which it is often the case that compulsorily acquired lands ended up in the hands of private profiteers. With this, it becomes untenable to think of neoliberalism as essentially an anti-state ideology. It emerges from these cases that the consolidation of neoliberalism actually requires an interventionist state, one that can, for instance, use its coercive instruments to avail land for capitalist development in agriculture.

To take seriously the current neoliberal conjuncture in the life of a post-colonial state like Uganda helps us to realise how such sweeping powers sought after via a law on Compulsory Land Acquisition can be excessively abused by this state. As it turns out in the few cases briefly explored above, the post-colonial neoliberal state cannot use Karl Polanyi's (2001) iconic phrase, champion society's 'self-protection' against the onslaught of capitalism. With issues as these in mind, the question before us remains whether or not, in a post-colonial neoliberal context, legalistic land reforms can be meaningful without state reform.

References

Ahikire J, Kanyesigye J, Nassali M, Nakayi R, Katushabe J, Pamara H (2017) Interrogating large-scale land acquisitions and land governance in Uganda: implications for women's land rights. Centre for Basic Research, Kampala

Akram-Lodhi AH, Kay C (2010) Surveying the agrarian question (part 1): unearthing foundations, exploring diversity. J Peasant Stud 37(1):177–202

Amanor KS (2012) Global resource grabs, agribusiness concentration and the smallholder: two West African case studies. J Peasant Stud 39(3-4):731–749

Amongi O (2019) Statement by Hon Minister of Lands, Housing and Urban Development on Compulsory Land Acquisition. The National Dialogue On Compulsory Land Acquisition In Uganda, Held on 21st March, 2019 At Skyz Hotel, Naguru. Available at Uganda Media Centre: https://www.mediacentre.go.ug/media/statement-ministry-lands-compulsory-land-acquisition (Accessed April 20, 2019)

ANARDE (2017) Constitutional Amendment Bill to the Article 26 of the Uganda Constitution: insights and challenges from field practice of land conflicts. Available: http://anarde.org/new2/wp-content/uploads/2017/10/ASF-ANARDE_UG_PolicyBrief_LandConflicts_201709.pdf

Bagchi AK (2000) The past and the future of the developmental state. J World-Syst Res 6(2):398–442

Banjwa A (2017) A critical analysis of the alternative energy-poverty discourse with a case of Kasese district in Uganda: New sites, actors, identities, language, and visions of power. Lund University Students' Publications. Masters Thesis. Available at: https://lup.lub.lu.se/student-papers/search/publication/8899585

Bernstein H (2002) Land reform: taking a long (er) view. J Agrarian Change 2(4):433–463

Bernstein H (2004) 'Changing before our very eyes': Agrarian questions and the politics of land in capitalism today. J Agrarian Change 4(1-2):190–225

Bonneuil C (2000) Development as experiment: science and State building in late colonial and postcolonial Africa, 1930-1970. Osiris 15:258–281

Borras SM Jr, Franco JC (2012) Global land grabbing and trajectories of agrarian change: a preliminary analysis. J Agrarian Change 12(1):34–59

Borras SM Jr, McMichael P, Scoones I (2010) The politics of biofuels, land and agrarian change: editors' introduction. J Peasant Stud 37(4):575–592

Borras SM (2001) State–society relations in land reform implementation in the Philippines. Dev Change 32(3):545–575

Borras SM, Backes S, Fyfe D, Herre R, Michele L, Mills E (2016) Land grabbing and human rights: The involvement of European corporate and financial entities in land grabbing outside the European Union. European Parliament, Directorate-General for External Policies Policy Department

Butler J, Athanasiou A (2013) Dispossession: the performative in the political. John Wiley & Sons

Carmody P, Taylor D (2016) Globalization, land grabbing, and the present-day colonial state in Uganda: ecolonization and its impacts. J Environ Dev 25(1):100–126

Chun L (2015) Rethinking land reform: comparative lessons from China and India. In: Mamdani M (ed) The land question: socialism, capitalism, and the market. Makerere Institute of Social Research, Makerere University

De Janvry A (1981) The agrarian question and reformism in Latin America. Johns Hopkins University Press, Baltimore

Doss C, Meinzen-Dick R, Bomuhangi A (2014) Who owns the land? Perspectives from rural Ugandans and implications for large-scale land acquisitions. Feminist Econ 20(1):76–100

Embassy of the Federal Republic of Germany (2019) Opening Remarks by H.E. Dr. Albrecht Conze, German Ambassador to Uganda National Dialogue on Compulsory Land Acquisition Skyz Hotel, Naguru, Kampala – 21 March 2019. Kampala, Uganda. Available: https://kampala.diplo.de/blob/2203310/30dac3949f40b3780da5c0aa036b14bc/national-land-diaologue-2019-speech-ambassador-conze-data.pdf (Accessed April 20, 2019)

Evans P (2014) The developmental state: divergent responses to modern economic theory and the twenty-first-century economy. In: Williams M (ed) The end of the developmental state? Routledge

Fanon F, Sartre JP, Farrington C (1963) The wretched of the earth. Grove Press, New York

FIAN (2016) Human Rights violations in the context of Kaweri Coffee Plantation in Mubende/Uganda. Available: https://www.fian.org/fileadmin/media/publications_2015/ParallelReport_UGA_CESCR54_E.pdf

Fine B (1999) The developmental state is dead—long live social capital? Dev Change 30(1):1–19

Grainger M, Geary K (2011) The new forests company and its Uganda plantations. OXFAM International, Washington DC

Hall R (2011) Land grabbing in Southern Africa: the many faces of the investor rush. Rev Afr Polit Econ 38(128):193–214

Hall R, Edelman M, Borras SM Jr, Scoones I, White B, Wolford W (2015) Resistance, acquiescence or incorporation? An introduction to land grabbing and political reactions 'from below'. J Peasant Stud 42(3-4):467–488

Harvey D (2007) A brief history of neoliberalism. Oxford University Press

Kafureeka L (1992) "The Dynamics of the Land Question and its Impact on Agricultural Productivity in Mbarara District, Uganda". CBR Working Papers, No.25

LANDNet (2019) National Dialogue on Compulsory Land Acquisition in Uganda. LANDnet, Kampala-Uganda. Available: https://www.landnet.ug/national-land-dialogue

LASPNET [Legal Aid Service Providers Network] (2019) Situational analysis on compulsory land acquisition management in Uganda. LASPNET Kampala

LEMU (2009a) Development, Land, Rights. Available at: http://www.land-in-uganda.org/assets/compulsoryacquisitiondoc2-development,landandrights.pdf

LEMU (2009b) Pressure from Development Actors and Private Developers. Available at: http://www.land-in-uganda.org/assets/compulsoryacquisitiondoc8-pressurefromdevelopmentactorsandinvestors.pdf
Lyons K, Westoby P (2014) Carbon colonialism and the new land grab: Plantation forestry in Uganda and its livelihood impacts. J Rural Stud 36:13–21
Mafeje A (1973) Agrarian revolution and the land question in Buganda. Institute of Social Studies Occasional Papers, No. 32
Mamdani M (2013) The contemporary Ugandan discourse on customary tenure: some theoretical considerations. MISR Working Papers No.13. Makerere Institute of Social Research
Mamdani M (2017) Citizen and subject: contemporary Africa and the legacy of late colonialism. Makerere Institute of Social Research, Kampala
Mamdani M (2019) Compulsory land acquisition: Huddles to deal with. Daily Monitor, March 26, 2019
Manji A (2006) The politics of land reform in Africa: from communal tenure to free markets. Zed Books
Martiniello G (2013) Land dispossession and rural social movements: the 2011 conference in Mali. Rev Afr Polit Econ 40(136):309–320
Martiniello G (2015) Rethinking the food question in Uganda: emerging debates on food sovereignty. MISR Working Papers No.18
Martiniello G (ed) (2017) Social struggles in Uganda's Acholiland: understanding responses and resistance to Amuru Sugar Works. In: World Scientific reference on natural resources and environmental policy in the era of global change: volume 2: the social ecology of the anthropocene: continuity and change in global environmental politics, pp 457–481. Available: https://www.iss.nl/sites/corporate/files/2017-11/BICAS%20CP%205-55%20Martiniello.pdf
Martiniello G (2020) Bitter sugarification: sugar frontier and contract farming in Uganda. Globalizations:1–17
MLHUD [Ministry of Land, Housing and Urban Development] (2017) Understanding land acquisition challenges that have necessitated the constitutional (Amendment) Bill, 2017. Kampala-Uganda
Moyo S (2006) The evolution of Zimbabwe's land acquisition. University of Zimbabwe (UZ) Publications/Michigan State University (MSU)
Moyo S (2011) Land concentration and accumulation after redistributive reform in post-settler Zimbabwe. Rev Afr Polit Econ 38(128):257–276
Moyo S, Yeros P (2005) The resurgence of rural movements under neoliberalism. In: Moyo S, Yeros P (eds) Reclaiming the land: the resurgence of rural movements in Africa, Asia and Latin America. Zed Books
Muhereza EF (2001) Ranchers and pastoralists: the restructuring of government ranching, Uganda. In: Salih MA, Dietz T (eds) African pastoralism: conflict, institutions and government. Pluto Press, London
Muhindo J (2017) Compulsory land acquisition in Uganda: an analysis of the proposed amendment of Article 26 of the constitution. ACODE Policy Briefing Paper Series No.47, Kampala
Nandy A (2010) State. In: Sachs W (ed) The development dictionary: a guide to knowledge as power. Zed Books
Oxfam Uganda (2018) An open Letter to Members of Parliament on Constitution (Amendment) Bill No. 13/2017. Available: https://uganda.oxfam.org/press_release/open-letter-members-parliament-constitution-amendment-bill-no-132017
Parliament of Uganda (2018) Report of the sectoral committee on legal and parliamentary affairs on the constitutional amendment bill, 2017. Parliament of Uganda, Kampala
Polanyi K (2001) The great transformation: the political and economic origins of our time, Vol 45. Beacon Press
Sachs W (2010) Preface. In: Sachs W (ed) The development dictionary: a guide to knowledge as power. Zed Books
Sachs W (2015) Planet dialectics: explorations in environment and development. Zed Books Ltd.

Shivji IG (1989) The concept of human rights in Africa. African Books Collective
Shivji IG (2007) Silences in NGO discourse: the role and future of NGOs in Africa. Fahamu/Pambazuka.
Shivji IG (2008) Accumulation in an African periphery: a theoretical framework. African Books Collective
Toulmin C (2005) The new tragedy of the commons. New Statesman 134:4731
Vertin C (2019) Land and land grabbing: the case study of the Neumann Kaffee Gruppe in Uganda
Walker C (2005) The limits to land reform: rethinking 'the land question'. J Southern Afr Stud 31(4):805–824
Williams M (2014a) Introduction. In: Williams M (ed) The end of the developmental state? Routledge
Williams M (2014b) Rethinking the developmental state in the twenty-first century. In: Williams M (ed) The end of the developmental state? Routledge
Young C (2004) The end of the post-colonial state in Africa? Reflections on changing African political dynamics. Afr Aff 103(410):23–49
Zeemeijer I (2011) Who gets what, when and how? New corporate land acquisitions and the impact on local livelihoods in Uganda. Masters diss., Utrecht University

The Struggle Continues: Namibia's Enduring Land Question

Henning Melber

Abstract With Independence in 1990, Namibia inherited a socio-economic structure that, in terms of land distribution, had anchored the colonial divide and rule under Apartheid: a white-owned commercial agricultural sector contrasted with communal areas based on regional-ethnic criteria. Constitutional principles accepted as the final step towards Independence and sovereignty excluded any expropriation without fair compensation and therefore contributed to limiting land restitution and redistribution. Since 1990, diversification has taken place in private land ownership in commercial agriculture. A growing number of black farm owners have benefitted from a redistributive land policy guided by state support for elite interests. In the communal areas, local traditional authorities and representatives of the central state administration abused control over land rights to further the privatisation of communal property in terms of its use. These land reform dimensions underlined the new pact among elites in independent Namibia in different ways and disclosed the class character of property relations and ownership related to land. But, in the absence of a coherent policy, even a neoliberal perspective and strategy is hardly visible. Government policy so far rather testifies more to the negligence of any meaningful land reform.

1 Introduction

With an area of over 824,000 km^2 and 2.5 million inhabitants, Namibia is a sparsely populated country. Embraced by the Namib desert along the Atlantic coast and the Kalahari in the East, only about 8% of its area is suitable for dry land cropping, due to the required minimum average annual rainfall of over 500 mm. Two-thirds of the country is classified as semi-arid and around a quarter as arid. Of the commercial

H. Melber (✉)
University of Pretoria, Pretoria, South Africa

University of the Free State, Bloemfontein, South Africa
e-mail: Henning.Melber@nai.uu.se

F. Mazwi et al. (eds.), *Capital Penetration and the Peasantry in Southern and Eastern Africa*, Advances in African Economic, Social and Political Development, https://doi.org/10.1007/978-3-030-89824-3_4

farmland (freehold agricultural land), 60% receives on average less than 300 mm of rain annually: 'In such an arid environment land ownership becomes much less of a crucial factor than in most countries'. (UNDP 1998, p. 46) Put differently: 'Although Namibian pride may not allow it, it has to be admitted that environmental conditions are generally poorly suited to agricultural production' (Mendelsohn et al. 2006, p. 72). An exception is a limited portion of land under irrigation, benefitting mainly specialised food production. The most prominent example is the vineyards near Aussenkehr along the southern border of the Orange river, producing mainly table grapes for the European market as a lucrative business for the foreign owners, with appalling conditions for the main seasonal local workforce (Smith 2020). Fruit and vegetables are produced under irrigation, often near dams such as the Hardap.[1] The so-called maize triangle in the northern part of central Namibia has—as its name suggests—commercial farming specialising in maize, which is highly vulnerable according to rainfall patterns. Millet is the more stable (and secure) locally produced corn (maize) in the northern communal areas. Other significant sources of income include commercial beef production for export to European, Chinese and American markets, with a significant drop in 2020 due to the effects of drought (Nembwaya and Erastus 2020).

The northern and north-eastern communal areas in which, despite an increased influx to the urban centres in the central parts, more than half of the population continues to make a living, benefit from a higher—but, because of the effects of climate change, increasingly unreliable—level of rainfall. Overall, communal land remains a key backbone of the country's economy. Over half of the population, mostly concentrated in these lands, depends on subsistence farming (crop and livestock). Subsistence farming is a key source of income for many families. The agricultural sector thus remains critical to Namibian household economies:

> According to the latest Namibian Statistics Agency (NSA) Labour Survey, agricultural production and directly linked economic activities provided a total of 167,242 jobs during 2018. This amounts to 23 percent of the total employed population in Namibia (Nangolo and Alweendo 2020, p. 3).

The government has an even higher figure to offer. As it states on its website (without any reference to the source for the data): 'Although arable land accounts for only 1% of Namibia, nearly half of the population is employed in agriculture'.[2] As

[1] Of late, the Neckartal dam further south (near Keetmanshoop as the next big town) was completed and, due to an exceptional rainfall season in 2021, filled to capacity as the country's (now by far) largest water reservoir, situated in one of the driest regions of the country. But the land earmarked for irrigation and agricultural production as a second step of the original plan could not be developed due to the lack of funds. The project hence remains for now a white elephant and another example of the inefficiency and waste of investments in infrastructure unable to be used (Grynberg 2021). With water in abundance, local people have not been empowered to use it for food production in one of the country's poorest regions.

[2] https://gov.na/the-land. However, employment in the definition used here is a very broad category. It includes people who work only very limited hours during a week with respect to households in the informal or subsistence sectors.

the figures show, Namibia's agriculture, despite the limited economic potential, remains highly relevant for the living conditions of a substantial part of the population. As with all other features of Namibian society, it still bears the traces of a century of settler-colonial rule, reproducing gross disparities.

In the dominant perception prevailing, the private possession of land (in the commercial farming sector) is associated with wealth generation. But aggregated data compiled in the mid-1990s suggests that the land utilised by the (hardly existing) 'average commercial farmer'[3] (and his/her labourers) is not yielding the high monetary income one might expect:

> If total value added by commercial agriculture (N$565 million in 1997) were evenly divided between the 6,337 farms, the average value added per farm would amount to about N $90,000, including wage bills to an average of six farm workers, return on capital employed, land rents and own labour (UNDP 1998, p. 45).[4]

Even at the advantageous exchange rate at the time, this translated (per farm unit) into merely the average per capita income of Namibians per annum. Hence, farming as such is certainly not a guaranteed road to wealth. This of course neither denies that there are much wealthier ranchers, nor puts into question that commercial farmers are usually much better off than most of those in the communal areas, whose average annual income was estimated (according to the same source) at about N$3000. The point is, however, that even among commercial (still predominantly white) farmers, land ownership cannot be automatically associated with a guaranteed secure existence, especially in times of drought, animal diseases or other constraints. When receiving the final report of the ancestral land commission in mid-2020 (see below), President Hage Geingob acknowledged the challenges landowners are facing: 'Some people think once they have land, they will be rich. But this is not so, the head of state said' (Beukes 2020).

Even a more nuanced understanding of the economic situation would not ease matters decisively and does not minimise the desire among the previously colonised to have the land stolen from their ancestors returned. More than a century of colonial rule has left not only scars but festering wounds (see Harring and Odendaal 2002; Hunter 2004; Von Wietersheim 2008). Notwithstanding the importance of land, in terms of the officially declared policy of national reconciliation, the land policy evolving since Namibia's Independence on 21 March 1990 (see Pankhurst 1995, 1996, 2000; Werner 2000, 2001, 2005; Kaapama 2007) remains ambiguous and half-hearted. It spans over two national land conferences in 1991 and 2018, illustrating the continued frictions, challenges and clashes of interests over how to address the structural legacies of the past. Lacking coherence and sufficient prioritisation, the policy is neither neoliberal nor transformative. It is, to a large extent, a sign of negligence by the government towards the rural poor. In this

[3]Farmers often own more than one registered farm.

[4]The Namibian Dollar is a non-convertible currency and pegged to the South African Rand.

context, this chapter engages with this policy over time,[5] during which time the dividing lines have slightly shifted from a category of 'race' to ethnicity and class.

2 The Long Shadows of Colonialism

Thirty years of German settler colonialism in South West Africa (1884–1914) paved the way for continued white minority rule under South African control. As summarised among others by Werner (1993), Melber (2000), and Wallace and Kinahan (2011), German colonialism created the infamous structures of an Apartheid society, in which the forced removal of the colonised people from their land in substantial parts of the country and its subsequent occupation by white settlers became an enduring and essential component of a past that remains alive in the present. The primary resistance against the foreign invasion triggered the first genocide of the twentieth century among the Ovaherero, Nama and Damara (as well as San communities) as the main occupants of the eastern, central, and southern regions of the country, where the survivors were forced from their land into so-called Native reserves within the part of the territory declared (since then for administrative purposes) a 'Police Zone' under direct colonial administration.[6] The negotiations initiated in 2015 between the German and Namibian governments to address the consequences of the crimes committed testify to the long shadow of colonialism and its past in the present (see Melber 2017, 2020b).

After Germany had to surrender control over the territory to South Africa during World War 1, land (dis)possession continued. The South African Apartheid regime's administration provided Afrikaans-speaking poor whites with a new existence as farmers in the occupied so-called fifth province. Land appropriations and resettlements took place until the 1960s. They were further systematised as part of the so-called Bantustan Policy. This consolidated the territorial entities (reserves) for each ethnic group under varying degrees of limited self-administrative structures, within a policy euphemistically called 'Separate Development'. The 1963 'Report of the Commission of Enquiry into South West African Affairs'—commonly known by the name of its chairman as the 'Odendaal Plan'—implemented a final physical segregation of groups based on ethnic classifications by means of further forced resettlements into 'homelands' (Wallace and Kinahan 2011).

Ever since then, the skewed distribution of land has remained largely untouched. According to data presented by the Namibia Statistics Agency (2018), land tenure was in 2018 composed of 23% state land, 35% communal land and 42% freehold

[5]It draws in part on some earlier engagements with the issue (Melber 2002, 2005, 2014, 2019).

[6]Notably, the majority of the population settled north of this Police Zone and was never moved from the land. Colonial-capitalist patterns of exploitation were established there in different forms of indirect rule. On the effects of the 'Red Line' separating the settler-colonial-controlled economy in the 'Police Zone' from the northern regions, see Miescher (2013).

land. As well, 97.7% of the 39.7 million hectares of commercial farms are owned by Namibians: 34 million hectares (86%) are privately owned, with government owning the remaining 5.4 million hectares (14%). About 70% (27.8 million hectares) of freehold agricultural land is owned by previously advantaged Namibians (the official nomenklatura for whites), with previously disadvantaged Namibians owning 6.4 million hectares (16%). Three per cent (1.2 million hectares) are owned by non-Namibians (more than half of them Germans, and more than a quarter South Africans). Since 1990, a total of three million hectares (comprising 496 farms) were acquired by the state under a National Resettlement Programme, allocated to 5352 beneficiaries (Namibia Statistics Agency 2018, p. 44). As Lenggenhager and Nghitevelekwa (2018) maintain: 'The pattern of land distribution and ownership reflects class inequality and perpetuates racial inequalities'. It is also a reminder of colonial dispossession, intoxicating the current social contract.

In November 2002, the then president of South West Africa People's Organisation (SWAPO) and Namibia's head of state Sam Nujoma granted an exclusive interview to the German journalist Thomas Knemeyer. The South African weekly *Mail & Guardian* (2002) published extracts.[7] Passages from this instructive dialogue document the sentiments and emotions characteristic of the ambiguities still influencing everyday interaction between the former colonisers and colonised:

Knemeyer: Another question which is on a lot of people's minds is the land question. Can you please give us the exact position of your government on this point?

Nujoma: I want this to be understood by everybody. Any corner of the Republic of Namibia is the property of the people of Namibia. It was invaded by German colonials from 1884 until 1915. They cut up our country. They never bought the land. So that is the prerogative of the people of Namibia, to decide who it belongs to. When you Germans were defeated, your country was divided in two. So why do you want to come and poke your nose into our affairs?

Knemeyer: 192 estates belonging to absentee landlords are now to be compulsorily purchased.

Nujoma: Certainly. We will not allow foreigners to own land who are not here. That is the decision of my government and the people of Namibia to expropriate land with fair compensation. Whether you like it or not!

The exchange dragged on and escalated further, documenting an enraged Nujoma's feelings of defeat, subjugation, humiliation and the wish for retaliation as an understandable temptation to restore human dignity.[8] Such desire for restoring

---

[7] Reprinted in full in Melber (2008, pp. 260–263).

[8] But despite the announced expropriation of 192 farms owned by absentee landlords (as decided shortly before this interview took place by the SWAPO Party Congress) being within Namibia's legal and constitutional framework, the directive was not implemented.

identity was a year earlier also emphasised by the Bishop Zephania Kameeta to the Evangelical Lutheran Rhenish Church in Namibia:[9]

> Our great grandparents died without seeing justice done to the land issue, our parents are dying in poverty with suffering engraved on their faces. They told us how they were living happily on their land, cultivating their crops and looking after their cattle. Together with their parents, they experienced the horror of their land being fenced around. [. . .] To remove the people from the land on which they have been living for generations, is to destroy and kill them, not only outside but also inside. [. . .] The violation of the land rights are the violation of the soul of the people, but its restoration is the resurrection of the soul of the people and life in abundance (Kameeta 2002, p. 29, 30).

Such an emotional, if not romanticising perspective, rooted in matters of identity, underlines that 'people's relationship to their environment is not only material, but also social and cultural' (Salih 1999, p. 163).

3 Whose Land?

When the anti-colonial liberation movement SWAPO, after an armed struggle for self-determination lasting 30 years, finally took over political power,[10] the new government faced expectations to transform society and address the structural imbalances. The process of decolonisation, however, has been one of controlled change as a result of a negotiated settlement (Melber and Saunders 2007). Core constitutional principles, ensuring fundamental civil rights, were designed in essence during the early 1980s by the so-called Western contact group. These rights included the recognition of existing property relations. The landowners at Independence, therefore, were legally entitled to their private property and protected by common law. This anchored to a large extent the socio-economic status quo at Independence, which in turn entrenched and perpetuated the social disparities created during the colonial period. It upheld and perpetuated private ownership at the time without reversing past injustices arising from forceful expropriation in colonial times.[11]

Bearing the process of negotiated change in mind, Sam Nujoma (2001, p. 419) paints a misleading picture when he suggests that, as a result of an imperialist conspiracy, Namibians were denied the opportunity to address the land issue

[9]Zephania Kameeta was a SWAPO Member of Parliament since Independence in 1990 and the first Deputy Speaker of the National Assembly; from 2001 until 2013, Bishop to the Evangelical Lutheran Rhenish Church in Namibia; and, between 2015 and 2020, Minister for Poverty Eradication and Social Welfare.

[10]In the process of transforming from a movement into a political party, SWAPO (also known as SWAPO of Namibia) was officially renamed Swapo Party. But SWAPO remains a commonly used acronym. Unless quoted otherwise, SWAPO is used throughout this chapter.

[11]It is interesting to note that in the parallel process of German unification, the former West German state expropriated private property in the former East Germany and returned it to previous owners with the argument that this is a corrective and legitimate restitution of earlier property relations which were violated by the East German state.

differently. As observed, 'land and property rights were never the subjects of public debate', and the 'aspect of the Bill of Fundamental Human Rights that gave guarantees to existing property owners received surprisingly little attention' during the deliberations and the ultimate adoption of the constitutional principles prior to Independence (Cliffe et al. 1994, p. 205, 215). This limited any form of transfer of ownership, since the Constitution stipulated that Articles 5 to 25 in its Chapter Three ('Fundamental Human Rights and Freedoms')[12] cannot be changed. As stated in Article 25(1):

> Parliament or any subordinate legislative authority shall not make any law, and the Executive and the agencies of Government shall not take any action which abolishes or abridges the fundamental rights and freedoms conferred by this chapter.

Next to civil and political rights, Article 16 includes the freedom and protection of property:

1. All persons shall have the right in any part of Namibia to acquire, own and dispose of all forms of immovable and movable property individually or in association with others and to bequeath their property to their heirs or legatees: provided that Parliament may by legislation prohibit or regulate as it deems expedient the right to acquire property by persons who are not Namibian citizens.
2. The State or a competent body or organ authorised by law may expropriate property in the public interest subject to the payment of just compensation, in accordance with requirements and procedures to be determined by Act of Parliament.

During the course of several generations, the ownership of land had changed as a result of legal transactions in many instances, and this complicated the matter further. Colonialism had introduced a legal system turning land into a commodity based on private property rights. It defined and regulated personalised ownership of land by means of individual title deeds, thereby transforming what was mainly a common good into private (settler) or public (state) ownership. Henceforth, the public interest was basically reduced to the interest of the colonial state and the European settlers.[13]

An additional complication was the challenge to define the point of departure for land restitution. Reversing the injustices emerging during historical processes requires determining when and under which circumstances change of land ownership became unacceptable. Was it only the introduction of registered private property titles in a deeds office marked the decisive shift under formally imposed

[12] See https://www.un.int/namibia/namibia/chapter-3-fundamental-human-rights-and-freedoms.

[13] As Thran (2014) argues, the private property titles created by German colonialism were not reversed by post-colonial land redistribution. Rather, private property had been reinforced through the forms of land transfer considered and practised under and since colonial rule. In its final consequence, appropriation of land therefore represents a continuity of the colonial property categories by only shifting the private ownership of specific parcels of land, while reaffirming the general claim to private ownership.

foreign rule? The southern African continent—like many other parts in the world—has been a region of intensive migration and hence also of continual changes in occupation and control of territories, originally inhabited by the Khoisan communities.

Signifying the centrality of the land issue, a major National Land Reform Conference took place early on, in 1991 (Republic of Namibia 1991). It adopted a far-reaching consensus document and recommended, among other things:

- Redistribution of commercial farmland, mainly on the basis of willing seller–willing buyer, with the government having preferential rights to purchase farmland for resettlement purposes.
- Introduction of a land tax.
- Reallocation of underutilised land.
- Limits to the size and number of farms made up of private-owned land.
- Elimination of foreign-owned land and absentee landlordism.
- In the communal areas (the former reserves), situated mainly in the northern regions and offering minimal rainfall for cultivating the land, disadvantaged communities (in particular the San) 'should receive special protection of their land rights' (Office of the Prime Minister 1991, p. 29).

As Schade (1992) pointed out, expectations were confronted with some sobering realities. The conference clearly stated: 'Given the complexities in redressing ancestral land claims, restitution in full is impossible' (Office of the Prime Minister 1991, p. 24). But restitution was not implemented at all. Rather, this vagueness allowed for widely differing interpretations and arbitrariness, thereby creating manoeuvring space for those who are in control over and execute the power of definition. Not surprisingly, since Namibian Independence, a certain ambiguity by the post-colonial authorities, especially towards the most marginalised indigenous minority groups, prevailed (Daniels 2003; Suzman 2002). State authorities have shown a large degree of unwillingness to accept land claims by local communities, as the case studies in Odendaal and Werner (2020) document.

As suggested by an insider, 'the difficulties involved in disentangling competing claims of lost lands provided an ideal political opportunity to broaden the category of beneficiaries of land reform to include those who were never dispossessed in the historical sense' (Werner 2002, p. 56). As director of the Ministry of Lands, Resettlement and Rehabilitation until the mid-1990s, Werner was able to gather first-hand insights. He points out that such controversies permitted the main base of SWAPO in the northern areas of former Ovamboland to be primary beneficiaries of redistributive measures. Hence the Land Conference 'provided the political legitimacy to rule out any ethnically specific claims to land, no matter how justified they might have been' (Werner 2002, p. 56). This explains why the government could, after a decade of Independence, refer to some 240,000 people on the waiting list for resettlement, mainly from the densely populated northern areas, where eviction from land never took place.

4 Land Policy as Policy Without Land

Despite the institutionalisation of a Ministry of Lands, Resettlement and Rehabilitation (since 2020 part of the Ministry for Agriculture, Water and Land Reform), the purchasing of farms was slow and inefficient. The ministry did not even spend the annual budget allocations for the purchase of land (Werner 2005, 2015a). By the mid-1990s, the Namibian authorities had acquired only some 100,000 ha of freehold land for redistribution – less than a handful of so-called commercial farms (Werner 2001, p. 272). After a decade of Independence, the farmland bought amounted to 54 farms totalling 341,000 ha (see the detailed overview in Werner 2000, pp. 45–48). The main problem in land acquisition was however not the reluctance of commercial farmers to abandon their property within the 'willing seller – willing buyer' policy. In contrast:

> By 2001 the government has been offered 759 commercial farms. A total of 505 of these farms were turned down, leaving them for sale in the private sector. The government has shown interest in 254 farms since 1991, or about one farm in three put on sale, but only actually purchased 97 for land reform purposes, only about 13% of the farms sold in Namibia over this ten-year period. (Harring and Odendaal 2002, p. 52)

The authors conclude that the strategy formulated in the 'White Paper of Resettlement Policy' of 2001 had failed not because of a lack of farms on the market. If the quality of the land on offer would not promote a meaningful redistributive effect by resettling people, it would actually support the argument that Namibia's climatic and environmental constraints simply do not encourage circumstances under which people would be enabled on a meaningful scale to make a decent living from the land.

Giving back land to a previous tiller (or actually herder) does not necessarily pay off when measured in terms of economic performance, and in some cases, not even in terms of self-employment. Field research exploring the results of some among the first farms utilised for resettlement purposes offered some sobering results. Most of the settlements remain dependent on food aid, do not receive the necessary support towards self-sufficiency and fail to meet the social welfare objectives (Gargallo 2010b). Where farms were used for resettlement purposes, beneficiaries were often unable to make a living due to a lack of capital and know-how (for a few prominent cases, see Melber 2019, pp. 76–77).

The most prominent case has so far been the farm Ongombo West 30 km northeast of Windhoek. It had successfully specialised in cut flowers exported to the European market. A dispute between the owners and workers triggered a legal battle in court. The case was closed in 2004 with a judgement defining the modalities of what became the first legal expropriation. The farm was subsequently used for resettlement purposes. But the infrastructure and production collapsed while people live in poverty dependent on support from neighbours (Jason 2021). Once contributing to exports, Gross Domestic Product (GDP) and revenue income, Ongombo

West has turned into a liability, a failure of land transfer and subsequent utilisation.[14] Such dismal performance testifies to a policy beset by incompetence. After all, there have been many largely ignored recommendations on how best to provide resettled farmers with meaningful opportunities to live from the land (Rothauge 2007; Odendaal and Werner 2010).

The main issue therefore remains—as in other parts of Southern Africa—not land, but poverty (Hendricks 2000). Revealingly so, neither Namibia's official Poverty Reduction Strategy, approved by Cabinet in 1998, nor the National Poverty Reduction Action Programme for 2001–2005 linked land reform to poverty reduction, which prompted the conclusion that:

> The Namibian Government does not view land redistribution as one of the major instruments in reducing poverty. In fact, there is an inexplicably pessimistic view expressed in the Poverty Reduction Strategy, namely that the agricultural base was too weak to offer a sustainable basis for prosperity (Sachikonye 2004, p. 74).

The challenge lies, as Cousins (2003, p. 308) points out, in dealing with an agrarian economy based on a highly skewed distribution of land as well as weak and insecure property rights for the majority of rural people. It remains:

> A festering wound on the body politic of post-liberation Southern Africa that will be healed neither through neglect nor the palliative of de-racialising commercial agriculture. Radical surgery is required, but, as Zimbabwe demonstrates so clearly, this must not itself threaten the life of the patient.

What has remained conspicuously absent from the government's land policy is the political will and vision to embark on a thought-through strategy with a clear focus. Instead, it translated to a large extent into a policy without land. What had been concluded already in 2005 remains a valid observation:

> The Namibian government should focus on a clear agricultural development policy that includes the restructuring of the existing commercial agricultural sector, improving agriculture on the communal lands through capital and skills investment, as well as a bold and creative policy of land reform and land resettlement in commercial and communal areas alike. This policy will be both expensive and involve a substantial government subsidy. Thus, it is not just 'land reform policy' that is expensive – all agricultural policy is (Odendaal 2005, p. 18).

5 Land Policy as Elite Land Grab

So far, Namibian land policy has not offered any meaningful improvements for the majority of the poor. Instead, it benefitted to a large extent the members of a new elite in various ways, both as regards the transfer of commercial farming land and the illegal occupation of communal land for individual private gains. Both forms of appropriation speak to the class nature of the Namibian post-colonial elite pacts.

[14] The misery was even televised by the National Broadcasting Company (NBC 2018).

5.1 *Commercial Farming*

Since the turn of the century, the contours of the allocation of land for the resettlement of members of communities from other regions than those where colonial expropriation took place became evident and a growing bone of contention. The first national land conference had stated: 'All Namibian citizens have the right to live wherever they choose within the national territory' (Office of the Prime Minister 1991, p. 28). But those being supported by the state authorities to settle on land taken from other groups fuelled inter-ethnic animosities (Gargallo 2010a). Descendants of those communities whose ancestors were robbed of their land by German and South African colonialism felt they remained on the margins while others closer to the government were given preferential treatment. They considered such redistribution as just another means of discrimination (Iikela 2018c).

Farming in Namibia has increasingly become 'a rich man's hobby' (Sherbourne 2003). It has partly been turned into a status symbol, and lifestyle choice for the urban middle and upper class of the new elite prepared to subsidise their farms from other principal sources of income. A government policy encouraging and supporting black Namibians as commercial farmers have at least initially to rely on heavy subsidisation. Land policy is—as it was in settler-colonial times—about pigmentation and ethnic belonging. Sherbourne (2004, p. 1) hence answers his hypothetical question 'Any Room for Economics'? as follows:

> While some have tried to argue that land reform is important to boost the country's economy and reduce poverty, in their hearts most people know that the land question is about race: black Namibians should own more of Namibia's commercial farmland. In reality everything else – agricultural output, the treatment of farm workers, poverty reduction, environmental sustainability – is very much secondary.

Trying to investigate the mounting complaints concerning the selective and privileged transfer of state purchased and subsidised land to a few privileged, Namibia's Ombudsman had demanded in May 2018 access to the list of resettlement farms and their beneficiaries. The ministry finally handed it over in October (Iikela 2018b). Since then, the Ombudsman has requested a clarification of resettlement criteria (Iikela 2018c), while members of the political opposition have questioned the list's authenticity and demanded a proper forensic land audit. Revealingly, a list compiled from legally required announcements in various print media between 2011 and early 2018 had several top government officials and high-ranking civil servants as beneficiaries resettled courtesy of the state on 99-year leaseholds throughout the country (Iikela 2018a). Despite their incompleteness, the records illustrate a haphazard reallocation of land guided by a dubious set of criteria. Beneficiaries were in many cases selected purely on the basis of being ethnically or politically (or both) close to those in political power. The form of transfer lacks any coherent socio-economic strategy with regard to agricultural production and productivity as an income- and employment-generating economic sector.

Partly as a result of the growing frustration among the Nama communities in the southern regions, the Landless People's Movement (LPM) registered as a new party in 2018. Its leader Bernadus Swartbooi[15] presented the political agenda at a party inaugural assembly (electoral college) in October 2019. He promised that LPM as governing party would amend laws so that:

> Our people have the land to be able to feed themselves. . . . We are a party that wants to get the land for our people, no matter what the law says. We go and change the laws. We want to get the basics right and get our people into agricultural production so that we can feed ourselves as a nation and export any surpluses that we produce here (quoted in Iikela 2019).

In the National Assembly elections held in November 2019, LPM became the second strongest opposition party (Melber 2020a). In the Regional and Local Authority elections of November 2020, it secured control over the two southern regions of //Karas and Hardap and a majority in all local authorities in both regions (Melber 2020c) and made inroads also in several towns and municipalities elsewhere as part of a major political earthquake shifting the ground away from SWAPO.

The gains by LPM underlined to some extent the frustrations expressed already, earlier on, in an Afrobarometer survey among 1200 Namibians during November 2017. Land reform was ranked as the third most important problem among respondents at 21% (the following unemployment with 66% and poverty/destitution with 34%), while 56% classified the land resettlement programme as not very or not at all effective (Isbell et al. 2019). It now remains a task for the new political office holders (in LPM) at central, regional and local levels to meet existing land expectations. In his speech during the National Assembly's debate of the annual budget 2020/21, Swartbooi on 2 June 2020, made extensive reference to his party's land policy priorities. He urged for agrarian reform,

> Redressing the past imbalances in the land dispensation. The restoration of the dignity of those Namibians who suffered genocide, who lost land, and who were subjected to white racism, which prohibited land ownership to black Namibians, is an urgent and long aspired human quest. . . . The polemic that land can only be given to those that have financial resources, and that the poorer Namibians are unable and incapable of producing on land . . . should be condemned by us all. Such anti-poor determinism against the vast majority of Namibians is toxic and nefarious in our young democracy (Swartbooi 2020, p. 11).

Commenting subsequently on the land reform ministry budget motivation speech in the National Assembly, Swartbooi on 15 June 2020 added:

> Black Namibians must enter the agrarian structure and among these blacks, we must be clear as to who must benefit from land reform . . . Land must be returned to those that lost land, and not be a generalised exercise of land acquisition and land allocation, without a political economic and sociological view of the land question (quoted in Tjitemisa 2020)

---

[15] Previously a SWAPO activist, he was a governor of the //Karas region and then the deputy minister for Land Reform. In 2016/17, his term of office ended with a fall out with minister Utoni Nujoma (a son of Namibia's first president) over the land policy and in particular the re-distribution of land in the southern regions to members of groups from other (northern) parts of the country. The controversy escalated and ended in his dismissal first from office, then from the National Assembly, and finally his departure from SWAPO (Immanuel 2017).

Given the paralysing impact of the Covid-19 pandemic on Namibian policy formulation and implementation, not least the reduction of parliamentary debates, not much is on record since then. But the success of the LPM will certainly depend to a considerable extent on its ability to influence not only discourse but also delivery.

5.2 *Communal Land*

The complexity of existing forms of land use and ownership goes far beyond the simple dichotomy of commercial and/or communal forms of land. Since about a third of some 2.5 million Namibians (estimation 2020) live on the communal lands in the northern parts of the territory, a meaningful land reform would have to address the issue of how to achieve effective ways and means of reducing poverty among the population living there:

> Given that some of the land north of the Red Line [i.e. outside the previous 'Police Zone'] is among the potentially most productive in Namibia, one could argue that the challenges to bring security of tenure, security of investment, equitable infrastructure and market participation to Namibia's communal areas is just as important to the land issue in Namibia as acquiring and redistributing commercial farmland that was expropriated during the colonial period (Fuller 2004, p. 86).

While this might entail advocating the introduction of title deeds and privatisation for the suggested benefit of the communities, it opens a can of worms as witnessed in the prevailing de facto process of appropriation of communal land as private property. This happens by fencing off communal lands as a land acquisition strategy in a process of further class diversification (Twyman et al. 2001). The local privatisation of communal land by illegal fencing marginalises the already marginalised and most vulnerable even further. While the government and the local authorities are not stopping this process with determination (and thereby act against those within their own rank and file), a deepening process of erosion of minimum security in livelihood for the rural poor takes place. As a result, 'the face of communal areas in Namibia will change forever with potential devastating consequences for the poorest of the poor in Namibia who mostly rely on access to the commonage for their livelihoods' (Odendaal 2011b, p. 24; see also Odendaal 2011a).

Residents of communal areas rely on the patronage of the traditional authorities—who in fact in most cases, cooperate closely with SWAPO or represent the party's interests. The evidence is the Land Bill tabled in 2010, which did not introduce any changes in the decision-making processes,

> Although this is absolutely necessary in view of the [recent] "land grabs" that have affected Namibia. Without improved accountability and transparency towards land right holders, people in communal areas will be vulnerable to the predations of international investors and their local allies (Werner 2010, p. 21).

By illegally fencing in the allocated land, the beneficiaries de facto privatised it as a form of 'elite land grabbing' (Odendaal 2011a). Between 2012 and 2015, close to 300 cases of illegal fencing of land in communal areas were recorded in five of the country's 14 regions (Tjitemisa 2018). A considerable portion of the best parts of communal land has been fenced off, largely tolerated by the authorities (sometimes with office-bearers being an active part thereof), despite demands to the contrary articulated already by the first National Land Conference as early as 1991.

The part-time pastoralism practised as a fashionable lifestyle of the post-colonial urban and rural elites in salaried employment adds to the pressure and increases the vulnerability of poor pastoral households.[16] As documented by Werner (2015b), reforms have created advantages for accessing communal tenure by ruling elites. These seek to abuse unclear provisions. Despite the absence of individual property titles, they use land exclusively individually for personal gains only, restricting grazing of livestock and access to water for own private purposes. Nghitevelekwa (2020) offers a more detailed engagement on this topic, pointing to the differences between land owners and land users through the introduction of long-term leasehold, while in a parallel process, customary land rights are gradually commodified:

> Although it operates illegally, an emerging land market in non-freehold areas opens new ways of accessing land through money transfers. This practice . . . raises the important policy question: how should the state deal with this illegal trading of customary land rights? (Werner 2020, p. xii).

6 Land Policy: From Failure to Failure?

After several postponements, the second land conference took place during the first week of October 2018. The Ministry for Land Reform provided access to most of the documents submitted.[17] Compared with the 24 resolutions adopted but barely implemented at the first land conference, many of the 176 resolutions now adopted—under altogether 40 different 'identified topical issues'[18]—offered more detailed follow-ups on the initial 1991 recommendations. As important additions, urban land and informal settlements received the long overdue attention (Remmert and Ndhlovu 2018; Lühl and Delgado 2018). Communal land also received more prominence. A resolution stressed the need for the protection of tenure rights, mainly in the interest of the poorest as victims of illegal land occupations, and condemned the ongoing privatisation of communal land by members of the new elite. Ancestral land claims and rights were also acknowledged. A final proposal suggested that 70%

[16] See the case study for the hinterlands of Fransfontein in the Kunene region by Schnegg et al. (2013) but, also earlier, Cox et al. (1998).

[17] Accessible online at: http://www.mlr.gov.na/land-conference1.

[18] Accessible online at: http://www.mlr.gov.na/documents/20541/638917/Second+National+Land+Conference+Resolutions+2018.pdf/15b498fd-fdc6-4898-aeda-91fecbc74319.

of resettlement farms would be reserved for descendants of people from communities who were robbed of their land, with 30% left for those coming from other regions (in itself already entailing preferential treatment). But the final resolution included war veterans from the ranks of SWAPO (including non-combatants) and their dependents in the group of people dispossessed through colonialism, which through the back door reintroduced a considerable number of potential claimants from the northern regions, from where by far most of the war veterans came (Lobo 2019).

The contrast between the declared goals and the realities was quite revealing.[19] progress report for the period until the end of November 2020 recorded 9 resolutions implemented and 142 'ongoing', with one 'pending' and 25 'already in existence' prior to the conference (Republic of Namibia 2020b, p. 1).[20] With reference to the progress report, Prime Minister Kuugongelwa-Amadhila disclosed that the government had, despite the recommendations, not abandoned the willing buyer-willing seller approach. In the two years since the conference, it had purchased 26 farms with a combined value of N$ 285 million. The legal(istic) reference to constitutional constraints appears as a convenient exit option to not engage in a proper examination of existing possible modalities to execute meaningful reforms in property relations and ownership of land in full compliance with the rule of law. This suggests that many in government remain distant to the expectations and desires of the descendants of those who under colonialism were robbed of the land. But as the success of the LPM and other parties shows, they are also voters. However, as observed by the director of the local Institute for Public Policy Research: 'No blueprint for a new Land Reform Act came out of the conference' (Iikela 2021).

The most noteworthy difference made so far is the formation of a Presidential Commission of Inquiry on Ancestral Land. In line with a resolution, it was appointed in February 2019 by President Geingob to offer further advice on restitution. Its report was submitted in July 2020, but only released into the public domain in January 2021. Its findings were not surprising to those who had with common sense observed the dynamics unfolding since Independence. As it emphasises, 'land was, and is, not just an economic resource, but also carries cultural and spiritual significance' (Republic of Namibia 2020a, p. XXVI). It also concedes that conflicting historical narratives among descendants of the indigenous communities and fluid social interactions make it impossible to define exact territorial boundaries for the various communities in the pre-colonial era. The report then shares diplomatically measured, but in no uncertain terms the critical views its authors came across during the numerous consultative meetings in all regions of the country:

[19] Reiterating the determination to end foreign ownership of land, ten days after the conference news leaked that a Russian oligarch, already in possession of three farms since 2013, had added another four to his Namibian empire in a questionable transaction agreed (but not disclosed) just ahead of the conference (for further details see Melber 2019, p. 79).

[20] The report notes that one resolution was not part of the original document.

> The rate at which land redistribution is taking place is perceived to be painfully slow, and thus falls far below the expectations of the majority of largely landless communities in the country, particularly the descendants of those that were mostly affected by colonial land dispossession.
>
> [...] There are limitations to land in general and agricultural land in particular, in relation to sustainable livelihoods by communities. This must, however, not be used as a pretext for denying the majority of communities who continue to face systematic economic exclusion from benefitting from the available opportunities for land ownership, access and utilisation.
>
> Although the Government adopted a well-intended land reform programme, this, however, lacks a robust environment to nurture and support it (professionally and financially) to propel historically disadvantaged Namibians to become agriculturally successful and to improve food security (Republic of Namibia 2020a, p. XXVIII).

It then acknowledges the perception that 'the process in its current form favours the rich, the powerful and the politically connected' and that beneficiaries were from '[r]egions regarded as having least been affected by past colonial land dispossession'. The Commission therefore finds that policies 'in their current forms are more 'individual' focused rather than 'community' focused' and 'lack adequate post-settlement support mechanisms' (Republic of Namibia 2020a, p. XXVIII, XXIX). Finally, it points out: 'if the Constitutional provisions are interpreted in a broad, expansionist and purposive manner, claims for ancestral land rights and restitution may be founded on our constitutional values' and that initiatives to restore social justice 'have not been adequately effective' (Republic of Namibia 2020a, p. XXX).

The Commission also offers a noteworthy interpretation of restorative justice by declaring that in 'international law, the term 'reparation' is used in a wide sense to refer to all those measures which include restitution, compensation and satisfaction that may be employed to redress the various types of harms that victims may have suffered as a consequence of certain crimes' (Republic of Namibia 2020a, p. XXVI). This seems to confirm the understanding established by court rulings that while the Namibian Constitution prohibits expropriation without just compensation, this does not turn it into a roadblock preventing land redistribution based on certain forms of legally enforced transfer within the rule of law.[21]

7 Conclusion: Land and Class

The government's land policy—or rather the absence of it—has so far mainly satisfied the appetite of the new black elite for securing their own private farms (or, in the case of communal land, its occupation and appropriation for individual gains). As a critical assessment two decades into Independence concluded:

[21] Already in 2008, a High Court judgment in 'Kessl versus the Ministry of Lands and Resettlement' (Glinz 2009), while dismissing the government's efforts to expropriate four farms of German owners, outlined clear guidelines on how to implement expropriation according to the rule of law (Harring and Odendaal 2008).

> The implementation of the Land Resettlement Programme seems to be riddled by numerous significant challenges which lead to procrastination of implementation. The same applies to the significant downgrading of the initiatives for integrated rural development and poverty reduction. . .[I]t is alleged that the "economics of affection" have found expression in the ties of political patronage, which are being exploited by some bearers of political office and bureaucrats alike as elaborate avenues for allocating preferential treatment to party stalwarts, as well as friends and relatives of the ruling elite (Kaapama 2010, p. 202).

In the end, then, land has become every bit as much a natural resource for individual acquisition by a new political class and its allies—be it for commercial farming or for the use of protected parks and reserves for tourism enterprises or other forms of utilisation through resource extraction—instead of being treated and protected as the country's collective natural wealth. In fact, it is yet another sad irony that so far, it has not been the (still predominantly white) commercial farmers who are most at risk in all this. Rather, it is the rural poor in the communal areas which are the most vulnerable.

A few days ahead of the second land conference, the editorial of a local weekly newspaper put the battles for land in its overall context as 'a smokescreen to cover-up continued elite control over not just the land, but all income-generating natural resources in Namibia'. As it pointed out:

> If an accurate look at who is receiving the resettlement farms, EPLs [Exclusive Prospecting Licenses], fishing quotas, affirmative action farm loans and other natural resource allocations is ever possible, we are convinced it will reveal not necessarily one ethnic group reaping all benefits but one socio-economic class gathering wealth (Windhoek Observer 2018).

This also brings to mind an observation by the late South African scholar Archie Mafeje, who during the early 1990s observed developments in Namibia while being based at the country's university. Far-sighted as he was, he concluded (as quoted in Sasa 2013, p. 41):

> The whole debate about land in Namibia is not about the livelihood of the dispossessed in the countryside but about how best to maintain the status quo. This could be true of white farmers, the government, as well as the black notables in the so-called communal areas.

References

Beukes J (2020) Land doesn't make you rich – Geingob. Namibian Sun, 27 July (https://www.namibiansun.com/news/land-doesnt-make-you-rich-geingob2020-07-27)

Cliffe L, Bush R, Lindsay J, Mokopakgosi B (1994) The transition to independence in Namibia. Lynne Rienner, Boulder, CO and London

Cousins B (2003) The Zimbabwe crisis in its wider context: the politics of land, democracy and development in Southern Africa. In: Hammar A, Raftopoulos B, Jensen S (eds) Zimbabwe's unfinished business. Rethinking land, state and nation in the context of crisis. Weaver Press, Harare, pp 263–316

Cox J, Kerven C, Werner W, Behnke R (eds) (1998) The privatisation of rangeland resources in Namibia. Overseas Development Institute, London and Windhoek

Daniels C (2003) The struggle for indigenous people's rights. In: Melber H (ed) Re-examining liberation in Namibia. Political culture since independence. Nordic Africa Institute, Uppsala, pp 57–63

Fuller B (2004) A Namibian path for land reform. In: Hunter J (ed) Who should own the land? Analysis and views on land reform and the land question in Namibia and Southern Africa. Windhoek, Konrad-Adenauer-Stiftung and Namibia Institute for Democracy, pp 83–86

Gargallo E (2010a) Beyond black and white: ethnicity and land reform in Namibia. Politique Africaine 120:153–173

Gargallo E (2010b) Serving production, welfare or neither? An analysis of the group resettlement projects in the Namibian land reform. J Namibian Stud 7:29–54

Glinz C (2009) The High Court of Namibia: *Günther Kessl v Ministry of Lands and Resettlement and 2 others. Case no. 27/2006 and 266/2006* – a test case for the Namibian land reform programme. Verfassung und Recht in Übersee 42(2):263–274

Grynberg R (2021) Namibian water torture. The Namibian, 26 March (https://www.namibian.com.na/100222/read/Namibian-Water-Torture)

Harring SL, Odendaal W (2002) 'One day we will all be equal'. A socio-legal perspective on the Namibian land reform and resettlement process. Legal Assistance Centre, Windhoek

Harring SL, Odendaal W (2008) KESSL – a new jurisprudence for land reform in Namibia? Legal Assistance Centre, Windhoek

Hendricks FT (2000) Questioning the land question. Agrarian transition, land tenure, and rural development in the former settler colonies of Southern Africa. In: Prah KK, Ahmed AGM (eds) Africa in transformation. Vol. 1: political and economic issues. Organisation for Social Science Research in Eastern and Southern Africa (OSSREA), Addis Ababa, pp 33–64

Hunter J (ed) (2004) Who should own the land? Analysis and views on land reform and the land question in Namibia and Southern Africa. Konrad Adenauer Stiftung and Namibia Institute for Democracy, Windhoek

Iikela S (2018a) Top Govt officials benefit from resettlement farms. The Namibian, 25 September (https://www.namibian.com.na/181732/archive-read/Top-Govt-officials-benefit-from-resettlement-farms)

Iikela S (2018b) Land reform releases resettlement list. The Namibian, 17 October (https://www.namibian.com.na/72315/read/Land-reform-releases-resettlement-list)

Iikela S (2018c) Govt ordered to clarify resettlement criteria. The Namibian, 22 October (https://www.namibian.com.na/182501/archive-read/Govt-ordered-to-clarify-resettlement-criteria)

Iikela S (2019) We will change the law and take the land. The Namibian, 7 October (https://www.namibian.com.na/193914/archive-read/We-will-change-the-law-and-take-the-land)

Iikela S (2021) Willing buyer-willing seller to stay. The Namibian, 20 January (https://www.namibian.com.na/98184/read/Willing-buyer-willing-seller-to-stay)

Immanuel S (2017) You are an idiot. The Namibian, 16 February (https://www.namibian.com.na/161373/archive-read/You-are-an-idiot)

Isbell T, Alweendo N, Moosa M (2019) Namibians look to social movement to prompt government action on land reform. Institute for Public Policy Research, Windhoek, https://afrobarometer.org/publications/ad289-namibians-look-social-movement-prompt-government-action-land-reform

Jason L (2021) Resettled farmers beg for handouts. New Era, 23 February (https://neweralive.na/posts/resettled-farmers-beg-for handouts)

Kaapama P (2007) Commercial land reforms in postcolonial Namibia. What happened to liberation struggle rhetoric? In: Melber H (ed) Transitions in Namibia. Which changes for whom? Nordic Africa Institute, Uppsala, pp 29–49

Kaapama P (2010) Politics of the land question in post settler colonial Africa: some comparative explorations of Zimbabwe, Kenya, Namibia and South Africa. In: Du Pisani A, Kössler R, Lindeke WA (eds) The long aftermath of war – reconciliation and transition in Namibia. Freiburg, Arnold Bergstraesser Institute, pp 171–214

Kameeta Z (2002) Land rights issues in Southern Africa with special focus on Namibia. In: Apelt W, Motte J (eds) Landrecht. Perspektiven der Konfliktvermeidung im Südlichen Afrika. Foedus, Wuppertal, pp 29–32

Lenggenhager L, Nghitevelekwa RV (2018) Why Namibians want fresh impetus behind land reform. The Conversation, 26 September (https://theconversation.com/why-namibians-want-fresh-impetus-behind-land-reform-103379)

Lobo PG 2019) In the wake of the Namibian Second National Land Conference. Agrarian South, 29 January (http://www.agrariansouth.org/2019/01/29/in-the-wake-of-the-namibian-second-national-land-conference/)

Lühl P, Delgado G (2018) Urban Land Reform in Namibia. Getting Ready for Namibia's Urban Future. Policy paper for submission to the 2018 National Land Conference Windhoek, 1-5 October 2018. Namibia University of Science and Technology, Integrated Land Management Institute, Windhoek, 14 August (http://dna.nust.na/landconference/submissions_2018/policy-paper-urban-land-reform-2018-final.pdf)

Mail & Guardian (2002) The art of saying absolutely nothing', 6 December

Melber H (2000) Economic and social transformation in the process of colonisation: society and state before and during German rule. In: Keulder C (ed) State, society and democracy: a reader in Namibian politics. Gamsberg Macmillan, Windhoek, pp 16–48 (2nd edition Windhoek, Konrad Adenauer Foundation 2010)

Melber H (2002) Contested territory: land in Southern Africa. The Case of Namibia. Journal, 50, Namibia Scientific Society, Windhoek, pp 77–85

Melber H (2005) Land and politics in Namibia. Rev Afr Polit Econ 32(103):135–142

Melber H (2008) We have not spoken at all about reparations. German-Namibian relationships: suppression or reconciliation? In: Zimmerer J, Zeller J (eds) Genocide in German South-West Africa. The Colonial War of 1904–1908 and its aftermath. Merlin Press, London, pp 259–273

Melber H (2014) Understanding Namibia. The trials of independence. Hurst, London

Melber H (2017) Genocide matters. Negotiating a Namibian-German past in the present. Stichproben Vienna J Afr Stud 33:1–24

Melber H (2019) Colonialism, land, ethnicity, and class: Namibia after the second national land conference. Afr Spectrum 54(1):73–86

Melber H (2020a) Geingob 2.0. Namibia's new government. J Namibian Stud 27:101–121

Melber H (2020b) Germany and Namibia: negotiating genocide. J Genocide Res 22(4):502–514

Melber H (2020c) Democracy beyond Swapo in Namibia. Democracy in Africa, 21 December (http://democracyinafrica.org/democracy-beyond-swapo-in-namibia/)

Melber H, Saunders C (2007) Conflict mediation in decolonization: Namibia's transition to independence. Afr Spectrum 42(1):73–94

Mendelsohn J, el Obeid S, de Klerk N, Vigne P (2006) Farming systems in Namibia. RAISON, Windhoek

Miescher G (2013) Die rote Linie. Die Geschichte der Veterinär- und Siedlungsgrenze in Namibia (1890er–1960er Jahre). Basler Afrika Bibliographien, Basel

Namibia Statistics Agency (2018) Namibia land statistics booklet. Namibia Statistics Agency, Windhoek

Nangolo M, Alweendo N (2020) Agriculture in Namibia: an overview. Institute for Public Policy Research, Windhoek

NBC (2018) Ongombo West a shadow of its former self, 3 October (https://www.nbc.na/news/ongombo-west-shadow -its-former-self.19018)

Nembwaya H, Erastus N (2020) Namibia's lucrative beef market at risk. The Namibian, 20 November (https://www.namibian.com.na/206519/archive-read/Namibias-lucrative-beef-market-at-risk)

Nghitevelekwa RV (2020) Securing land rights. Communal land reform in Namibia. University of Namibia Press, Windhoek

Nujoma S (2001) Where others wavered. The autobiography of Sam Nujoma. Panaf Books, London

Odendaal W (2011a) Elite land grabbing in Namibian communal areas and its impact on subsistence farmers' livelihoods. Institute for Poverty, Land and Agrarian Studies/School of Government, University of the Western Cape (Policy Brief 33)

Odendaal W (2011b) Land Grabbing in Namibia: A Case Study from the Omusati Region, Northern Namibia. Paper presented at the International Conference on Global Land Grabbing at the Institute of Development Studies, University of Sussex, 6–8 April

Odendaal W, Werner W (2010) Financing resettlement and securing tenure: are leasehold agreements the key to success? Livelihoods After Land Reform, Policy Brief no. 2 (https://assets.publishing.service.gov.uk/media/57a08b04ed915d3cfd000a9e/60332_Financing_Resettlement.pdf)

Odendaal W, Werner W (eds) (2020) "Neither here nor there". Indigeneity, marginalisation and land rights in post-independence Namibia. Legal Assistance Centre, Windhoek

Odendaal, W.A. 2005. Confiscation or compensation? An analysis of the Namibian commercial agricultural land reform process. Legal Assistance Centre, Windhoek. https://www.lac.org.na/projects/lead/Pdf/odendaal.pdf

Office of the Prime Minister (1991) National Conference on Land Reform and the Land Question. Consensus Document, Windhoek (http://www.mlr.gov.na/documents/20541/290353/Conference+Consensus+Document+%28Booklet+and+Programme%29.pdf/dfa21c58-1112-49e8-b22e-54d09e77cf52)

Pankhurst D (1995) Towards reconciliation of the land issue in Namibia: identifying the possible, assessing the probable. Dev Change 26(3):551–585

Pankhurst D (1996) A resolvable conflict? The politics of land in Namibia. Department of Peace Studies/University of Bradford, Bradford. (Peace Research Report 36)

Pankhurst D (2000) Unravelling reconciliation and justice? Land and the potential for conflict in Namibia. Peace Change 25(2):239–254

Remmert D, Ndhlovu P (2018) Housing in Namibia: rights, challenges and opportunities. Institute for Public Policy Research, Windhoek

Republic of Namibia (1991) National Conference on Land Reform and the Land Question. Windhoek, 25 June – 1 July 1991. Volume 1: Research Papers, Addresses and Consensus Document. Prepared by the Namibian Economic Policy Research Unit on behalf of the Office of the Prime Minister. Windhoek: Namibian Economic Policy Research Unit

Republic of Namibia (2020a) Report of the Commission of Inquiry into Claims of Ancestral Land Rights and Restitution. Office of the Prime Minister, Windhoek (https://opm.gov.na/archive/-/document_library/BFb3E1XtpdEc/view_file/1079542)

Republic of Namibia (2020b) Progress report (October 2018 – November 2020) on the Implementation of the Resolutions of the 2nd National Land Conference. Office of the Prime Minister, Windhoek. (https://opm.gov.na/documents/97540/1000168/Progress+Report+2nd+NLC+2+December+2020.pdf/33cfea9f-a48b-20d5-36a8-6b9ac6fccc47)

Rothauge A (2007) Overcoming barriers to the productive resettlement of Namibians. Agricola, pp 28–32 http://www.nbri.org.na/sites/default/files/Agricola_2007_No17_04_Rothauge.pdf

Sachikonye LM (2004) Land reform in Namibia and Zimbabwe: a comparative perspective. In: Hunter J (ed) Who should own the land? Analysis and views on land reform and the land question in Namibia and Southern Africa. Konrad-Adenauer-Stiftung and Namibia Institute for Democracy, Windhoek, pp 64–82

Salih M (1999) Environmental politics and liberation in contemporary Africa. Kluwer, Dordrecht/Boston/London

Sasa M (2013) Namibia: landless in the land of the brave. New Afr 47(525):38–41

Schade K (1992) Die Ergebnisse der Landkonferenz in Namibia: eine Relativierung geweckter Hoffnungen? Afr Spectrum 27(3):303–336

Schnegg M, Pauli J, Greiner C (2013) Pastoral belonging. Causes and consequences of part-time pastoralism in North-western Namibia. In: Bollig M, Schnegg M, Wotzka H-P (eds) Pastoralism in Africa. Past, present and futures. Berghahn, New York and Oxford, pp 341–362

Sherbourne R (2003) A rich man's hobby. Institute for Public Policy Research (IPPR Opinion no. 11), Windhoek

Sherbourne R (2004) Rethinking land reform in Namibia: any room for economics? Institute for Public Policy Research (IPPR Opinion no. 13), Windhoek

Smith S (2020) Grape crop brings in millions but farmworkers live a harsh life. Daily Maverick, 14 December (https://www.dailymaverick.co.za/article/2020-12-14-grape-crop-brings-in-millions-but-farmworkers-live-a-harsh-life/)

Suzman J (2002) Minorities in independent Namibia. Minority Rights Group International, London

Swartbooi B (2020) Budget Debate 2020. LPM Response to the Minister of Finance. National Assembly, 2 June

Thran M (2014) "Rassengerechtigkeit" und Fetischisierung von Land. Kritik der Landreform in Namibia. Tectum, Marburg

Tjitemisa K (2018) Ohangwena tops illegal fencing charts. New Era, 5 October (https://neweralive.na/posts/ohangwena-tops-illegal-fencing-charts)

Tjitemisa K (2020) Agrarian reform must be a tool for redressing poverty – Swartbooi. New Era, 17 June (https://neweralive.na/posts/agrarian-reform-must-be-a-tool-for-redressing-poverty-swartbooi)

Twyman C, Sporton D, Thomas D, Dougill A (2001) Community Fencing in open rangelands: self-empowerment in Eastern Namibia. Rev Afr Polit Econ 28(87):9–26

UNDP with UN Country Team (1998) Namibia human development report 1998. Environment and human development in Namibia. United Nations Development Programme, Windhoek

Von Wietersheim E (2008) *This Land is My Land'. Motions and Emotions Around Land Reform in Namibia*. Friedrich Ebert Stiftung, Windhoek

Wallace M, Kinahan J (2011) A history of Namibia. from the beginning to 1990. Hurst, London

Werner W (1993) A brief history of land dispossession in Namibia. J South Afr Stud 19(1):135–146

Werner W (2000) Agriculture and Land. In: Melber H (ed) Namibia: a decade of independence 1990-2000. Windhoek, Namibian Economic Policy Research Unit, pp 29–48

Werner W (2001) The land question in Namibia. In: Diener I, Graefe O (eds) Contemporary Namibia: the first landmarks of a post-apartheid society. Windhoek, Gamsberg Macmillan, pp 259–272

Werner W (2002) Land reform and land rights in Namibia. In: Apelt W, Motte J (eds) Landrecht. Perspektiven der Konfliktvermeidung im Südlichen Afrika. Foedus, Wuppertal, pp 51–72

Werner W (2005) Our land we farm. An analysis of the Namibian commercial agricultural land reform process. Legal Assistance Centre, Windhoek

Werner W (2010) Missed opportunities and fuzzy logic: a review of the proposed land bill. Institute for Public Policy Research, Windhoek

Werner W (2015a) 25 years of land reform. Namibia University of Science and Technology, Land, Livelihoods and Housing Programme 2015-2018, Windhoek. Working Paper No. 1 (http://ilmi.nust.na/sites/default/files/2015-WERNER-25-Years-of-land-reform-in-Namibia-A4.pdf)

Werner W (2015b) Tenure reform in Namibia's communal areas. J Namibian Stud 18:67–87

Werner W (2020) Foreword. In: Nghitevelekwa RV (ed) Securing land rights. Communal land reform in Namibia. University of Namibia Press, Windhoek, pp xi–xii

Windhoek Observer (2018) The dispossessed vs elites, 28 September (https://www.observer.com.na/index.php/editorial/item/10443-the-dispossessed-vs-elites)

Land Reform or Continued Social Exclusion? Land Occupations, State Responses and Neoliberal Policies in Southern Malawi

Justin Alinafe Mangulama and Jin Wu

Abstract The last five decades have witnessed an increasing number of peasants encroaching onto idle tea estate land in Thyolo district, in southern Malawi. In drawing upon a study of this district, this chapter argues that state responses to land occupations remain contradictory. Malawi's 2002 land policy advocates for redistributive land reform. At the same time, however, the state has actively promoted the Malawi Investment Policy, which encourages land expropriation for foreign capital. Repressive measures that include policing, punitive fines and arrests of peasants, stirred the land occupations further, rather than inhibiting them. The state remains in a dilemma, whether to optimise local votes from the peasants or side with white agrarian bourgeois interests for capital accumulation via a rent scheme. The chapter points to the tension-riddled character of neoliberealism, as shown through accumulation at one pole and impoverishment of the majority at the other pole.

1 Introduction

Land occupations in Malawi remain an understudied topic. This is so despite the rising number of peasants occupying 'idle' private or public land in the country for either settlement or social reproduction purposes. In the southern region of Malawi, land occupations are rampant, especially in the tea-growing districts of Thyolo and Mulanje. In drawing upon a study of these districts, this chapter argues that state responses to land occupations remain contradictory—including Malawi's 2002 land policy, which advocates for redistributive land reform. While advocating for this, the

---

J. A. Mangulama (✉)
College of Humanities and Development Studies, China Agricultural University, Beijing, China

Department of Development Studies, The Catholic University of Malawi, Nguludi, Malawi
e-mail: jusmangulama@cau.edu.cn

J. Wu
College of Humanities and Development Studies, China Agricultural University, Beijing, China
e-mail: wjin@cau.edu.cn

F. Mazwi et al. (eds.), *Capital Penetration and the Peasantry in Southern and Eastern Africa*, Advances in African Economic, Social and Political Development, https://doi.org/10.1007/978-3-030-89824-3_5

state has—simultaneously—actively promoted the Malawi Investment Policy, which encourages land expropriation for foreign capital. Repressive measures that include policing, punitive fines and arrests of peasants, stirred the land occupations further, rather than inhibiting them. The state remains in a dilemma, whether to optimise local votes from the peasants or side with white agrarian bourgeois interests for capital accumulation via a rent scheme. The chapter points to the contradictory character of neoliberalism, as shown through accumulation at one pole and impoverishment of the majority at the other pole.

2 Malawian Agricultural Sector and the Land Question in Neoliberal Context

The land question is becoming an increasingly important issue regarding Malawi's political economy because 85% of Malawians remain directly or indirectly employed in the agricultural sector. The Malawi economy is predominately agricultural, with about 80% of the population living in rural areas. Agriculture contributes 90% to export earnings for the country, 39 per cent to the Gross Domestic Product (GDP) and 65% to total rural income (Kanyongolo 2005; Chinsinga 2016). In 2013, Malawi's manufacturing sector contributed only 10.7% to GDP. The main industries are food processing, construction, consumer goods, cement, fertiliser, ginning, furniture production and cigarette production (Malawi Government 2016a, b). The service sector accounts for 51.7% of Malawi's GDP. Notable industries are tourism, retail, transport, education, health services, telecommunication, and the banking sector. In 2014, agriculture, industry and service sectors made up 33, 17 and 50% of Malawian GDP, respectively (World Bank 2016).

Access to arable land by the rural poor is a huge problem in many areas in Malawi. This is due to the fact that land ownership is highly skewed, with a limited number of estate farmers owning huge tracts of land and the majority of the peasantry being landless or land-short. This is a huge problem in rural Malawi, where access to land is paramount for achieving some form of sustainable livelihoods. Overall, 55% of peasant farmers cultivate on less than one hectare of land, while there are about 30,000 estates cultivating from 10 to 500 ha of land (Chirwa 2004; Chinigo 2015). This problem is particularly prevalent in the tea-growing areas in southern Malawi, where huge areas of land are owned by tea plantation farmers, leaving the poor with limited or no land (Chinigo 2017; Chinsinga 2011). In Thyolo and Mulanje districts specifically, average peasant households cultivate less than 0.4 ha of land, and evidence exists that the amount of land continues to shrink due to increasing land shortages (Chinigo 2017). This casts doubt on the possibility of alleviating poverty for the landless poor since it is very difficult to access industrial employment in the context of the weak manufacturing sector. As well, though the service sector contributes more to Malawi's GDP than agriculture, it employs fewer people.

Like many other African countries that were colonised by Western countries, Malawi's national economic policy conforms to the neoliberal model and has for some time. This entails the placing of significant emphasis on private sector initiatives for economic growth, with government (and non-governmental organisations) acting only in a facilitative role. The dominance of this approach since 1981 has been due largely to the adoption of Structural Adjustment Programmes (SAPs) under the auspices of the International Monetary Fund (IMF) and the World Bank, which have made liberalisation a key condition of foreign assistance (especially in donor aid). Such assistance, however, has been critical to the sustenance of the Malawian economy, which had experienced a severe decline in the late 1970s and early 1980s due to various factors, including drought in the 1980–1981 season, a rise in interest rates on international financial markets, and the closure of the Beira-Nacala trade corridor, which had provided a cost-effective outlet for landlocked Malawi (Kanyongolo 2005). Some of the objectives of the SAP and ensuring neoliberal initiatives for agriculture in Malawi included diversification of the export base, ensuring appropriate price and incomes policy to offer adequate incentives to peasants, expanding the role of the private sector in the marketing of agricultural produce, and increasing the efficiency and incomes of smallholder farmers.

The SAP in Malawi expired in the 1990s, but the Malawian government continues to employ other neoliberal economic policies up to the present day. The initial SAP was designed to reduce government expenditure in order to free up money for debt servicing, and the rural poor suffered the dire consequences of this. For peasants, for example, it led to the removal of fertiliser subsidies in 1984, deregulation of fertiliser marketing in 1990, and liberalisation of burley tobacco production. On the plus side, the burley tobacco liberalisation led to an increase in the number of peasant farmers growing burley tobacco, and peasants rapidly became the main producers of burley tobacco (accounting for about 70% of national production) (Chirwa 2004). But, overall, the removal of farm input subsidies worsened the situation of peasant households, as production became constrained due to the inability to purchase necessary farm inputs.

Over time, the neoliberal economic thrust found normative expression in the liberal constitution of 1994. This guaranteed the right to private property and placed limitations on the functions and powers of the state. Despite the passing of the new constitution and neoliberal economics, national economic growth has remained limited. According to the government, this has been due in large part to external shocks, inconsistent implementation of reforms, fiscal policy slippages and the narrow base of production capacity (Kanyongolo 2005). At the same time, and in the context of neoliberal reforms, Malawi has formulated and implemented a number of land policies in favour of redistributive land reforms.

However, it is clear that little has been achieved. Powerful landed groups and descendants of the British colonial masters continue to control huge swathes of land, with land grabbing now being the order of the day. In 2019, the Malawi government conceded that there is chaos in land administration throughout the country, and the poor rural majority is paying the price for this (Chimjeka 2019). Land grabs for purposes of settlement and cash crops exist. Foreign countries (especially China,

India and Pakistan), multinationals, and foreign citizens are scrambling for land in Malawi. At the same time, the government has simply failed to resolve the colonial legacies that left hundreds of thousands of peasants in southern Malawi land poor. Meanwhile, neoliberal practices continue to manifest themselves (including in land administration), with the government taking a backseat and showing an unwillingness to take charge of land issues at the expense of the interests of the rural poor. As the following sections demonstrate and explain, meaningful policies in favour of redistributing land have not materialised, given the powerful interests and influence of the landed bourgeoisies.

3 Malawi Land Policies from Colonial Era to Present (1963–2020)

Malawian land policies can be grouped into three eras: the colonial era, Kamuzu Banda's post-independence authoritative rule, and multiparty democracy. The colonial land policy can be attributed to the surge in the number of Europeans who flocked to Malawi for trade and other ventures between 1790 and 1860. In 1889, the British Government established a protectorate in southern Malawi, which legitimised the colonisation efforts (Holden et al. 2006; Silungwe 2005). The influx of Europeans trekking to Malawi led to an increase in the demand for land for agriculture, more especially estate agriculture. The 'army' of Europeans that arrived in Malawi started to maneuvre in deceitful ways to access land from the locals (Boeder 1984). They accumulated land through 'agreements' with traditional chiefs, a behaviour and form of transaction that remains a contested topic even in present-day Malawi (Chinigo 2017). So, since the 1890s, when Malawi became a British protectorate, a dual agrarian structure was established with estate farming operating alongside peasant farming (Machira 2007; Peters and Kambewa 2007). This system also prevailed in other colonial states in Africa (Moyo 2007), where policy favoured large-scale commercial and estate agriculture as opposed to peasant agriculture. Chinigo (2015) asserts that this was done on the pretext that revenues from estate agriculture would stir growth in the other sectors of the economy. This hardly happened, as an 'incomplete capitalism' emerged, which created a dispossessed proletariat with neither a job nor land.

A twist of events was witnessed in 1965 when the Malawi Congress Party (MCP) government (under Banda) passed the 1965 Land Act. This Act, as Silungwe (2005, p. 24) demonstrates, legitimised the colonial status quo in land tenure regimes. It confirmed that Malawi had three categories of land: customary land—which did not give the Natives[1] enforceable rights; public land—which belonged to the government; and private land—which consisted of private land (and the land that was 'dubiously' obtained through the issuance of 'Certificates of Claims') (Holden et al.

[1] Local Malawians at times have also been termed 'Natives' in this chapter.

2006). All this was happening amidst, and despite, resistance from the peasantry. Despite promises by President Banda, the land question was not addressed under his authoritarian reign.

In the period after 1993, there was a transition from the MCP one-party rule (authoritarian regime) to multiparty democracy. Many were hopeful that with the adoption of multiparty democracy, the Malawian land question would be solved once and for all. It never happened (Holden et al. 2006). Hence, many were of the view that the land policy of 2002 would not only be drafted but implemented as well to reflect the reality that peasants in southern Malawi were land poor. The 2002 Policy stated that it 'would free up land to local Malawians in areas where land conflicts were rampant, and the situation was critical' (MLPPS 2002, p. 12). As well, under the 2002 Malawi Land Policy, the government ceased to grant 'freehold land tenure to non-Malawians'. The white colonial farmers were also instructed to relinquish land or partner with Malawians in their estates or acquire Malawian citizenship. This seemed to be a progressive move on the part of the government, but meaningful land reform did not take place.

4 Tea Estates: Idle Land and Social Exclusion

Land conflicts in Africa are not a new phenomenon. As of 2000, land-related conflicts escalated in Zimbabwe, Côte d'Ivoire, Nigeria's Delta region, and elsewhere in Africa, including Malawi (Moyo 2007; Chinigo 2015). The surge in land-related conflicts in Africa portrays the failure of African states to decisively deal with the land development nexus. Therefore, it is not surprising that, in 2018, British settlers still owned enormous tracts of land in southern Malawi, which were forcibly acquired in the 1890s during the colonial era. Racially, white farmers of British origin continue to own the majority of the tea estates in Thyolo, Malawi.

The land shortage situation is pronounced in southern Malawi in particular as, in the central and northern regions, limited land redistribution did take place, and local Malawians have some access to farmland. Most populated districts in Malawi are in the southern region where ironically, there is an artificial shortage of land due to failed land reform implementation. Though the actual figures of land covered by estates in Mulanje and Thyolo[2] district remain unknown, it is reported that 75% of arable land is covered by the tea estates plantations in Thyolo (Chinigo 2017).

The population in this southern area continues to grow, and thus the population density increases likewise, with the region also characterised by meagre wages on the part of wage-workers. Peasants in these two districts continue to resist land alienation in favour of the estates' agricultural activities, by encroaching on idle

[2] In this chapter, 'southern Malawi' and 'Thyolo and Mulanje districts' have been used simultaneously because many of the tea estates in southern Malawi are found in these two districts. The living conditions among the peasantries in these two districts are similar.

land. Despite their contribution to the country's GDP, capital investments by tea estates on large tracks of land have not only alienated the people from the means of production but also from the tea-economy itself. Colonialism in Malawi did little to incorporate rural Malawians into the plantation economy, and this condition has 'recreated the material and symbolic conditions appropriate for people to reconstitute themselves as peasants' (Chinigo 2015, p. 97). From an economic and social point of view, the two districts are dramatically segmented between, on the one hand, large-scale, mechanised, export-oriented and foreign-owned tea estates enjoying freehold rights over land and, on the other, peasant farmers (and the majority of landless poor) working on small parcels of customary land.

Evidence shows that tea estates in Thyolo and Mulanje do not necessarily place all their hectares of land into productive use. Over 24,000 hectares remain idle in Thyolo alone, which peasants are occupying. While owned by the white-owned estates, this land is idle as it is not under cultivation. This occupied land, idle or not, can be used as collateral to secure loans from local banks by the estate enterprises. Chinigò (2016) reports that the tea estates are reluctant to share the land with the landless out of fear that the land will be permanently lost to the latter. Tea as a commodity fetches lucrative and stable prices on the world market, although there are price fluctuations. Hence, it is not surprising to see power relations being played out and in favour of estates given their ownership, access and control of the land.

Peasants in the Thyolo and Mulanje tea-growing districts continue to struggle when it comes to accessing arable land. Memories are still fresh of a group of over one thousand farmers who stormed the usually quiet streets of Thyolo Boma on 15 January 2014, marching towards the offices of the district assembly. Government authorities in the southern region were aware of the tension in the district, and police were well-prepared to act on any troubles. This was not the first time for farmers to clash with officials and security agents, as land disputes in the tea plantation areas begun as early as the 1930s. In 1953, more than ten people were killed in a clash between peasants and AJ Tennet (an estate 'owner'), also known as the 'Tennet massacre'. Any particular incident is just a tip of the iceberg, as clashes between the people and tea estate[3] owners are the order of the day.[4] The land question in southern Malawi is clearly not only an important and very sensitive one, as it is also a highly politicised topic (Chinigo 2015, 2017). Efforts to resolve the land issue in southern Malawi have involved seemingly never-ending discussions by land policymakers, but decades have gone by, and only minimal practical measures have been put in place to respond to the area's land tensions.

The Malawi Constitution prohibits any type of encroachment on private estate land. However, the land occupations in southern Malawi continue to increase at an alarming rate, and there are always stories of land clashes and/or occupations in Thyolo. Much scholarly literature on land occupations has largely focused on the

---

[3]In Malawi, the term 'tea estate' is used synonymously with 'tea plantations'.

[4]The most recent clash between peasants and tea estate owners was on 23 July 2020. Security guards killed a peasant in a standoff in Mbeluko Village close to Thyolo Sports area in Thyolo.

legality of the occupations, tenure regimes, and the recent land grabs in Malawi.[5] However, this chapter does not discuss the legality of the land occupations in southern Malawi. Rather, it looks into state and local level responses to land occupations in Malawi. The chapter also highlights how neoliberal policies (re) shape the state responses (or non-responses) to these land occupations.

5 Theoretical and Methodological Considerations

The state remains one of the key stakeholders when it comes to land deals. It remains pivotal in responding to political processes like land occupations in privately owned land. State responses (or non-responses) to political processes like land occupations have consequences for the concerned conflicting parties (in this case, landed estate owners and the landless black majority). In this regard, the state should not be conceived as an actor with a unified voice and internal consistency in its agenda; rather, the state itself is a site of struggle over resources, power and authority among its various constituents (Moore 1993; Watts 1989; Hall et al. 2015).

Some of the notable scholars who have examined and explained the role of the state in land deals include Watts (1989), Wolford et al. (2013), Burnod et al. (2013), Peters (2013) and Moreda (2017). Based on fieldwork in rural Ethiopia, Moreda (2017, p. 1) concludes that states' role in land deals entails a 'strategy of enforcing political authority over territory and people'. While this is true, the state is also subject to contestation. As Watts (1989, p. 4) claims, '[t]he State [can] be opened as a theatre where resources, property rights and authority are confronted'. Beyond this, there is an analytical need to consider the state's internal processes, which involves 'unbundling the State, viewing government and governance as processes, people and relations' in gaining a better understanding of the state's position regarding land acquisitions and occupations (Wolford et al. 2013, p. 189). More specifically, Wolford et al. (2013, p. 191) emphasise the 'need to learn more about the nature of states themselves; ... the intentions of specific actors, as well as the capability of government agencies and the political cultures that influence the direction from policy to practice'.

Thus, the study adopts the view that the state is central in any discussion concerning rural land politics. It recognises and views the state as a blend of 'multiple actors, factions and aspirations, many competing directly for political power' (as expressed by Hall et al. 2015, p. 475, quoted in Mamonova 2016, p. 36). By adopting this view, it unmasks the dynamic situation on the ground in

[5] Many studies on land related conflicts have centred on the green-belt initiative (GBI) in Salima, Malawi. Here, the Government of Malawi has appropriated land to foreign capitals for sugar and mango production. The Green-Belt initiative has forced hundreds of peasants into landlessness, qualifying it as a 'modern-day land grabbing' venture orchestrated by the state.

rural southern Malawi, including the incoherence of state policies and contradictory practices at different governmental levels.

This study was conducted to understand state and local level responses to land occupations in southern Malawi, and it also considered how neoliberal policies reshape state responses (or non-responses) to the land occupations. The study largely employed a qualitative research design in order to ensure a comprehensive understanding and interpretation of the phenomenon under investigation. In this respect, the gathering of narratives was of particular significance for this study. The study was conducted in Chibwana and Chaona villages in Thyolo District in the southern region of Malawi. The study villages were selected because they were located outside the Comforzi tea estate.[6] Many peasants who were occupying idle land from the tea estates were residing in these villages.

Data collection took place over a period of seven months between 30 January to 30 August 2018. Some respondents were followed up in the period between January and June 2020 to obtain further clarification on emerging issues in the study. In total, we interviewed 60 households in Chaona Village and 50 households in Chibwana Village. This included 33 female-headed households (representing 30% of the total) and 77 male-headed households (representing 70%). We discontinued interviews in the villages once we realised that we had reached saturation point in terms of the evidence collected. We also interviewed 15 other peasant households that did not occupy land in the tea estates. The aim was not for comparison per se but to have an in-depth understanding of alternative narratives about state responses to land occupations in the region. Apart from the peasants, data was also collected from key informants: District Land Officials, Ministry of Lands and urban Housing Officials, representatives from Peoples Land Organisations, Catholic Commission for Justice and Peace (CCJP); Senior Estate Tea Managers, Ministry of Agriculture officials, Malawi Police Service, Legal Practitioners, scholars, non-governmental organisations, political cadres and Village Chiefs. Data was analysed using a thematic approach and narrative methods.

6 State Responses to Land Occupations in Thyolo

The state's response to the land occupations in Thyolo entails two sets of policies and programmes, that is, general policies (marked by contradictory tendencies) and more localised policies to address specifically the political processes in Thyolo. These are examined in turn.

[6] This is in fact only one of the tea estates studied by the researchers.

6.1 Contradictory State Policies

In order to address land ownership and access inequalities, the Malawian government drafted the 2002 Land Policy. In general, the 2002 Policy aimed at redistributing land in favour of the marginalised peasantry. This did not happen, in part because there was no enabling legislation in place to facilitate this. As well, any redistribution initiative was curtailed by the presence of neoliberalism, with its demands for respecting property rights (including the property of the tea estates owned under freehold land tenure). In this context, the government also adopted the Malawi Investment Promotion Policy and the ensuing Malawi Investment and Promotion Act (2012). As the land occupations and conflicts in Thyolo involve local people and private investors, Malawi's investment policy further complicates the situation by promoting and facilitating foreign investments in landholdings in the country. The policy places no restrictions on the size of the investment, the source of funds or whether products are destined for export or for the domestic market. As well, domestic investors are encouraged to join with foreign investors to pursue joint investment opportunities in Malawi (see Malawi Investment and Promotion Act 2012).

A very good example of land transfers in Malawi is the Green Belt Initiative (GBI), a government initiative to transfer more than 1 million hectares of land to investors alongside Lake Malawi. Although the actual number of hectares that have been transferred to investors is not clear, it is alleged that hundreds of thousands of smallholders have lost communal land to GBI investors (Chinsinga et al. 2013). Another example is that, in 2009, the government signed off 55,000 hectares of irrigable farmland to the government of Djibouti in exchange for unspecified support for the construction of a Malawian inland port (Chingaipe et al. 2011). With soft conditions for investment available, Malawi has seen a problematic flocking of foreigners 'investing', in that the quality of investors is compromised. There has been an outcry from indigenous Malawians that a significant number of foreigners (especially from Asian countries) are involved in low-level petty production and trading, which falls short of meaningful investment. For peasants dispossessed through the larger land investments (like the GBI), land occupations arise on private or public land for agricultural purposes.

Another important policy related to these events is the Agricultural Policy. The main aim of the Malawi National Agricultural Policy is 'to achieve sustainable agricultural transformation that will result in significant growth of the agricultural sector, expanding incomes for farm households, improved food and nutrition security for all Malawians, and increased agricultural exports' (Malawi Government 2016b, p. 9). For the Agriculture Ministry, this entails increasing 'agricultural exports' on a massive scale ('by 50 percentage') while, simultaneously, promoting peasant farmers as indicated in the notion of 'farm households' (Malawi Government 2016b, p. 11). This policy remained unclear on the origins of the agricultural exports, whether from peasant farmers or from the large-scale capitalist farms (such as tea enterprises), or both. However, the policy intention signals capitulating to prescriptions of international organisations such as the World Bank and IMF, which have been promoting export-oriented crops at the expense of food crop production. Such policies have been shown elsewhere to have adverse implications for food self-sustenance, leading to a high food import bill (Chambati et al. 2018).

Intriguingly, these neoliberal trends have not spared the state. In Thyolo district, the government recognises that the District Council was in dire need of land for infrastructural development. Tea plantations exist throughout the district, and there is simply no further room for expansion of the district's public infrastructure. When asked, the Acting Lands Officer for Thyolo District had this to say:

> We tried to lease land from the estates for the construction of a bus terminal but the estates told the government to pay Mk20 million Kwacha.[7] The ministry of Local Government did not approve this and the project did not see the light [of day]. In addition, we have another project to construct a football stadium at the centre of Thyolo district. The council has failed to secure land from the neighbouring tea plantation.

This revelation shows that neoliberal policies have not only contributed to the marginalisation of the peasants in the region, but have also undercut state operations and capacities.

6.2 Community Based Rural Land Development Programme (CBRLDP)

In relation to localised state responses, one of the most practical and targeted state responses to the land occupations and related processes in southern Malawi has been the Community Based Rural Land Development Programme (CBRLDP), popularly (and locally known) known as '*Kuzigulira Malo*'. The CBRLDP was a World Bank-funded project aimed at resettling 15,000 households from Thyolo and Mulanje districts (sending districts) to Mangochi, Machinga and Balaka districts (also known as host/receiving districts). In terms of land redistribution, the programme was founded on the neoliberal philosophy, namely, willing seller (estate farmers) and willing buyer (peasants). The host districts (Balaka, Machinga and Mangochi) were selected for this programme because white farmers in Thyolo refused to offer their estates for sale for redistribution to the peasants (Chinigo 2015). The peasants initially wanted to buy land from the tea estates in Thyolo, but the estate owners were not willing. This means the peasants had to buy land (most of it not suitable for agriculture) in other districts like Mangochi.

Our study found out that 99 interviewed peasant households (representing 90 per cent of the sample) were beneficiaries of the CBRLDP back in 2004–2005. They indicated that they had been resettled in Balaka or Mangochi districts in the eastern region of Malawi. However, they returned to their former villages in Thyolo District. The research established that 80% of the households that had returned to their former

[7] Mk20,000,000 was equivalent to USD 27,200 at the time of the field work.

villages did so solely due to lack of social amenities in the resettled lands, like roads, transportation, hospitals, maize mills, and markets to trade agricultural surplus. The majority of the returnees also lamented that they had only had bumper yields in the first three years of settlement but, thereafter, they experienced poor harvests. The reasons for the poor harvests varied. For some peasants, it was because they were allocated infertile soils (not suitable for crop farming). Overall, 85% of the 99 households indicated that the land bought for them in the host districts was infertile. Other returnees highlighted that they had exhausted the 1050 USD relocation package, and they had no extra income to purchase farm inputs. A total of 79% of the returnees also stated that peasants from the surrounding areas invaded their new farmlands claiming ownership, forcing the resettled peasants to leave. In the end, the peasants did not benefit from the programme. Many returned to their original district, and land poverty and marginalisation continued due to the ongoing neoliberal policies.

6.3 *Land Resettlement Schemes in Thyolo*

Apart from CBRLDP, another localised policy response in Thyolo has been the purchase of estate land by the government to be redistributed to the locals to ease the land tensions. From our study, 15 peasants indicated that they had been beneficiaries of the land resettlement scheme within the estate land. One peasant, however, lamented:

> The government bought land in Makande Estate. We were all promised that we would get land. I was surprised and equally excited when I got message from the Traditional leader that we had been granted a piece of land. Only 7 households in the whole of this village got the land from Makande. Though many people in this village do not have land, they did not get any land from the redistribution exercise. I was also surprised that many of the people who we share land boundaries at Makande estate are relatively rich people.[8]

From the interviews with the beneficiaries of land resettlement in Makande, one certain fact is that many people from the villages did not benefit under the programme. Historically, land resettlement on estate land is not a new phenomenon. There have been several estates that were bought by the state and redistributed to the peasants previously. However, neoliberalism demands respect for property rights. This means that if the tea estate owners do not want to sale their estates for redistribution, land resettlement as a state response is jeopardised. Drawing upon the necessity of willing sellers under neoliberalism-conditioned land policy, most of the tea estates in Thyolo refused to offer their land for redistribution in Thyolo.

[8] Interview with Makande Estate land beneficiary household, Chibwana Village, Thyolo. 20 August, 2020.

It can be briefly added that some tea estate owners sometimes provide money to local village leaders in order to 'sensitise' their subordinates (i.e. villagers) not to encroach on tea estate land.

6.4 *Repressions, Policising and Fines*

The study discovered that a further local state response in Thyolo has been repression. This happens in three ways. The majority of the respondents in Thyolo (95%) indicated that they had either experienced or witnessed fellow peasants being arrested and/or put in jail. The police do this on instructions from either the white farmers or the District Authority. One peasant had this to say:

> I have witnessed various farmers being arrested by police in this village. I for one was arrested in 2014 alongside Peoples Land Organisation officials.[9]

The researchers are able to corroborate this peasant's claim about the number of peasants who have been arrested from the villages. Information from the Thyolo Police Department under the Ministry of Internal Affairs showed that it was common for police to be involved in the land conflicts between peasants and white farmers in the area. One policeman agreed with the peasant's argument about the scale of arrests:

> It is true we have dozens of cases at our unit. The bone of contention is that the peasants are encroaching into the idle land belonging to the estates. All necessary laws are followed in every arrest we have made so far.[10]

The study also noted that the state increased the amount of money the peasants needed to pay as 'bail bond' for the peasants to be released. About 80% of the respondents agreed that 6 months prior to the fieldwork, the 'bail bond' was increased from Mk10,000 to Mk25,000 ($11.40 to $34). As one peasant farmer said:

> What is more puzzling is that Police Bail is free, but Thyolo Police make us pay huge sums of money if they arrest us. They say it's a strategy to make sure they limit the number of landless poor occupying the estate land. However, the numbers continue to increase, hence the strategy is not that effective. This too cannot stop us from occupying more land.[11]

Another (third) tactic that has been employed by the state is to work with the white farmers to destroy grown crops on the estate land. One villager spoke in a frustrating manner about this state tactic:

> This pains me a lot. They wait when we are about to harvest. They slash all the maize down in my field. For the sugarcane and cassava, they did not just slash the crops, [as] they actually

---

[9] Interview with former arrestee and land occupant in Chaona Village, Thyolo District, Malawi 02 April, 2018.

[10] Interview with Thyolo District Police Officer, Thyolo Malawi. 5 April, 2018.

[11] Interview with Peasant Farmer, Chibwana Village, 28 July 2018.

> collected them for their own consumption. We do not relent. When they slash the crops today, the next day we go to clear the land and replant.[12]

Clearly, then, the state has utilised multiple methods (repression, policing and punitive fining) as localised ways of deterring would be land occupants from encroaching onto the tea estates.

A debate exists scholarly about state repression and peasant protests (Ondetti 2006). On the one hand, repression tends to discourage protests and activism; on the other hand, repression at times stirs protest and encourages even those who were not involved in the first place to join the protests. In the case of peasants in Thyolo, the evidence suggests that the number of peasants occupying tea estate land continues to increase despite the localised methods of closing down the protests via coercion. Hence, repression has not been effective. It is also relevant to highlight that neoliberal reconfigurations in rural Malawi have deepened the economic hardships of peasants, and this spurs on the latter to access land (even illegally) for livelihoods purposes. As discussed earlier, the state's attempts to resolve land woes in the region, especially through the CBRLDP, have utilised neoliberal approaches which hinder land redistribution. Peasants in Thyolo do not have access to land, and the tea estate economy is unable to absorb the rural poor as a labour force. Further, outward migration to urban areas may simply involve transitioning from rural poverty to urban poverty. The 'invisible hand' of neoliberalism is squeezing the Thyolo peasantry, leaving them with occupations as perhaps the most viable option.

7 Land Occupations, Land Alliances and Electoral Politics

Notable alliances have been formed among peasants and local land movements to fight for land access in Malawi, especially in the southern region. Chief among them is the Peoples Land Organisation (PLO), a local land movement that seeks to defend and promote peasant land rights. The PLO has been advocating for the redistribution of idle estate lands to the peasant farmers in Thyolo and Mulanje. However, its main goal goes beyond land, as it also seeks to address the free labour that the forefathers of the peasants had provided to the estates in the form of land rent. Its headquarters are at Chipironi in Thyolo. The PLO's main leaders are former senior government workers[13] who have significant knowledge about land policies, human rights and the state constitution. Its membership consists of more than 10,000 peasant households in Thyolo and Mulanje, where it plans to force the state to restitute 24,000 hectares of unused private land belonging to the white farmers to the peasants. It has organised peasants to occupy idle land, for instance, at Comforzi estates in 2014. What the PLO has lacked, though is placing sufficient pressure on the landed estate owners

[12] Interview with Peasant Farmer, Chaona Village, Thyolo, Malawi. 03 August 2018.

[13] The President for PLO during the time of the field study was Vincent Wandale, who was a senior government worker in the Ministry of Agriculture, Irrigation and Water Development.

and the state to redistribute idle land in the estates. Since 2014, PLO failed to organise a substantial number of peasants to occupy this idle land. Despite the PLO not achieving its objectives, it empowered local peasants to individually occupy the tea estates' idle land.

In addition, PLO has called for the succession of Thyolo and Mulanje from Malawi so as to become an independent state. The media (both social and print) have gone to town publicising the PLO's intention to succeed from Malawi and form its own government (Chinigo 2015). The call for succession though seems to be just one tactic used by the PLO to put more pressure on the Malawi government to restitute unused estate land in Thyolo and Mulanje. But it has tended to muddy and confuse the land conflicts because, instead of tackling the matter at hand (landless peasants), the state machinery has focused its energies on propaganda about the PLO and its attempts to break up the country through its succession plans.

Besides the PLO, the Catholic Commission for Justice and Peace (CCJP) is a non-governmental organisation in Malawi, which works to improve the welfare of people especially in access to justice. At the time of the study, the CCJP had a project in Thyolo and Mulanje to assist farmers to improve crop yields in the 'land that they already possess'. A total of 65 households in the study (representing 59% of the sample) indicated that they were beneficiaries of CCJP-sponsored projects with the aim of improving the livelihoods of peasants in Thyolo. The CCJP had noble intentions to discuss with the government and the tea estate owners to act as a guarantor—it wants the estates to release some land for lease for a period of 2–5 years to the landless poor in Thyolo and Mulanje, where they would be able to grow crops at least for survival. Whether this will be successfully launched remains unclear.

Finally, there are important links between land reforms and electoral politics in the southern region of Malawi. Many politicians promise peasants that, once they are elected into political positions, they will influence policy and implement redistributive land reforms. This has been the case especially from the dawn of multiparty democracy in 1993–1994. The narrative has been coming from all levels of political offices (including presidential aspirants, Members of Parliament and ward councillors) in the region—all with the strident claim that 'after you vote us into power, we will implement distributive land reform'. Deceitfully, the politicians utilise the plight of the poor landless people from the southern region in exchange for votes. Certainly, their promises do not go beyond political podiums. Even if they were firmly committed to doing so, the neoliberal structuring of rural Malawi (and the power of the tea estate owners) would likely undermine their efforts.

8 Conclusion

This chapter has focused on the contradictory land-related policies and approaches which have worked to the advantage of the current landed-bourgeoisie in Malawi. The 2002 redistributive land policy was never implemented, and state-orchestrated land grabs continue through, for instance, the GBI. Even with the implementation of the localised CBRLDP, the neoliberal 'willing buyer- willing seller' philosophy (as designed and implemented) has failed to offer a permanent solution to the widespread social exclusion in Thyolo, Malawi. It is an undeniable fact that the land occupations in southern Malawi express the challenges which peasants face daily because of the neoliberal restructuring of rural Malawi in terms of both land injustices and economic hardships. Though the state itself at times suffers from the logic of neoliberalism, and that this might generate tensions within the Malawian state, it is aligned broadly with foreign capital and the local white agrarian bourgeoisie. Simultaneously, local land movements like the Peoples Land Organisation and non-governmental organisations are either weak or have limited capacity to act on land matters forcefully or successfully. Despite this, there is strong reason to believe that land occupations will continue to characterise southern Malawi.

References

Boeder RB (1984) Silent majority: a history of the Lomwe in Malawi, 1st edn. Africa Institute of South Africa, Heer Printers, Pretoria

Burnod P, Gingembre M, Ratsialonana RA (2013) Competition over authority and access: international land deals in Madagascar. Dev Chang 44(2):357–379

Chambati W, Mazwi F, Mberi S (2018) Agrarian accumulation and peasant resistance in Africa. Inclusive Development in Africa Edition: First Publisher: AISA/CODESRIA

Chimjeka R (2019) Chaos in land management. The Times Newspaper. 23rd November, 2019

Chingaipe H, Chasukwa M, Chinsinga B, Chirwa E (2011) The political economy of land alienation: exploring land grabs in the green belt initiative in Malawi, A Research Report for the FAC-PLAAS Country Study: University of Western Cape, South Africa

Chinigo D (2015) Re-peasantization and land reclamation movements in malawi. Afr Aff 115(458):97–118. https://doi.org/10.1093/afraf/adv057

Chinigò D (2016) Rural radicalism and the historical land conflict in the Malawian tea economy. J South Afr Stud 42(2):283–297. https://doi.org/10.1080/03057070.2016.1141514

Chinigo D (2017) Contested extractivism. In: Engels B, Dietz K (eds) Contested extractivism, society and the state. Palgrave Macmillan

Chinsinga B (2011) The politics of land reforms in Malawi: the case of the community based rural land development programme (CBRLDP). J Int Dev 23:380–393

Chinsinga B (2016) The Green Belt initiative, politics and sugar production in Malawi. Journal of Southern African Studies

Chinsinga B, Chirwa E, Chingaipe HM, Chasukwa B (2013) The political economy of land grabs and land reforms in Malawi. J Agric Environ Ethics 13:47–80

Chirwa EW (2004) Access to land, growth and poverty reduction in Malawi. Consult Working Paper WC/03/04, University of Malawi, Chancellor College, Wadonda August 2004. Available at: http://www.wadonda.com/land0304.pdf

Hall R et al (2015) Resistance, acquiescence or incorporation? An introduction to land grabbing and political reactions 'from below'. Journal of Peasant Studies 42(3-4):467–488. https://doi.org/10.1080/03066150.2015.1036746

Holden S, Kaarhus R, Lunduka R (2006) Land policy reform: the role of land markets and women's land rights in Malawi. Noragric Report No. 36

Kanyongolo FE (2005) Land occupations in Malawi: challenging the neo-liberal legal order. In: Moyo S, Yeros P (eds) Reclaiming the land: The resurgence of rural movements in Africa, Asia and Latin America. Zed Publishers, London, pp 118–141

Machira S (2007) A case study on designing, piloting and scaling-up a land redistribution programme in Malawi. Available at: http://sarpn.org/documents/d0002698/Land_redistribution_Malawi.pdf. Accessed 20 Mar 2020
Malawi Government (2012) Malawi investment and promotion act. Lilongwe, Malawi
Malawi Government (2016a) Customary land act. Lilongwe, Malawi
Malawi Government (2016b) Malawi National Agricultural Policy. Lilongwe, Malawi
Mamonova N (2016) Rethinking rural politics in post-socialist settings. Dissertation. Erasmus University Rotterdam
MLPPS (2002) Malawi national land policy. Ministry of Lands, Physical Planning & Surveys, Lilongwe
Moore DS (1993) contesting terrain in Zimbabwe's eastern highlands: Political ecology, ethnography, and peasant resource struggles. Econ Geogr 69(4):380–401
Moreda T (2017) Large-scale land acquisitions, state authority and indigenous local communities: insights from Ethiopia. Third World Q *38*(3):698–716
Moyo S (2007) Land in the political economy of African development: alternative strategies for reform. J Afr Dev XXXII(4):1–34
Ondetti G (2006) Repression, opportunity, and protest: explaining the takeoff of Brazil's landless movement. Latin Am Polit Soc 48(2):61–94
Peters EP (2013) Land appropriation, surplus people and a battle over visions of agrarian futures in Africa. J Peasant Stud 40(3):537562
Peters P, Kambewa D (2007) Whose security? Deepening social conflict over customary land in the shadow of land tenure reform in Malawi. J Mod Afr Stud 45:447–472
Silungwe CM (2005) Customary land tenure reform and development: A critique of customary land tenure reform under Malawi's National Land Policy, Warwick Law School, Dissertation for Master of Laws in Law in Development
Watts M (1989) The agrarian question in Africa: debating the crisis. Progress Human Geography 13(1):1–41
Wolford W, Borras SM, Hall R, Scoones I, White B (2013) Governing global land deals: the role of the state in the rush for land. Dev Change 44(2):189–210
World Bank (2016) Malawi Poverty Assessment Report

Part III
Agricultural Policies Under Neoliberalism

Gender, Household Food Security and Neoliberal Decimation of the Grain-Producing Peasantry in Zimbabwe

Newman Tekwa and Happymore Tekwa

Abstract With over half of the Zimbabwean population now facing food hunger, this could be juxtaposed to the 1980s' dirigiste period when the state boosted peasant maize production (as a proportion of national maize output) from 3.6% in 1979/80 to 35.6% in 1984/85. Since then, though interspersed with brief periods of heavy state involvement in the 2000s, Zimbabwe has undergone three decades of economic liberalisation from a Structural Adjustment Programme (SAP) in the early 1990s to the current Transition Stabilisation Programme (TSP). The gendered effects of decades of agricultural market liberalisation on peasant households in the country remain inadequately documented and analysed. In this chapter, we first consider the extent to which the shift from dirigisme to liberalisation affected integration, efficiency and competitiveness in the agricultural sector. We examine the distribution of benefits of market liberalisation across different scales of agricultural production in addition to interrogating how female peasants have fared in these economic restructuring processes relative to men, primarily in relation to food security. We argue that liberalisation negatively impacted peasant maize production and curtailed the dual role of peasant households, leading to gender-differentiated knock-on effects for household food security. This highlights the crucial role of the state in ensuring national and household food sufficiency.

1 Introduction

The 1980s saw indicators of economic trouble arising across much of sub-Saharan Africa, manifesting in the form of deteriorating balances of trade, depleting foreign currency reserves and rising external indebtedness (World Bank 1981). A World

N. Tekwa (✉)
College of Graduate Studies, University of South Africa, Pretoria, South Africa

H. Tekwa
Department of Agriculture, Environment and Natural Resource Management, Midlands State University, Gweru, Zimbabwe

F. Mazwi et al. (eds.), *Capital Penetration and the Peasantry in Southern and Eastern Africa*, Advances in African Economic, Social and Political Development, https://doi.org/10.1007/978-3-030-89824-3_6

Bank publication known as the Berg Report (of 1981) challenged the existing policy regimes and prescribed a development strategy for sub-Saharan Africa based on agricultural market liberalisation (Baden 1998; Mkandawire and Soludo 1998; World Bank 1981). Agriculture was the centrepiece of the iconoclastic and dogmatic prescriptions contained in the Berg Report, with recommendations pointing to the reduction in states' monopsonistic position in agricultural input and output markets and the removal of food subsidies, price controls and state credit facilities to agriculture (Moyo 2011; Mkandawire and Soludo 1998; Zulauf and Irwin 1997; World Bank 1981; Razavi 2007). This structural adjustment programme (SAP) represented the emerging ascendency of the self-interested neoliberal economic agenda of globally-dominant finance capital, which entailed moulding the economic policies of pliant governments and the subsequent loss of policy space by African governments regarding sovereign economic policy (Patnaik 2011; Patnaik 2003).

Forced implementation of this global capitalist agenda (through for instance conditional loans) was accompanied by a substantial drop in basic food output and availability per head in sub-Saharan Africa (Patnaik 2003). With developing countries urged to boost agricultural export production, Patnaik (2011) makes reference to the inverse relationship between producing for exports and maintaining domestic food grain availability, not only in colonial times but also during the post-colonial trade liberalisation period in developing countries broadly (Patnaik 2011). Resultantly, the food grain importation bill for the African continent rose exponentially as countries sought to compensate for the declining domestic food production following the mal-integration of the peasantry into global capitalist value chains (Patnaik 2011; Moyo 2011; Chambati et al. 2018).

Departing from SAPs' imposed food security policy framework, involving a focus on agricultural production for export, we argue that food security requires enhanced food sufficiency based on national and household production (Moyo 2011). As cautioned by Ghosh (2010), sustainable national food security requires increasing domestic production of food to eliminate dependency on imports. This is not merely a matter of choice but also a policy imperative with huge strategic implications (Ghosh 2010). In the extroverted neoliberal definition of food security, strategic public grain reserves are considered as irrational as countries could import food as and when needed (Moyo 2011). The effect of this cannot be divorced from the problematic food security situation prevailing in most developing countries, particularly Africa.

A contemporary food security analysis of Zimbabwe reveals that the number of people facing food crisis in Zimbabwe increased by 40% from 5.5 million in 2019 (FAO 2019) to 7.7 million people in 2020 (World Food Programme 2020). This entails an exponential increase in food insecurity in the country and is a major social policy issue requiring urgent policy attention. Further, Anseeuw et al. (2012) assert that the food security landscape in Zimbabwe transitioned from a mere 'accessibility problem' in the 1980s to 'an accessibility and availability problem' from the 1990s onwards. This is largely because the national maize output post-1990, until recently, never exceeded 2 million tonnes, which is considered to be the basic national food requirement (Anseeuw et al. 2012, p. 50). Maize productivity trends post fast track land reform remained subdued in the 2000s despite substantial funding, as the policy framework neglected the peasantry in favour of medium- and large-scale producers (Moyo et al. 2009). This is the case, although there exists enhanced food production and security at the household level, particularly for (fast track) resettled small-scale farmers, except in periods of drought (Tekwa 2020; Moyo et al. 2009).

2 Statement of the Problem

The current situation of 7.7 million people in Zimbabwe (over 50% of the population) facing food hunger exemplifies an agrarian crisis of significant magnitude. This is particularly so when juxtaposed to the 1980s when the state boosted peasant maize production (as a proportion of national maize output) from 3.6% in 1979 and 1980 to 35.6% in 1984 and 1985. With the increasing dominance of global finance capital and concomitant loss of policy space for African governments, the current food security framework was reconfigured to accommodate and indeed prioritise a market-based notion of national and household food supply and access. Interrogating the effect of this neoliberal reconfiguration on the relative importance of domestic national food (maize) production vis-à-vis reliance on donors and commercial grain imports and aid dependency for food insecurity at the national and household level remains imperative. From a gender perspective, the ways in which female peasants in Zimbabwe have fared in neoliberal restructuring processes, primarily in relation to household food security, has been absent in many analyses. The disastrous integration of peasant farmers into the global capitalist system had led to rising food insecurity with a concomitant negative effect on the well-being of peasants, particularly women.

Using a gendered political economy perspective, we sought answers to the following questions with specific reference to Zimbabwe:

- How exactly has global capitalism reconfigured a conceptualisation of the food security policy framework in de-emphasising domestic-based food sufficiency based on national and household production?
- To what extent has the attendant shift from dirigiste to private sector-led agricultural policies led to declining food production and rising food imports, particularly maize?
- How has this affected national and household food security and the dual role of peasant households as grain producers and consumers?
- In what ways have female peasants fared in this economic restructuring process, particularly in terms of household food security and well-being?

Secondary data analysis research, a method involving the use of existing data to address research questions, was a key research method adopted for the chapter. This was complemented with primary data drawn from part of the first author's PhD thesis, with the research conducted in 2016. There are several advantages of using already-existing data, including a good fit with the researcher's own research aims

(Johnson 2014). The two secondary data sets pertinent to this study comprised the number and value of agricultural credit by farming sector and maize production trends in Zimbabwe pre- and post-1990. These data were drawn from Agricultural Finance Corporation (AFC) documents and the then Ministry of Agriculture, Mechanisation and Irrigation Development, respectively.

The rest of the chapter on Zimbabwe is structured as follows. First, we offer a literature review highlighting the adverse incorporation of peasant farmers into global capitalist markets and the extent to which neoliberalism reconfigured the concept of food security, with disastrous effects on food sufficiency in developing countries. This is followed by a discussion of empirical trends counterposing peasants' food supply response during the first decade of independence vis-s-vis the gendered impact of neoliberalism on household food production and food security in the post-1990 period. Before concluding the chapter, a brief section highlights the role of the state in household food security, particularly for peasants in the context of land reforms.

3 Adverse Global Incorporation of Peasants

We adopt a political economy perspective, an analytical framework that places emphasis on the relations and distribution of resources among different actors—in this instance, peasants in relation to global finance capital. We interrogate the integration of the former into global markets under neoliberalism (Chambati et al. 2018; Patnaik 2011). Within the neoclassical vision of the economy, market integration denotes a progressive process, as it is a process of combining separate (local, national and regional) economies into a larger (global) economic region for the benefit of all (González-Rivera and Helfand 2001). The envisaged integration of markets includes trade liberalisation policies which, in Zimbabwe post-1990, entailed the removal of tariff and non-tariff barriers to trade, alongside the state's decreasing presence in the movement of goods and factors of production (Koester 2000).

From a Marxist political economy perspective, this process entails the opening up of developing economies to the interest of global finance capital under the pretext of economic restructuring (Patnaik 2003). The attendant agricultural land-use patterns reflect the neoliberal emphasis on export production to satisfy market demands in the global North at the expense of food grain production for domestic consumption in developing nations (Patnaik 2011, 2003). This has led to a dramatic rise in importation of exceptionally low-priced and heavily subsidised grain from countries of the global North by countries of the global South (Moyo 2011; Patnaik 2011, 2003). Ironically, the same countries 'lecturing' developing countries to remove subsidies continue to subsidise their own farmers, resulting in excess supply problems and coercing countries of the Global South to open their markets to imported grain. This has the potential of undermining the production capacities of local farmers in the South (Patnaik 2003). The net effect on incomes, livelihoods and food security of millions of grain-producing peasants, including women, is far reaching (Chambati et al. 2018).

Noteworthy, the incentives and pressures to adjust emanating from integration into global capitalist markets can lead to the disappearance or contraction of previously highly protected groups in the economy, including peasant farmers in the global South (Prugl et al. 2012; Knetter et al. 2001; Koester 2000). This is particularly so because integration into global capitalist markets provides a leeway for external global factors and interests to exert increasing influence on domestic outcomes (Mkandawire and Soludo 1998; Knetter et al. 2001; Koester 2000). As highlighted by Patnaik (2003), liberalisation of trade and opening up of markets, which constitute the hallmark of global market integration, entails the importation of depressing effects from the global market into domestic economies with concomitant effects on small-scale producers, particularly peasants (Patnaik 2003). Such continued peasant mal-integration into unequal trade relations within the world capitalist system also entrenches domestic inequities leading to a crisis of peasant reproduction manifesting in the form of persistent food insecurity (Moyo 2011).

The neoclassical perspective on prices and market efficiency is problematic, as it defines an abstract situation where prices in input and output markets, including agriculture, are subject by necessity to laws of supply and demand (Lundy et al. 2004). This implies doing away with dirigiste policies of price and income determination, with the role of the government reduced to regulation under an unfettered market system that elevates the role of the private sector in growing the economy (Koester 2000; Lundy et al. 2004; Zulauf and Irwin 1997; Buccola 1989). Preceded by a period characterised by heavy state intervention in the economy, in the Zimbabwean case, this involved the dismantling of all forms of state support (including public-mandated commodity marketing boards) to ensure that global capitalist market forces determine agricultural commodity prices (Poulton et al. 2002; Sibanda and Makwata 2017). This raises crucial questions about the ability of different categories of farmers, located at different scales of production and technological use, in taking advantage of the new markets.

The assumption of perfect competition among all market actors in a capitalist global economy, irrespective of size and scale of operations, represents one shortcoming of neoclassical economics (Knetter et al. 2001; Zulauf and Irwin 1997). Such competitiveness in global capitalist markets is attained supposedly through specialising in specific comparative advantages in order to survive and thrive (Knetter et al. 2001; Zulauf and Irwin 1997). This relates back to the fallacies of Ricardo's two-country two-commodity theory of comparative advantage that has been used as a basis for developing countries to open up for free trade purposes while specialising in the production of agricultural export commodities at the expense of local food production (Patnaik and Moyo 2011; Moyo 2011). While the ability of peasant farmers and peasant women in particular to withstand growing international competition is questionable, it was considered price competitive and less costly for developing countries to import grain from the North despite bloating governments' indebtedness in the South (Moyo 2011; Whitehead undated). The overall trend, though, has been decreasing food production in Africa and escalating food insecurity in the region.

3.1 Gender, Household Food Security and Neoliberalism

The term 'gender' is a key theoretical and conceptual innovation of feminist scholarship for explaining persistent inequality between women and men (Scott 1986). A gender analysis is not concerned only with women but also with the social, cultural, economic and political structures conditioning the different roles played by women and men in the family and the community (Spieldoch 2007). Extending this to processes of economic change, gender structures and hierarchies in other social institutions (notably markets) are also of significance (Tsikata 2015; Razavi 2007). With reference to a neoliberal reconfigured concept of household food security that led to extroverted African agriculture (Moyo 2011), a deep theoretical issue relates to understanding the profound gendered outcomes of this on food security at local household and community levels (Patnaik 2011). Thus, gender remains a valuable analytical tool in understanding social relations of agrarian change, particularly with regard to peasant household food security in Africa (Tsikata 2015; Baden 1998; Adekambi et al. 2019).

The domination of global finance capital, as exemplified by the shift in government policies towards greater market orientation, trade liberalisation and reduction in state controls and protection, had the potential to put the squeeze on vulnerable groups (Karshenas 1997). In fact, there have been significant adverse effects arising from such economic restructuring on peasant women, including on their household food production (Awimbula and Tsikata 2010). As well, gendered barriers to female mobility in new state-supported export-oriented sectors worsen the position of peasant women as financial resources are shifted to these sectors (Karshenas 1997; Spieldoch 2007). As witnessed in many developing countries, this has had concomitant adverse effects on the welfare and food security of female-headed peasant households in particular. Deregulation was accompanied not only by declining agricultural commodity prices on the world market but also declines in per capita food production (especially for women) on the African continent (Patnaik 2011; Moyo 2011). The outcomes of these processes were twofold. First, depressed export earnings crippled the capacity of African governments to import food grain to supplement deficits in domestic production (Anseeuw 2012). Secondly, at the local level, this created a food insecurity crisis with a pronounced gendered dimension. Food aid programmes are implicitly being used as hidden grain markets allowing the North to unload its overproduced grain onto the South (Spieldoch 2007, p. 16). This has the real possibility of undermining the food security situation of peasant farmers, with women most affected as key producers of the world's staple foods.

4 Dirigiste Policies in the First Decade of Zimbabwe's Independence (1980–1990)

This section examines the peasant grain supply response to independence in Zimbabwe during the first decade (1980–1990) and the attendant national food sufficiency situation with a surplus for export. This stands contrary to the neoliberal decline in domestic food production, increasing food insecurity at the national and household level and persistent food aid dependence post-1990. In the following section, we outline the disastrous neoliberal policies that transitioned the country from a surplus maize exporting country to a deficit grain importing country with gendered effects at the household level, particularly peasant households.

While the 1980s marked a landslide introduction of neoliberal reforms (including agriculture) across much of the developing world (Prugl et al. 2012), Zimbabwe appeared to be an oxymoron contradicting the prevailing popular neoliberal doctrine (Masiyandima et al. 2011; Chambati et al. 2018). Against a tide in the resurgence of market optimism and liberalisation, for a decade policy makers in Zimbabwe relentlessly pursued a dirigiste economic doctrine and approach to economic development, justified as a basis for the prevention of market failures (Mkandawire and Soludo 1998; Brett 2005). The successes recorded in the first decade of independence were such that: 'As late as 1998, the IMF acknowledged that Zimbabwe was ... a corporatist state ... composed of ... trained and committed intellectuals.... who simply did not share the reformers' belief in the efficacy of the market' (Botchwey et al. 1998, quoted in Brett 2005, p. 3).

As an outcome of its dirigiste agricultural policies, the country was considered one of Africa's agriculture and food security success stories, in particular, due to the peasant supply/production response to state-supported agricultural market incentives (Brett 2005). Concurrently, famines were ravaging across the continent, killing millions of people in Ethiopia between 1984 and 1985 (Gwara 2011). For Zimbabwe, two flagship state interventions deserve particular attention. They comprised state interventions for peasant participation in agricultural credit markets through the Agricultural Finance Corporation (AFC) and a public grain procurement, storage and distribution system exemplified by the Grain Marketing Board (GMB) (Poulton et al. 2002).

4.1 *Peasant Participation in Agricultural Markets*

Increasing the number of peasants receiving agricultural credit through the Agricultural Finance Corporation (AFC) was one of the new government's agricultural policy priorities during the first decade of independence (Poulton et al. 2002; Anseeuw et al. 2012; African Development Bank 1992; Pandey and Ramnarayan 1994). Initially established under colonialism in 1971 as a public enterprise, until 1978, the main clientele of the AFC comprised less than 3000 white commercial farmers holding land under freehold (Pandey and Ramnarayan 1994). This excluded the majority black population in Tribal Trust (now called communal) lands holding no title to any land (Rusike and Sukume 2006).

With the amendment of the Agricultural Finance Act in 1979, the AFC has expanded to service all sectors of the farming community to include peasant farmers in communal and resettlement areas. In its five-year plan beginning in 1981, the AFC set an ambitious goal of giving agricultural loans to 65,000 farmers by 1985 (Pandey and Ramnarayan 1994, p. 48). Among the many credit schemes offered by the AFC, as part of its social responsibility initiative, two credit schemes are germane to this study: namely, the Small Farm Credit Scheme (SFCS) and the Resettlement Credit Scheme (RCS). The former, which began in 1981, had a principal objective of providing agricultural finance to communal and small-scale commercial farmers. The latter, introduced in 1982, targeted peasant farmers resettled under the government's first land resettlement programme. Taking cognisance of the risk inherent in extending agricultural credit for the development of rural areas, as part of its social policy objectives, the government underwrote the risk of losses and the net cost of lending to peasant farmers (African Development Bank 1992).

The number of peasant farmers receiving agricultural credit through the AFC increased from a mere 18,000 in 1980/81 to over 77,000 in the 1986/87 agricultural season, with loans provided at a subsidised interest rate (Poulton et al. 2002). The 1986/87 agricultural season marked the peak of loans extended to peasant farmers (communal and resettlement farmers combined) with 91, 392 peasant farmers accessing agricultural credit loans through the AFC (Zumbika 2006; Anseeuw et al. 2012). Highlighting the government's commitment to service peasant farmers residing in the communal areas during the first 10 years of independence, the ratio of the value of loans extended to the communal sector relative to the large-scale (mainly white) commercial sector increased from 4.5% in 1980/81 to 63.1% in the 1987/88 agricultural season. The gendered nature of the Zimbabwean state's agricultural policies, by privileging male heads of households, is clear (Baden 1998). However, in 1983, the AFC commendably decided to finance female peasant farmers on the same terms as men. With an estimated 50% of small-scale farms headed by women, this suggests that the bulk of the beneficiaries of this state-facilitated non-collateralised agricultural credit in Zimbabwe were women (Anseeuw et al. 2012; Eicher 1995).

4.2 *Public Grain Procurement, Storage and Distribution Infrastructure*

State interventions also affected peasant access to agricultural output markets in Zimbabwe as part of the latter's efforts to stimulate the peasantry's grain supply response.

During the dirigisme period of the early 1980s, agricultural output markets were dominated by parastatals or state enterprises, with the Grain Marketing Board (GMB) monopolising grain procurement, storage and distribution (Poulton et al. 2002). The GMB (created through the Grain Marketing Act No. 31 was originally the Maize Marketing Board set up by the Maize Control Act of 1931 (Ndlela and Robinson 2007). The GMB was responsible for the marketing of maize, soya bean, wheat, sunflower, coffee (controlled products), sorghum, millet and groundnuts, including edible beans (regulated products) (Poulton et al. 2005). As part of the integration of peasant farmers located historically out of reach of agricultural output markets, the government deliberately sought to extend marketing services into remote areas as part of its social and strategic objectives (Ndlela and Robinson 2007). Pre-independence, only three depots served peasant farmers in communal areas.

After independence, the public grain intake network in communal areas was extensively expanded from 3 to 10 depots (between 1980 and 1985) and subsequently increased to 37 depots by 1991 (Poulton et al. 2002). This was in addition to numerous seasonal buying points meant to receive grain from peasant farmers (Ndlela and Robinson 2007; Masters and Nuppenau 1993). The latter increased from only 5 to 148 (buying points) between 1980 and 1985, with the majority located mainly in the drier southern parts of the country (Eicher 1995). The target was to ensure a grain procurement station within 8–10 km of every peasant farmer, including women (Government of Zimbabwe 1982, cited in Masters and Nuppenau 1993). This was in addition to the establishment of public grain storage facilities with the potential to hold over 2 million tons of grain (Poulton et al. 2002).

Further, a system of pan-territorial and pan-season pricing effectively subsidised peasant production in remote areas. Pan-territorial pricing policy includes the payment of uniform producer prices throughout the country, an essential income transfer policy. Such price incentives were meant to stimulate peasant grain production in remote surplus regions in Zimbabwe through an implicit transport subsidy (Jayne and Nuppenau 1993). Pan-seasonal pricing policy encompasses the setting of producer and consumer prices annually with an implicit policy objective to encourage centralisation of stocks as opposed to farm grain storage (Poulton et al. 2002). This entailed pre-planting pricing, and pre- and post-harvest pricing, which performed a critical function in the dirigiste economic regime. Pre-planting pricing policy included the announcement of producer prices before the season's planting with the policy objective of boosting producer incentives. This reduces the risk of uncertainty, enabling farmers to make decisions based on known relative prices (Poulton et al. 2002).

4.3 *Peasant Supply Response, National Food Security and Peasant Households' Dual Role*

This set of policy instruments worked well in a controlled market environment, particularly in favour of grain-producing peasants located in remote parts of the country. This was coupled with a prohibition of private movement of controlled products (particularly maize) so as to solidify the income transfer mechanism in favour of the peasantry (Jayne and Nuppenau 1993). The outcome was a tremendous grain production supply response spearheaded by peasant farmers (Eicher 1995; Brett 2005). In this regard, it is noticeable that an intimate relationship between agricultural finance, agricultural production and food security in Zimbabwe has been highlighted recently in the literature (World Bank 2019; Masiyandima et al. 2011).

With regard to the provision of agricultural credit, the AFC was the main operational arm of the government's financial policy in the agricultural sector and the single largest credit institution servicing the sector (Sithole 1990). Historically, no other organisation had ever extended agricultural loans to the communal and resettled agricultural sub-sectors at such levels as the AFC (Pandey and Ramnarayan 1994). To highlight the strategic importance of AFC loans to peasant farmers, by 1985, the loan credit from the AFC covered 2/3rds of the value of inputs purchased by peasant farmers (Chisvo 2000, cited in Poulton et al. 2002).

With increased access to agricultural credit, sales of hybrid maize seed to communal farmers increased from 4600 tons in 1980/81 to 15,000 tons in 1985/86 with an annual growth rate of 27% throughout the first decade (Poulton et al. 2002). Resultantly, by the early 1990s, 100% of the peasant maize area was planted with hybrid maize seed (Eicher 1995). As well, access to non-collateralised AFC loans tripled total annual consumption of inorganic fertilisers by peasant farmers from 27,100 tons between 1975–1979 to 97,200 tons between 1980–1984, subsequently rising to 119,000 tons in the period 1985–1989 (Poulton et al. 2002).

Maize deliveries to the GMB by sector (peasant or commercial) show a massive increase in peasant deliveries during the 1980s, with these deliveries doubling while commercial deliveries stagnated. With maize producer prices set at attractive levels, the 1985 bumper harvest meant that the GMB maize stocks reached 2 million tons for the first time. By 1987, peasant marketed maize surplus reached 60% of deliveries to the GMB, with large-scale farmers beginning to shift their production to higher value uncontrolled horticultural crops (Poulton et al. 2002; Stanning 1989). The overall net result of Zimbabwe's agricultural policies during the 1980s was national food sufficiency and autonomy (Brett 2005). Due to the expanded peasant access to credit, higher state-guaranteed maize producer prices and an assured market, Zimbabwe generated a reliable maize surplus and exported maize for 19 out of 21 years between 1970 and 1991 (Eicher 1995; Anseeuw et al. 2012). The country's self-sufficiency ratio of maize reached 212% in 1985, earning the late former President Robert Mugabe the African Leadership Award in 1988 (Gwara 2011). This meant that maize stocks represented an amount equivalent to 2 years of domestic consumption at that time (Eicher 1995; Brett 2005). The dual role of peasant households as both producers and consumers is not often adequately highlighted in the market integration literature. As well, normally, missing in official peasant production statistics is production for use value, where peasant households produce for own consumption (Tekwa 2020) or non-excludable consumption (Buccola 1989). Maize sold to agricultural output markets by peasant farmers has been rightfully termed 'marketed maize surplus', suggesting that it is over and above 'retention,' that is, the amount of grain retained for household consumption (Poulton et al. 2002; Stanning 1989). While this highlights the dual role, the motivation to produce tends to vary. As well, a gender perspective reveals that women mainly produce for the household, thus contributing to household food security as opposed to profit driven male production tendencies (Baden 1998). At the same time, the paradoxical food security situation comprising pockets of food insecurity at the household level in the midst of national production surplus must be acknowledged (Anseeuw et al. 2012), with this problem being the inevitable outcome of distributional rather than production failures.

5 Post-1990 Neoliberal Turn in Zimbabwe: From Dirigisme to Liberalisation

The shift from a tightly controlled corporatist economy, accompanied by a restructuring of agricultural input and output markets, led to a crisis in the 1990s (Brett 2005). This represented an almost complete reversal of state-directed or dirigiste policies (Patnaik 2003). The introduction of marketing principles, namely market integration, price efficiency and market competitiveness within Zimbabwe's agricultural credit markets and publicly subsidised grain marketing services, did not leave peasant maize production unscathed.

5.1 Liberalisation of Agricultural Credit Markets Post-1990

Liberalisation saw the restructuring and commercialisation of the AFC accompanied by the introduction of high-interest rates and tight monetary policies that seriously curtailed lending to peasant farmers. While challenges faced the AFC Small Farms Schemes, including managerial and loan supervision problems, external factors, particularly the effect of poor agricultural seasons, led to high default rates. The 1990s witnessed a significant reduction in the number and value of loans extended to the peasant sub-sector. Hence, the number of peasant farmers receiving AFC loans plummeted by over 800% from a peak of 77,526 loans in the 1986/87 season to 9214 loans in the 1997/97 season. Correspondingly, the value of loans decreased by over 60% from a peak of \$60 million in 1987/88 to \$26.4 million in the 1991/92 season when the Economic Structural Adjustment Programme (ESAP) was first introduced

(Poulton et al. 2002, p. 32). Admittedly, the ratio in the value of AFC loans was tilted in favour of large-scale farmers even during the period of dirigiste policies (with the highest being peasant loans to 2/3rds the value of commercial loans in the 1987/88 season). However, post-1990, the gap widened significantly as the peasant sector was considered risky by the same institutions that supported it in the 1980s (Pandey and Ramnarayan 1994, p. 50).

Under the pervasive neoliberal ideology post-1990 (and beyond), it was argued that the household-based benefits of financing peasant farmers were below the national social-economic benefits of such an intervention (Masiyandima et al. 2011). Left with no access to agricultural finance, peasant farmers felt compelled to approach commercial banks to access agricultural credit (Anseeuw et al. 2012). Such attempts were not particularly successful, with banks often rejecting the peasantry's loan applications. The key reason (at 60%) for rejection was the sheer lack of collateral on offer by peasant households, with the gendered effects being very telling (Masiyandima et al. 2011, p. 16).

The intersectionality of race and gender within agricultural credit markets of former settler economies provides a critical lens for understanding the social nuances of economic liberalisation regarding peasant farmers in Zimbabwe. With much of the agricultural finance collateralised in the 1990s, liberalisation impacted female peasant farmers most severely as they lacked not only freehold title to any piece of land but also any physical registered property in their name to use as collateral. Resultantly, with the demise of the AFC that provided non-collateralised agricultural credit to male and female peasants, the latter could not compete on par with men in liberalised agricultural credit markets (Pandey and Ramnarayan 1994).

It can safely be concluded that liberalisation severed peasant integration in agricultural input markets as many cut back, for instance, on inorganic fertiliser purchases, due to reduced access to agricultural credit (Tibugari et al. 2019; Sithole 1990). This was coupled with the reduced access to improved seed due to weak and unpredictable demand resulting from the dismantling of agricultural marketing boards and the ensuing high prices in rural areas, which in turn, arose from the introduction of price and market efficiency principles within agricultural input markets (Poulton et al. 2002; Sibanda and Makwata 2017; Patnaik and Moyo 2011). With price and distribution controls on fertilisers removed by 1995, the prices of agricultural inputs in remote areas skyrocketed due to logistical and related transactional costs (Chinyemba et al. 2006; Gonzalez et al. 2001; Mkandawire and Soludo 1998). The situation was exacerbated by collusion in the pricing of hybrid seed maize by seed housing companies with prices beyond the reach of peasant farmers (Tibugari et al. 2019).

5.2 *Integration, Efficiency and Competitiveness in Maize Grain Markets*

While the publicly subsidised grain marketing services were not fully liberalised, GMB's large-scale grain movement, storage and wholesaling were gradually deregulated and opened to private traders (Anseeuw et al. 2012). As part of bringing efficiency in agricultural output markets, all 'so-called' uneconomical maize depots serving peasant farmers located in remote parts of the country were closed (Ndlela and Robinson 2007). The contradictory opening up of grain markets to private trading alongside the maintenance of pan-territorial pricing policies saw private traders encroaching GMB's least-cost markets for maize procurement, thereby compelling the latter to procure maize from remote locations at a greater cost (Ndlela and Robinson 2012). This was coupled with the establishment of the Zimbabwe Agricultural Commodity Exchange (ZIMACE), a crucial institutional part of agricultural liberalisation in Zimbabwe (Muir-Leresche and Muchopa 2006). ZIMACE was a private sector initiative that acted as a source of information on supply and demand conditions in agricultural commodities except for tobacco and horticultural crops. Trade volumes through ZIMACE increased at a rate of 35% annually as commercial farmers took advantage of the liberalised agricultural marketing system (Poulton et al. 2002). Resultantly, by 1997, GMB share of domestic maize sales declined to 10% as ZIMACE provided a major alternative channel for large-scale grain sales (Muir-Leresche and Muchopa 2006; Baden 1998).

While medium and large-scale traders (including large-scale commercial farmers) benefitted from economic reform of public grain procurement, certain tendencies worked contrary to the interests of peasant farmers, particularly females (Jayne and Nuppenau 1993, p. 314). Female peasant farmers' market integration was the first to be severed with the scaling down of government marketing services provided by grain depots located in marginal areas, due to now high transaction costs associated with participating in agricultural output markets (Chinyemba et al. 2006; Gonzalez et al. 2001). While ZIMACE took on nearly the entire trading in maize grain up until the end of the decade, the minimum ZIMACE transaction volume was set at a minimum of 5-tons. This excluded female peasant participation in agricultural output markets due to their lack of economies of scale (Baden 1998; Zulauf and Irwin 1997). Stripped of any government protection, many peasant farmers in Zimbabwe, particularly females, soon faced an increasingly difficult future in agriculture (Lundy et al. 2004, p. 9), as noted below.

5.3 *Gender, Liberalisation and the Food Crisis*

Despite receiving a relatively smaller share of AFC loans, peasant contribution to total maize output had always exceeded that of large-scale farmers. Illustratively, for the period 1997/98, large-scale farmers received 77% of the value of AFC loans relative to 13.6% extended to communal peasant farmers. Though agricultural credit from the AFC covered almost 2/3rds of the value of inputs purchased by peasants before neoliberal restructuring, the figure fell to 1/3rd by 1991, declining further to 1/5th by 1995 (Poulton et al. 2002, p. 47). This means that the extent of neoliberal restructuring of the AFC effectively resulted in the contraction of peasant agriculture in Zimbabwe, with gendered knock-on effects on national and household food security (Prugl et al. 2012).

Neoliberal reforms to the GMB, particularly the closure of grain depots in marginal areas, the subsequent removal of pan-territorial and pan-seasonal prices, and integration of maize grain markets (Ndlela and Robinson 2007, p. 20), worsened the vulnerability of female households regarding food insecurity. A large proportion of peasant households in Zimbabwe, as indicated, are located in remote regions typically not within easy reach of agricultural output markets. The social policy objective of ensuring that every peasant farmer is within 8-10 kilometres of a depot effectively subsidised grain-producing peasants and facilitated their participation in agricultural output markets (Masters and Nuppenau 1993; Government of Zimbabwe 1982; World Bank 1981). The neoliberal scaling down of government grain marketing services in remote regions increased peasant transactional costs associated with participating in agricultural output markets (Adekambi et al. 2019, p. 615). This was coupled with peasant farmers' lack of capacity, particularly females, to adjust and respond to the changing incentives that came with liberalisation (Mkandawire and Soludo 1998). Inadvertently, such scaling down resulted in increased food insecurity and poverty among disadvantaged groups mostly women and children (Chinyemba et al. 2006, p. 639).

The gendered effects on household food security emanating from the removal of pan-territorial and pan-season pricing policies (which acted as income transfers to remote production regions) were severe (Poulton et al. 2002). Female peasant farmers were the hardest hit, as they not only lacked the capacity to transport their produce to the market; as well, they were effectively severed from market integration, and their maize grain production was curtailed (Moyo 2011). The increased risk emanating from uncertainty around maize producer prices and the absence of an assured market provided by the GMB thus took a toll on the food security situation of the grain-producing peasantry, particularly females (Chinyemba et al. 2006).

The close nexus between 'own production' and household food security within peasant households is central to peasant women and food security. In a survey of rural households in northern Zimbabwe, Stanning (1989) found maize retention for household consumption within grain-producing peasant households to account for 13% of available supplies, with over 75% of maize marketed to the GMB (Stanning 1989, p. 262). With maize accounting for over 50% of the calories consumed in Zimbabwe (Muir-Leresche and Muchopa 2006; Eicher 1995), the dual role of peasant households as producers and consumers cannot be emphasised. Own production and consumption of unprocessed grain remain a key source of calories for female peasant households in Zimbabwe due to gendered income-related constraints in accessing food through the market (World Bank 2015; Moyo 2011). With maize grain produced by over 90% of peasant households constituting their main source of calories, neoliberal restructuring curtailed the dual role of peasant households as producers and consumers (World Bank 2015). Resultantly, the country regrettably transitioned from a surplus maize exporting country to a deficit grain importing country with access to food reflecting gendered class-based income inequalities (Moyo 2011; FAO 2019).

6 Land Reforms, Gender and Household Food Security Post-2000

Noticeably anti-neoliberal in form, in 2000, Zimbabwe implemented an expropriatory land redistribution programme (fast track) that saw the government acquiring over 10 million hectares of former freehold white commercial farm land and redistributing it to a variegated group of beneficiaries under lease and permissory tenure (Moyo et al. 2009; Tekwa 2020). As an improvement on land redistribution programmes of the 1980s and 1990s, research on fast track indicates that 18% and 12% of land allocations in the A1 and A2 fast track models went, respectively, to women in their own right (Chiweshe et al. 2014, p. 6; Utete 2003; GoZ and SIRDC 2007, cited in Tekwa 2020, p. 152). Fast track reconfigured the agrarian structure in Zimbabwe to one in which small-scale family farms constitute over 90% of the landholdings (Cousins 2013, p. 122; see also Moyo et al. 2009; Moyo 2011). Nevertheless, as Moyo (2011) argues, this expropriatory land reform (which led to expansive land redistribution and structural changes in agrarian relations) remained tied to a broader neoliberal policy framework, particularly finance capital's dominance in seed supply, technology and credit (Moyo 2011). In this regard, there emerged an important contradiction between the objectives of fast track and the overall policy framework post-2000, leading to inconsistencies in the country's development path, with gendered knock-on effects in terms of agricultural productivity and national and household food security (Tekwa 2020).

6.1 Policy Inconsistences and Food Production

While the 1990s were largely characterised by liberalisation, the period 2000–2008 saw a marked return to regulation with the government heavily involved in agriculture (Anseeuw et al. 2012). Unlike the dirigiste period of the 1980s, however, government interventions post-2000 were averse to smallholder farmers, including small-scale A1 fast track beneficiaries.

For instance, the declining trend in agricultural credit support towards smallholder farmers witnessed in the 1990s continued into the post-2000 fast track period. Thus, the number and value of loans extended to peasant farmers by the AFC declined by 23.1% and 86.9%, respectively, between the period 2000 and 2002

(*Agriculture and Economic Review*, cited in Zumbika 2006, p. 341). The same source revealed a decline in the ratio of loans extended to peasant farmers relative to that extended to commercial farmers, plummeting from 2: 3 in 1987/88 to a ratio of 1:7 in the 2001/2002 agricultural season. This is despite the significance of small-scale farmers to agricultural output in the first decade of independence (Poulton et al. 2002; Stanning 1989). Indeed, in 2005, the then Portfolio Committee on Lands, Land Reform, Resettlement and Agriculture acknowledged that the agricultural financing facilities that existed were tailored for large-scale commercial farming at the expense of smallholders (Anseeuw et al. 2012). Though receiving much of government's agricultural support, the average contribution of commercial farmers to total national maize production for the period 2001–2007 never exceeded 1/8th of the total requirement (pegged at 2.2 million metric tons).

The years from 2009 to 2013, covering the period of the Government of National Unity (GNU), saw the adoption of a mixed approach, partly liberalising agricultural inputs and output markets (Anseeuw et al. 2012). Post-GNU, the government reverted to interventionist approaches with increased public expenditure on agriculture (World Bank 2019). However, the World Bank, in its review of public expenditure with a focus on agriculture, commented that 'despite substantial funding agriculture production did not pick up the key reason being the neglect of the small-scale communal and resettled farmers' (World Bank 2019, p. 35). As a result of the policy inconsistencies and the misplaced neoliberal emphasis, national food security was never achieved—as agricultural production, particularly maize, remained subdued (World Bank 2019). Resultantly, food insecurity became a permanent feature of the country's food security landscape (Anseeuw et al. 2012). The hostility of the current economic blueprint, the Transitional Stabilisation Programme (TSP), towards public expenditure in agriculture in favour of private sector initiatives contradicts the kind of dirigiste policies that led to a peasant-led 'agricultural revolution' in the 1980s.

6.2 Role of State and Household Food Security

Drawing upon empirical work that forms part of the first author's PhD fieldwork, we highlight, using micro level data, the counteractive effect of the redistributive land reforms (i.e. fast track) on gendered food insecurity at the household level. The study was conducted in one remote district to the south-east of the country (Masvingo province) and comprised an investigation of household food security status across three study sites, two resettlement sites (A1 and A2 farming areas[1]) and one communal area site. The latter acted as a control or counterfactual group to benchmark the effect of fast track on neoliberal-induced food insecurity by the gender of

[1] A1 farms (family farms) consisted of 5 to 10 ha of arable land, while A2 are the larger farms or farm plots above 20 ha.

the household head. Three important dimensions were identified to comparatively investigate rural households' food security by gender across the three sites. The first dimension (existence of food shortage) was adopted as an indicator, while the other two dimensions, the household's main source of food grain (maize) and household cultivable land size, were adopted as predictors of food (in)security at household level.

With regard to the existence of household food shortages, none of the participating households in the A2 study site reported experiencing household food shortages, including those headed by women. In the A1 study site, a meagre 9.1% reported experiencing household food insecurity. This contrasts markedly with non-land reform households located in the control study site (communal area), where the majority of the fast track land reform beneficiaries, particularly A1 beneficiaries, came from. In the control group, over 80% of participating households reported experiencing household food shortages, with 81.0% and 84.2% for male- and female-headed households, respectively. This suggests a severe food security crisis at the household level within much of the communal areas in Zimbabwe (World Food Programme 2020). These findings confirm that the status of food security in Zimbabwe varies spatially (by region or area) and socially (gender and income) (World Bank 2019).

On the first predictor of food security at the household level, a household's main source(s) of food grain, three important sources of food grain for rural households were investigated, namely, own production, purchase and food aid/safety nets. Notably, all participating households in the A1 farming areas reported 'own production' as their main source of food grain, particularly the staple maize (World Bank 2015). Resultantly, no A1 households in the study reported the purchase of maize grain to satisfy household calorie needs. In the A2 farming areas, despite no provision made officially for the cultivation of other food crops (including maize) on the predominantly sugarcane plots, 23.5% of participating households reported 'own production' as their main source of food grain. The allocated plots and irrigation water were *exclusively* for the cultivation of a specialised crop (sugarcane) and no other (*Key Informant Interview, Field Extension Officer, Tongaat Hulett Zimbabwe, 24 September 2016).* Contrastingly, a mere 5% of households in the control group (i.e. communal area) reported 'own production' as their source of food grain.

Owing to their high incomes following integration into the high-value (sugar cane) commodity chains, 75% of households in the A2 sugarcane farming areas reported 'purchase' as their main source of food grain. 'Purchase' was the second most important source of food grain for communal area households, reported by a quarter of them. While an equal number of male- and female-headed households in the communal areas reported 'purchase' as their second most important source of food grain, female-headed households are likely to find it more difficult to use the market as their source of food due to gender inequalities in income. The last source investigated, that is, 'safety nets/food aid' was more revealing on the counteractive effect of redistributive land reforms on gender-based neoliberal effects on household food security. With none of the fast track land reform households (A1 and A2) reported the use of 'safety nets/food aid' as their source of calories, it represented the main source of food grain (after 'purchase') in the communal control group. Over 70% of the participating communal households reported safety nets, particularly food aid, as constituting their main source of calories. This resonates with the claim by Moyo (2010) that neoliberal restructuring only served to increase food imports and food aid dependency in countries of the global South (Moyo 2010, cited in Moyo 2011, p. 62).

The available household cultivable land explains the large discrepancies relating to use of 'own production' as a source of food grain between the communal control group and resettlement households, particularly the A1 farmers. Further, it also contributes to understanding the different gendered experiences in household food shortages. In the communal areas, the available household cultivable land size averaged 2.78 ha compared to 16.6 ha and 21.3 ha in the A1 and A2 resettlement study sites, respectively. Juxtaposing the household food security situation in the A2 farming areas and the communal areas, it seems clear that households become food insecure when they lack not only the means to produce 'own food' but also access to income to purchase food. The last point highlights the important role of the state in counteracting the gendered neoliberal effect on household food security, particularly for the peasantry, through gender-equitable redistributive land reforms. In contrast to agrarian reforms that seek to integrate the peasantry into unequal world food systems, the critical role of the state in enhancing the participation of the peasantry for food sufficiency at the national and household levels remains imperative (Moyo 2011).

7 Conclusion

The current food crisis in Zimbabwe and its gendered characteristics at the household level has its origins in the 1990s' neoliberal dismantling of the dirigiste agricultural policies and institutions arising during the first decade of independence. This policy shift not only curtailed the dual role of peasant households but also severely affected the food security situation of peasant households.

Key findings indicate that access to agricultural finance, grain output markets and favourable producer prices in the first decade of independence not only boosted peasant maize production and marketed surplus but also enhanced national food sufficiency and household food security, particularly for the peasantry. Liberalisation of agricultural credit markets and closure of many GMB 'uneconomical' rural depots in the 1990s led to a significant decline in peasant consumption of inorganic fertiliser and hybrid maize seed use. This curtailed the dual role of peasant households as grain producers and consumers, severely affecting the food security situation of female-headed households, which constitute the majority of peasant farmers. The penultimate outcome was the decimation of the grain-producing peasantry with hunger and its gendered dimensions, becoming a seemingly permanent feature of Zimbabwe's food security.

The current economic blueprint advocates and pursues policy and institutional reforms for a private sector-led economy. On the contrary, we argue for a return to the peasant-focused state-led agricultural policies of the first decade if the persistent food crisis is to be averted. This is crucial as it has become apparent that post-2000, and despite substantial funding, agricultural production has failed to pick up due to the neglect of the peasantry. As presented in the case study of the fast track land reform programme, the role of the state in reversing the ongoing agrarian crises and promoting the participation of the peasantry for purposes of national and household food self-sufficiency is not only a matter of choice, as it has important policy and strategic implications.

References

Adekambi SA, Ingenbleek PTM, van Trijp HCM (2019) The role of market learning in the market integration of African smallholders. Afr J Bus Manage 13(18):613–621

African Development Bank (AfDB) (1992). Zimbabwe line of credit to Agricultural Finance Corporation: Project Performance Evaluation Report (PPER), 09 September 1992

Anseeuw W, Kapuya T, Saruchera D (2012) Zimbabwe's agricultural reconstruction: Present state, ongoing projects and prospects for reinvestment. Technical Report. Working Paper Series No. 32, Development Bank of Southern Africa. Halfway House, South Africa

Awimbula M, Tsikata D (2010) Economic liberalisation, changing resource tenures and gendered livelihoods: a study of small-scale gold mining and mangrove exploitation in rural Ghana. In: Tsikata D, Golah P (eds) Land tenure, gender and globalisation research and analysis from Africa, Asia and Latin America. Zuban: New Delhi, India

Baden S (1998) Gender issues in agricultural liberalisation. Topic Paper Prepared for Directorate General for Development (DGVIII) of the European Commission. BRIDGE Report No 41, January 1998. Institute of Development Studies, Brighton

Botchwey K, Collier P, Gunning JW, Hamada K (1998) From a group of independent persons appointed to conduct and evaluation of certain aspects of the enhanced structural adjustment facility. IMF, Washington

Brett EA (2005) From corporatism to liberalisation in Zimbabwe: economic policy regimes and political crisis 1980-1997. Crisis States Programme, Working Paper Series No. 1. Crisis States Research Centre, London School of Economics

Buccola ST (1989) Pricing efficiency in agricultural markets: issues, methods, and results. Western J Agric Econ 14(1):111–121

Chambati W, Mazwi F, Mberi S (2018) Agrarian accumulation and peasant resistance in Africa. CODESRIA, Dakar, Senegal, pp 1–32

Chinyemba MJ, Muchena ON, Hakutangwi M BK (2006) Women and agriculture. In: Rukuni M, Taonezvi P, Eicher C, Munyuki-Hungwe M, Matondi P (eds) Zimbabwe agricultural revolution revisited. University of Zimbabwe Publication, pp 631–650

Chisvo M (2000) Reaping the whirlwind economic liberalisation and food security. In: Zimbabwe Catholic Institute for International Relations (CIIR). United Kingdom

Chiweshe MK, Chakona L, Hellicker K (2014) Patriarchy, women, land and livelihoods on A1 farms in Zimbabwe. J Afr Asian Stud:1–16

Cousins B (2013) Smallholder irrigation schemes, agrarian reform and 'accumulation from above and below' in South Africa. J Agrarian Change 13(1):116–139

Eicher C (1995) Zimbabwe's maize-based green revolution: preconditions for replication. World Dev 23(5):805–818

FAO (2019) GIEWS Update, Zimbabwe. The Food and Agricultural Organisation. Rome, Italy. 14 October 2019
Ghosh J (2010) The political economy of hunger in 21st century India. Econ Polit Weekly 45 (44/45):33–38
González-Rivera G, Helfand SM (2001) Economic development and the determinants of market integration: the case of the Brazilian rice market. University of California, Department of Economics, Riverside
Government of Zimbabwe and Scientific and Industrial Research and Development Centre (SIRDC) (2007) National A2 land audit report. Preliminary report. Harare
Government of Zimbabwe (1982) Transitional National Development Plan: 1982/83-1984/85, vol 1. Amalgamated Press (Pvt) Ltd, Harare
Gwara S (2011) An estimation of price and non-price factors affecting maize supply response in Zimbabwe. MSc. Thesis. Department of Agricultural Economics and Extension, University of Zimbabwe. December 2011
Jayne TS, Nuppenau E-A (1993) Maize market reform in Zimbabwe. Food Policy:308–315
Johnson MP (2014) Secondary data analysis: a method which time has come. Qual Quant Methods Libr 3:619–626
Karshenas M (1997). Economic liberalization, competitiveness and women's employment in the Middle East and North Africa. SOAS, University of London
Knetter MM, Matthew J, Slaughter MJ (2001) Measuring product-market integration. In: Blomstrom M, Goldberg LS (eds) Topics in empirical international economics: a festschrift in Honor of Robert E. Lipsey. University of Chicago Press, pp 15–46
Koester U (2000) Market integration: how it works. In: Burrell A, Oskam A (eds) Agricultural policy and enlargement of the European Union. Wageningen Press, Wageningen, pp 21–34
Lundy M, Gottret MV, Cifuentes W, Ostertag CF, Best R, Peters D, Ferris S (2004) Increasing the competitiveness of market chains for smallholder producers: manual 3: territorial approach to rural agro-enterprise development. International Centre for Tropical Agriculture (CIAT)
Masiyandima N, Chigumira B, Bara A (2011) Sustainable financing for agriculture in Zimbabwe. ZEPARU Working Paper Series (ZWPS 02/10). Zimbabwe Economic Policy Analysis and Research Unit, March 2011
Masters W, Nuppenau E-A (1993) Pan-territorial versus regional pricing for maize in Zimbabwe. World Dev 21(10):1647–1658
Mkandawire T, Soludo CC (1998) Our continent, our future: African perspectives on structural adjustment. Council for the Development of Social Science Research in Africa (CODESRIA). Dakar, Senegal
Moyo S (2011) Primitive accumulation and the destruction of the African peasantry. In: Patnaik U, Moyo S (eds) The Agrarian question in the neoliberal era: primitive accumulation and the peasantry. Pambazuka Press, Dakar
Moyo S, Chambati W, Murisa T, Siziba D, Dangwa C, Mujeyi K, Nyoni N (2009) Fast track land reform baseline survey in Zimbabwe: trends and tendencies, 2005/06. African Institute for Agrarian Studies (AIAS), Harare
Moyo S (2011) Three decades of agrarian reform in Zimbabwe. J Peasant Stud 38(3):493–531
Muir-Leresche K, Muchopa C (2006) Agricultural marketing. In: Rukuni M, Tawonezvi P, Eicher C (eds) Zimbabwe's agricultural revolution revisited. University of Zimbabwe Publication, pp 299–320
Ndlela D, Robinson P (2007) Distortions to agricultural incentives in Zimbabwe. Agricultural Distortions Working Paper 39, December 2007. World Bank, Washington DC
Pandey IM, Ramnarayan S (1994) Agricultural finance corporation, Zimbabwe. Vikalpa 19(2):47–60
Patnaik U (2003) Global capitalism, deflation and agrarian crisis in developing countries. UNRISD Social Policy Paper Series 2003

Patnaik U (2011) The agrarian question in the neoliberal era. In: Patnaik U, Moyo S (eds) The Agrarian question in the neoliberal era: primitive accumulation and the peasantry. Pambazuka Press, Dakar

Poulton C, Davies R, Matshe I, Urey I (2002) A review of Zimbabwe's agricultural economic policies: 1980 –2000. ADU Working Paper 02/01 March, 2002

Prugl E, Razavi S, Reysoo F (2012) Gender and agriculture after neoliberalism. Report of A Workshop Organised by the United Nations Research Institute for Social Development (UNIRSD), 19-20 July 2012, Geneva, Switzerland

Razavi R (2007) Liberalisation and the debates on women's access to land. Third World Q 28(8):1479–1500

Rusike J, Sukume C (2006) Agricultural input supply. In: Rukuni M, Taonezvi P, Eicher C, Munyuki-Hungwe M, Matondi P (eds) Zimbabwe agricultural revolution revisited. University of Zimbabwe Publication, pp 279–298

Scott JW (1986) Gender: a useful category of historical analysis. Am Hist Rev 91(5):1053–1075

Sibanda V, Makwata R (2017) Zimbabwe post independence economic policies: a critical review. Lambert Academic Publishing, Saarbrucken, Germany.

Sithole LN (1990) Agricultural finance corporation workshop on de centralisation of rural finance, case study – agricultural finance corporation (AFC) – Zimbabwe. Paper Presented at the Decentralisation of Rural Finance Conference, 22–26 October 1990, Cotonou, Benin

Spieldoch A (2007) A Row to Hoe: the gender impact of trade liberalisation on our food system, agricultural markets and women's human rights. Friedrich Ebert Stiftung, Geneva

Stanning J (1989) Smallholder maize production and sales in Zimbabwe: some distributional aspects. Food Policy:260–267

Tekwa N (2020) Gender, land reform and welfare outcomes. PhD Thesis. University of South Africa

Tibugari H, Chikasha T, Manyeruke N, Mathema N, Musara JP, Dlamini D, Mapuranga R, Mapanje O, Banda A, Parwada C (2019) Poor maize productivity in Zimbabwe: can collusion in pricing by seed houses be the cause? Cogent Food Agric 5(1):1–13

Tsikata D (2015). The social relations of agrarian change. IIED Working Paper. IIED, London

Utete CMB (2003) Report of the Presidential Land Review Committee, under the Chairmanship of Dr Charles M.B. Utete. Volumes 1 and 2: Main Report to his Excellency the President of The Republic of Zimbabwe, Presidential Land Review Committee (PLRC). Harare

Whitehead A (undated) The gendered impact of liberalisation policies on African Agricultural economies and rural livelihoods. Prepared for the UNRISD Report Gender Equality: Striving for Justice in an Unequal World, Draft Working Document. UNRISD. Geneva, Switzerland

World Bank (1981) Accelerated development in sub-Saharan Africa: an Agenda for action. The World Bank, Washington DC

World Bank (2015) Spatial integration in Zimbabwe product markets. The World Bank, Washington DC

World Bank (2019) Zimbabwe public expenditure review: with a special focus on agriculture. The World Bank, Washington DC

World Food Programme (WFP) (2020) Urgent international support needed to prevent millions of desperate Zimbabweans plunging deeper into hunger. World Food Programme 8 April 2020. Rome, Italy

World Food Programme (WFP) (undated) PDPE Market Analysis Tool: Market Integration

Zulauf CR, Irwin SH (1997) Market efficiency and marketing to enhance income of crop producers. OFOR Paper Number 97, 04 October 1997

Zumbika N (2006) Agricultural finance: 1990–2004. In: Rukuni M, Taonezvi P, Eicher C, Munyuki-Hungwe M, Matondi P (eds) Zimbabwe agricultural revolution revisited. University of Zimbabwe Publication, pp 339–353

Smallholder Farmer Empowerment and Neoliberalism: Examining the Current Institutional and Policy Arrangements in Zambia

Sam Mwando

Abstract Agriculture supports the livelihoods of up to 70 per cent of the Zambian population. The rural population is characterised by poorly developed monetary economies and markets with inadequate infrastructure and weak institutions for supply chain development, as needed for agricultural intensification and productivity. This is despite the structural adjustment and liberalisation programmes of the early 1990s, which were hyped as the precursor to incentivising foreign direct investments and reigniting the wheels of economic growth in Zambia. Thirty years on, economic liberalisation policies, including for the agricultural sector, continue to exist, albeit in altered and haphazard form. The failure to liberalise the agricultural sector fully, with piecemeal, start-stop and frequency policy reversals, has tended to depress any possible returns and raised risks for smallholders associated with private sector investment. As well, the weak institutional support for smallholder farmers, despite some state support, has inhibited the capacity of smallholders to enhance their agricultural production and rural livelihoods. Because of this, neoliberal agricultural policies have failed to empower smallholders in Zambia. This chapter examines and highlights this agricultural trend, including through a case study in the Chibombo district.

1 Introduction

To improve development outcomes, the majority of sub-Saharan countries have tended to situate and emphasise agriculture as the backbone of their economy. Work by Cimai et al., for instance, estimate that 85 per cent of the Zambian population, especially in the country's southern parts, base their livelihoods on

S. Mwando (✉)
Department of Land and Property Sciences, Namibia University of Science and Technology, Windhoek, Namibia
e-mail: smwando@nust.na

F. Mazwi et al. (eds.), *Capital Penetration and the Peasantry in Southern and Eastern Africa*, Advances in African Economic, Social and Political Development, https://doi.org/10.1007/978-3-030-89824-3_7

agriculture. Smallholder[1] farmers form 54.7 per cent of Zambian's population of 18,921,000, with many being women (Habanyati et al. 2020). The agricultural sector alone employs directly and indirectly more than half (70 per cent) of the total rural labour force (Hazell et al. 2010; Kamara et al. 2019; Murisa and Helliker 2011). Smallholder farmers in Zambia mainly produce food crops such as maize/corn (the national staple food crop), sorghum, millet, cassava (a staple in northern Zambia) and groundnuts. Other equally important smallholder crops include cotton, beans, rice, tobacco, sugar cane and vegetables. Overall, 80 per cent of smallholder Zambian farmers cultivate maize[2] as the principal food crop. The cultivation of maize has over the years received preference over all other crops in terms of the various subsidy interventions (Ministry of Agriculture and Co-operatives 2004; World Bank 2012).

For the larger part of the past thirty years, scholars, development practitioners and the state have been singing the following chorus: '[T]he agricultural sector contributes to household food security that is reflected in its prioritisation in the development agenda'. For the past fifteen years, agriculture's contribution to Gross Domestic Product (GDP) has hovered around six per cent, with 2019 seeing only a 2.7 per cent contribution to GDP (IAPRI 2020; PMRC 2020). In spite of its meagre contribution to GDP, the sector still commands an important effect on the broader macro-economy. It is undeniable that agriculture lies at the heart of the development process, and smallholder farmers are seen as the driving force of economic growth, poverty reduction and food security. By engaging in both farm and non-farm activities, smallholders generate up to sixty per cent of the total rural income (PMRC 2020). Additionally, the country is endowed with agriculturally fertile lands, abundant water, and a favourable climate for diverse agricultural products, along with a fast-growing urbanisation process that can offer a ready market for farm produce.

Despite the various donor-driven and government subsidies to empower smallholder farmers, Zambian agricultural growth has been sluggish, with the rural poverty level continuing to increase at an alarming rate (World Bank 2012; Phiri et al. 2020). Regardless of the government's efforts being regarded as promoting empowerment, most smallholder farmers continue to languish in poverty, since these subsidies are treated as typical loan schemes and systems. For instance, in 2010, the moderate poverty rate in rural areas was 74 per cent, with rural areas home to 80 per cent of Zambia's poor. Poverty rates are particularly higher among the 20 per cent of those smallholder households headed by women and among those headed by elderly men and women (Heinemann et al. 2011). According to Chibomba (2017), 68 per

[1] The term smallholder refers to those farmers with limited resource endowments in comparison to other groups of farmers. Merely defining and characterising smallholder farmers by land size (less than two hectares) and use of land tends to limit the broader understanding of smallholder farms, such as land quality, productivity, and income generated from production. Despite their large numbers, smallholder farmers in Zambia, as in many other sub-Saharan African countries, tend to be a weakly organised and represented constituency.

[2] Maize is the staple food for Zambia.

cent of Zambians have reported cases or incidences of stunting and malnutrition, as well as substantial agricultural product wastage due to low storage and preservation capacities. In this regard, the meaningful empowerment of small-scale Zambian farmers in the country would address poverty and food security, and also their resilience in the face of natural disasters such as droughts, floods, and famines.

Key questions arise about smallholder farmers, including their capacity to be food secure and even transition into commercial farmers. These and related questions continue to elude policy makers and development practitioners alike, particularly in the context of neoliberalisation. As fittingly argued by Wedig and Wiegratz (2018: 2), '[t]he neoliberal restructuring of African agriculture through the structural adjustment programmes from the 1980s onwards had debilitating effects on smallholders who experienced reduced access to finances, technologies and supporting infrastructure'. At its core, some of the major policies of structural adjustment that directly or indirectly affected the agricultural sector were: removal of exchange rate controls, opening up of economies to foreign direct investment, the elimination of price controls, and the privatisation of state-owned enterprises (Harrison 2019).

This chapter examines the extent to which government policies and programmes have assisted in the empowerment of subsistence farmers in Zambia. This entails a case study approach using data from the Chibombo district in Zambia, including gender-separated vignette questions about agricultural support to smallholder farmers. Specific objectives are twofold. First, to investigate the current Zambian government's subsidy programmes and evaluate its efficacy in empowering smallholder farmers; and, secondly, to consider the extent to which subsidy programmes, initiatives and institutions contribute to the empowerment of smallholder farmers. The results from the study could assist policy makers, the private sector and development agencies to develop effective and appropriate empowerment strategies.

2 Agricultural Policy Trends

Historically, only a few countries achieved rapid economic growth at their early stages of development without substantial growth in agriculture (Hazell et al. 2010), with a strong agricultural sector having positive implications for the urban and national economies more broadly. In this sense, as De La Torre Ugarte and Dellachies (2006) argue, the agricultural sector has been the cornerstone of industrial and economic development for most nations while also contributing to poverty reduction and food security. To put this into context, Badiane and Makombe (2014) assert that a 1 per cent incremental growth in agriculture raises growth outside the agriculture sector by up to 1.32 per cent, through multiplier effects. There is a significant consensus that poverty reduction in Zambia, as in many low-income countries, can only be achieved if development efforts and policy are clearly focused on smallholder rural farmers (Otieno 2007).

Admittedly, there is a small but increasingly strong voice that asserts that a biased and 'romanticised' policy focus on smallholder farming will keep the agricultural sector in Zambia and elsewhere on the historical trajectory of mediocre growth (Collier and Dercon 2014). Advancing this argument, this pessimistic school of thought maintains that, rather than focusing on small-scale farming, policymakers should encourage investment in commercial farming (Sitko and Jayne 2014). They make three arguments against smallholder farms:

> First, larger farms are in a better position to feed rapidly expanding cities in Africa than millions of small-scale farmers with little or no surplus to sell. Second, these farms can provide remunerative employment to people unprofitably engaged in semi-subsistence agriculture. Finally, larger farms are in a far better position than small-scale farms to adopt and adapt technologies to local contexts, thereby allowing them to maintain yield growth over time. (Sitko and Jayne 2014: 194)

Other critics add that smallholder farmers face a number of challenges that limit their productivity, such as (i) lack of information about production methods and market opportunities, (ii) lack of necessary financial reserves and collateral to access credit, and (iii) smallholders who operate near subsistence (subsistence farmers) are more risk averse than commercial farmers (Minot 2007).

It is certainly the case, as USAID contends, that 'decades of conventional government and donor assistance to promote rural development through micro-project assistance and input subsidies to smallholder households have had little lasting effect on rural poverty and in some cases have even perpetuated it'. In the case specifically of Zambia, the government, in its national agricultural policies, highlights that rural poverty is still very high and that any growth and gains made within the agricultural sector have not been widely inclusive of smallholder farmers (Ministry of Agriculture 2013; PMRC 2020). However, as this chapter seeks to demonstrate, the challenge relates to the context, constitution and character of smallholder support schemes and not to the schemes per se.

2.1 Neoliberal Restructuring

As started earlier, neoliberal policy reforms in Africa were designed to remove market distortions in order to allow the production and circulation of goods to be dictated by a self-regulating market (Sitko 2006). In Zambia, the government adopted a neoliberal approach to the agricultural sector after buckling to external pressures and by dismantling its subsidy system for maize production and marketing and for food production more broadly in the early 1990s. As with the neoliberal agricultural programme in Africa in general, this entailed a two-pronged package: one towards liberalisation and deregulation of markets, and the other towards the withdrawal of the state from direct support to farmers (Oya 2007).

In this context, the African (and Zambian) development policy landscape has radically evolved over the years (Jomo and Von Arnim 2012). While certain aspects of policy pronouncements may have been fashioned to suit and benefit local, national economies, many others only marginally, if at all, sought to improve (or improved) the socio-economic fortunes of smallholder farmers. It is well known that the debt crises of the 1980s provided an opportunity for the Bretton Woods Institutions (BWIs) to broaden the power of the neoliberalisation agenda and impose it on recalcitrant governments through policy conditionalities for providing desperately needed credit. In Zambia, the genesis of market liberalism coincides with the period of the collapse of the Soviet empire that globally ushered in the introduction of multiparty democracy while simultaneously liberalising economies (Rakner 2003).

The policies upon which the Zambian agricultural sector is currently predicated can be traced as far back as the early 1980s. Forty years ago, the infamous Berg Report made the following observation regarding the focus that developing countries ought to put on smallholder farmers in Africa. Although smallholder farmers accounted for the bulk of agricultural output, their potential had not been realised. Further, raising the output and income of smallholder farmers was the best way to meet the necessities of rural communities, such that policy attention to smallholders was the most cost-effective way to raise outputs and reduce poverty than other alternatives at the time. The above observations still hold true today in Zambia, as in many other African countries, but now with a neoliberal thrust.

Prior to 1991, at the dawn of multiparty democracy in Zambia, the main elements of government policy intervention were fixed producer prices, transportation and storage subsidies, consumer price subsidies, and subsidies on agricultural inputs and credits (Wichern and Chiwele 1999). Hence, the state provided significant support to smallholders. These policies were designed to have a double-edged effect: on one hand, guaranteeing a higher income to small-scale farmers in rural areas and, on the other, providing cheap staple foods to the urban population. Huge financial commitments by the Zambians were disbursed annually (from 1964) to sustain this model, which proved unsustainable over the long term.

Fast forward to 1992, with the new government at the helm, major institutional reforms took place and, still today, these continue to guide the planning and organisation of the agricultural sector. These neoliberal reforms included the following:

- Decontrolling of prices and major reductions of subsidies to provide proper market signals.
- New monetary and fiscal policies to dampen inflation.
- Market-based exchange and interest rates to lower indirect taxation.
- Privatisation of parastatals to improve the efficiency of markets, and.
- Deregulation and removal of many governments control to promote private sector investment and activity in competitive markets, including the opening of markets to international competition (Dorward et al. 2004; Wichern and Chiwele 1999: 21).

These liberalisation policies (in the form of structural adjustment programmes) from the early 1990s, and their misapplications, are not short of critics (Dorward et al. 2004; Kherallah et al. 2000; Jayne et al. 2014). A major criticism is that market liberalisation makes the unrealistic assumption of perfect functioning markets devoid of externalities, including in developing nations like Zambia, and no other causes of market failure as well as constant return to scale. Strident neoliberalism also entailed the uniform application of policies (including agricultural policies) to all developing countries, without recognising the significant differences between them. In this sense, the policy diagnosis was founded on a sweeping generalisation of agricultural sector failures across the developing world. Another criticism against liberalisation policies has been the weak institutional framework for market-led development.

In this context, the Agricultural Sector Investment Programme (ASIP) was established in the mid-1990s in Zambia in order to support the liberalisation of the agricultural sector (Wichern and Chiwele 1999). This programme was to be implemented alongside improvement in the domestic supply of agricultural inputs and in the marketing of products (on domestic and international markets). It was also to entail the economic pricing of goods, the reduction of subsidies, and the privatisation of state-owned agricultural enterprises, such as the now defunct National Agricultural Marketing Board, popularly known as NAMBoard. This phenomenon is not unique to Zambia. By 1995, most Input Subsidy Programmes (ISPs) in African countries were phased out or scaled down substantially.

However, by 2005, most of the ISPs had been revived under the pretext of 'smart subsidies'. Jayne et al. (2018) allude to a number of major factors for the resurgence of agriculture subsidies in Africa. First of all, many African governments never really accepted the tenets of structural adjustment and accepted them only under duress from the BWIs. Secondly, they soon realised that subsidies were politically popular and appropriate response to former colonial policies that discriminated against smallholder farmers. Thirdly, around 2000, many African countries experienced a relaxation of their foreign debt burden, and this eventually freed up financial resources to reinstitute, among other policies, agricultural subsidies. Finally, the global food price crisis in 2007 and 2008, and the fear of looming food shortages, prompted many African nations to finance ISPs to ensure national food self-sufficiency.

Perhaps the re-introduction of subsidies for smallholder farmers in Zambia, and indeed for many other African countries, is best encapsulated by the work of Oya (2007: 291), who rightly concludes that

> [M]ore than 20 years of neoliberal agricultural experience in sub-Sahara Africa have taught us that allowing market forces to work under conditions of high risk and poor and unevenly distributed resources, in an international context of volatile and dumped world prices, can condemn most peasant farmers to a permanent state of vulnerability and uncertainty.

There have been varying degrees of implementation of structural adjustment programmes across Africa, including partial implementation and policy reversals—the latter is generally applicable to the Zambian context.

2.2 Smallholder-Led Strategy

Evidence from Asia and Africa continues to show that agricultural transformation and mass poverty reduction require a smallholder-led strategy (Muyanga and Jayne 2017), with relevant and sufficient support from the state.

In this regard, after a decade (the 1990s) of not assisting smallholder farmers, the Zambian government reintroduced—initially–a temporary Agricultural Support Programme in the form of loans or credit. From 1997/1998 to 2001/2002, the Fertiliser Credit Programme (FCP) was launched (Mason et al. 2013; Ministry of Agriculture 2013). Smallholder farmer beneficiaries were obligated to make an initial payment of 10 per cent of the cost of fertiliser (ranging between 200 and 800 kilogrammes), with the balance of 90 per cent to be offset at harvest time. Farmers were to access the fertiliser through farmer cooperatives. As is the case with the majority of input support schemes, farmers needed to fulfill certain requirements in order to benefit from the programme (Chapoto et al. 2012; Mason et al. 2013). For example in terms of fertiliser support, this is specifically for:

> (i) Small-scale farmers cultivating less than 5hactares of land; registered with the Ministry of Agriculture and Livestock (ZMoAL) and actively engaged in farming; (ii) members of a farmer organisation that had been selected to participate in Fertiliser Input Support Programme; and (iii) not concurrent beneficiaries of the Food Security Pack Programme; (iv) financial ability to pay the farmer share of the input costs, that is, 200 kg fertiliser bag and 10 kg hybrid maize seed; (v) the capacity to cultivate a minimum of 1 hectare of land. (de la Fuente et al. 2017: 10)

Subsequent to the FCP, other programmes have been formulated and implemented. Various state ministries, notably Agriculture, Land and Natural Resources, and Community Development and Social Services, have led these. For instance, the cash-based Fertiliser Support Programme (FSP) was launched in the 2002/2003 farming season, with the aim of improving the supply and delivery of fertiliser at subsidised rates (50 to 75 per cent). Mason et al. (2013: 6) note that the overall goals of the FSP were 'improving household and national food security, incomes, and accessibility to agricultural inputs by smallholder farmers through subsidies'. The provision of subsidised fertiliser was prompted by the low loan repayment rates under the FCP as well as significant droughts in the last two agricultural seasons. And the severe droughts in the 2000/2001 and 2001/2002 farming seasons that had adversely affected smallholder farmers.

As a response to increasing political pressures and rising rural poverty, the Zambian government reintroduced farm input subsidies to stimulate farm-level fertiliser application, enhance food security, improve household income and alleviate poverty (Chibwana et al. 2012; Marenya et al. 2012). The FSP was later rebranded as the Farmer Input Support Programme (FISP). This programme was similar to FSP except that the quantities of fertiliser provided were halved. As well, 10 kilogrammes of hybrid maize seed (at 50 to 60 per cent of cost price) became available to smallholders. In addition, small quantities of seeds for other crops were included later (in 2012/2013), such as rice, sorghum, and groundnuts. Despite the addition of more crops, smallholder farmers were restricted to receiving inputs for one crop only (Mason et al. 2017).

In responding to some of the inefficiencies and criticisms of FISP, the Zambian government in 2015/2016 piloted the FISP electronic voucher system (e-voucher) in 13 districts of the country and, in 2017, rolled out the programme national wide (consisting of more than 106 districts). The e-voucher was valued at US$210 (400 Zambian Kwacha farmer contributions and 1700 Zambian Kwacha government contributions). This initiative was implemented through a pre-paid VISA card redeemable for crop, livestock, or fisheries inputs or equipment (Chikobola and Tembo 2018). Other projects which seek to enhance the productivity and income of smallholders, and even to put them along a viable commercial path, include Enhanced Smallholder Agribusiness Promotional Programme, Sustainable Intensification of Smallholder Farming Systems in Zambia, and Smallholder Productivity Promotion Programme (Benhammouche and Skinner 2016).

At the same time, the Zambian government gave increasing prominence to the commercialisation of the smallholder sector by way of out-grower (contract farming) schemes as a way to integrate small-scale farmers into the national economy (Matenga 2017). Contract farming may be defined as agricultural production carried out according to a prior agreement in which the farmer commits to producing a given product in a given manner, and the buyer commits to purchasing it (Minot 2007). The common commodities under out-grower schemes are the traditional smallholder export commodities (tobacco, cotton, and sugar), new export crops (fresh vegetables, paprika, castor seed) and a range of food crops (maize, sunflower, soya, cowpea, groundnuts, sorghum) (Stringfellow 1996). In the case of Zambia, in 2004, between 35 and 40 per cent of Zambia's nearly one million smallholder farmers were participating in out-grower scheme arrangements. Cotton, tobacco and paprika were nearly 100 per cent produced through the smallholder contract farming system (Matenga 2017). These schemes, which are not discussed in greater detail in this chapter, are meant to offer certain solutions to smallholders with reference to lack of information, credit, and market risk.

Despite these initiatives (ISPs), targeting mainly maize cultivation, Zambia continues to operate in a neoliberal policy environment implicitly. This speaks to the disjuncture within the agricultural policy landscape. Although neoliberal policies demand that markets self-regulate with minimal state intervention where necessary, the state continues to reactively intervene in the agricultural sector, especially at the subsistence agricultural level. Among the different farmer categories in the country, smallholder subsistence farmers are the least resilient and the most vulnerable to the external forces that affect the agricultural sector. Hence, they form the largest constituent who is in dire need of empowerment programmes.

Despite the re-introduction of the limited agricultural subsidies for smallholder farmers, there are numerous challenges that still confront smallholders. In fact, the majority of government support programmes no longer exist, including access to credit, extension services and the provision of rural infrastructure, such that smallholder farmers have been left to their devices. Because of this, many smallholder farmers have tried to venture into non-farm activities to make ends meet.

2.3 Smallholder Challenges

Currently, the subsidy programmes are significant in terms of their sheer volume. Zambia allocated approximately 32 per cent of its agricultural sector expenditure to Input Support Programmes (Mason et al. 2017) and 47 per cent of the government's agricultural sector poverty reduction programme spending (Mason et al. 2013). Despite all these initiatives and the institutional arrangements supporting them, smallholder farmers in Zambia experience ongoing challenges.

For instance, even though the eligibility criteria are clear, there have been cases where farmers that have the capacity to purchase both seed and fertiliser at commercial rates have been offered these benefits (Chikobola and Tembo 2018). This is in contradiction to the spirit of the policy to support the 'vulnerable but viable' smallholder farmers in Zambia (de la Fuente et al. 2017; Mason 2018). Another concern with the programmes, which generally have targeting criteria requirements of between 0.5 and 5.0 hectares, is that they exclude the poorest and landless households. They are indeed scathing criticisms of the state and its involvement in input support programmes in Zambia as encapsulated in the statement below:

> The heavy involvement of the republic of Zambia in the procurement and distribution of input subsidies under the traditional mode of delivering FISP provided fertile grounds for corruption, rent seeking and racketeering, and stifled competitive private-sector participation in input marketing, including the focus of this programme was mainly on maize, which restrained agricultural diversification. (Chikobola and Tembo 2018: 194)

More broadly, it has been argued that the support programmes tend to have limited investment in key agricultural growth drivers such as research and development, extension, feeder roads and appropriate irrigation infrastructure' (IAPRI, 2020: 78).

Poor agricultural planning in Zambia, alongside limited government investment and agricultural education, is linked to low production and declining productivity among smallholder farmers. In particular, governments' low investments represent one of the most severe challenges affecting Zambia's agricultural sector. Agricultural spending by the Zambian government formed 13.6 per cent of the national budget (by 2011), with 80 per cent spent going to farm inputs (Swanepoel et al. 2015). The remaining 20 per cent is distributed across other agricultural production-oriented processes, including disaster management and extension services, finances for subsidised loans, agricultural grants, and policy planning and implementation. Further, policies mainly revolve around maize farming, inhibiting the development of other agricultural practices and thereby agricultural diversification.

Lack of empowerment represents an immense challenge in small-scale farming, increasing poverty and reducing productivity and disaster resilience. Since independence in 1964, many programmes have been implemented in Zambia, intending to empower the agricultural activities of smallholder farmers, but without sustained success. For example, since the 2000s, Zambia has pursued Fertiliser Support programmes and Security Packs subsidy programmes (Phiri et al. 2020), but the productivity effectiveness and transformative effects remain unclear among smallholder farmers. Equally, the Agricultural Support Programme (ASP) under the Ministry of Agriculture has been linked to empowering female smallholders, but its success appears minimal or at least unsubstantiated.

3 Case Study

The research reported in this study used a case study approach to understand the extent to which smallholder farmers are empowered or not by the Zambian state. The field study was conducted in Shangala village of Chibombo district in the central province of Zambia, located 35.9 kilometres to the west of the capital city of Lusaka. Chibombo is a farming district with a mixture of commercial and smallholder farmers where cotton, maize, wheat and livestock rearing dominate. A number of factors influenced the choice of the study. First, the area falls within an agro-ecological zone which allows for the cultivation of a myriad of crops. Second, due to its accessibility to the major road network and its proximity to the ever-growing urban centre of Lusaka and Kabwe, there is a huge market for the produce of the farmers in the study area. Finally, smallholder farmers in this area are eligible to receive subsidies from the state, but the private sector also plays an active role in determining the pertinent agricultural value chains. In this light, farming in the study site ought to be thriving, given the many positive attributes as well as the availability of arable soils and water. To this end, Shangala village, in particular, was selected for the study to gain a reasonable understanding of the empowerment of smallholder farmers.

The fieldwork was conducted between 24 March and 20 April 2021 in collaboration with Mr. Sonwell Shakami of the University of Zambia. Upon entry into the community, we contacted the village headman to establish the full list of households. A total of 108 households were identified. Overall, 46 heads of households were sampled and interviewed using a semi-structured questionnaire. All study participants were of the majority age. To supplement this survey, unstructured interviews were also conducted with some smallholder farmers. The data collected was mainly of a qualitative nature. The interview questions covered such areas as educational background, marital status, membership in organised farming groups, ownership and access to land and productive assets. I used python and DisplayR to analyse the data for the study. Data that solicited textured responses were contextually examined using sentiment analysis to generate a more complete, meaningful and useful understanding of smallholder farmers in the study area. Participants whose responses were incomplete were excluded in the data analysis. Table 1 provides an overview of key evidence arising from the study, which is discussed below. It should be noted

Table 1 Evidence from Study

	Characteristics	Frequency ($N = 46$)	Percentage
Gender	Female	13	28.3
	Male	33	71.7
Age	24.5	10	21.7
	34.5	11	23.9
	45	11	23.9
	Above 60	14	30.4
Marital status	Single	2	4.3
	Married	40	87
	Widower	1	2.2
	Widow	2	4.3
	Never married	1	2.2
Qualification	College degree	1	2.2
	Grade 12	12	26.1
	Grade 9	12	26.1
	Primary school	21	45.7
Smartphone ownership	Yes	12	26.1
	No	34	73.9
Experience in farming (years)	< 2	3	6.5
	2–5	12	26.1
	6–10	7	15.2
	> 10	24	52.2
Do you receive any support from the state	Yes	23	50.0
	No	23	50.0
Access to loan facility	Yes	3	6.5
	No	43	93.5
Bank account holder	Yes	2	4.3
	No	44	95.5

that these smallholders are not engaged in contract farming, either with the state or through private companies.

3.1 *Profile of Respondents*

Out of the 46 household heads surveyed, 33 or 72 per cent were male and 13 or 28 per cent female. The minimum age was 24.5, and the maximum was 60, with a mean of 41. More than 50 per cent were in the age range of between 34.5 and 45. An overwhelming majority (40 or 87 per cent) of the respondents were married.

Furthermore, all the sampled respondents had some level of education with a minimum of primary school education. Nearly half of respondents (21 or 46 per cent) have only attained primary education. This study is consistent with similar studies, which also show that the typical smallholder in Zambia only attains a primary school education. There was also a statistically significant number of respondents (24 or 52 per cent) with 10 years' experience in farming.

A striking result is the number of respondents without smartphones, accounting for 34 or 74 per cent. The finding from this study indicates that respondents mainly use their mobile phones to make or receive calls. There is ample evidence that suggests that access to smartphones has the potential to improve farmer's skills and knowledge and facilitate information sharing and the marketing of agriculture produce to a wider market. Smartphones and their applications could help farmers to access relevant information that can empower them to achieve improved farming techniques.

The landholding or farm sizes owned ranged from 2 hectares to more than 5 hectares with a mean of 4 hectares. However, the majority of respondents owned more than 5 hectares. In the sampled survey, as indicated, male household heads predominate (33 or 72 per cent), and, by extension, they own most of the land. This is related to the patriarchal character of most rural African communities in Zambia. Results also show that the respondents with larger tracts of land also tend to own more livestock (with plenty of land for cultivation and pasture for animals).

3.2 Access to Credit and Labour Needs

Related studies show that improving access to credit is often regarded as one of the key elements in increasing smallholder productivity and reducing poverty. Work by Adugna and Heidhues (2000), and Binswanger and Khandker (1995) show that access to finance can ease the liquidity constraints of smallholder farmers and improve their risk-bearing capability. According to Sebatta et al. (2014), farmer access to agricultural finance is still dismally low in many parts of Zambia. There are a number of reasons for this state of affairs, but mainly the reluctance of financial institutions to lend to smallholders in the agricultural sector because of the latter lack collateral. From this current study, there are a number of factors that limit the farmers' access to credit, such as the low level of education, problematic access to information and limited engagement in off-farm activities. Additionally, despite the fact that almost all the respondents in the study own their land, albeit customarily, they are not able to access credit using land as collateral—ultimately, the land is state land.

A dominance of smallholders (43 or 93 per cent), representing 30 males and 13 females, reported that they did not have any access to credit through the conventional channels of financial lending institutions. This situation exists despite the fact that most respondents have surplus land to cultivate. Whenever they need extra money to fund farm activities, they turn to their only option—family and friends. M.M., a 54-year-old female farmer, bemoaned the lack of credit to expand her agricultural activities by highlighting that 'there is so much potential for people to become bigger farmers, but without help from the lending institutions, it is practically impossible to move from being peasant farmers to commercial farmers'.

With respect to labour needs, respondents overwhelmingly (34 or 74 per cent) reported that they either use family or hired labour to prepare, cultivate and sell agricultural produce. For smallholders in particular with landholdings of more than five hectares, labour is required for the following tasks: (i) land preparation, (ii) planting, (iii) weeding, (iv) harvesting and (v) livestock care. The growth and expansion of these smallholder farmers are closely linked to the availability of affordable labour, including family labour. As one of the respondents noted, 'households with large families of more than ten people cultivate more and make more money than those with fewer young people that you can use to engage in farm activities'. This observation goes to show that farming practices are still very much labour intensive and highly rudimentary in many ways. In addition, even though the majority of the respondents (32 or 70 per cent) indicated that they consider farming as a business and many (36 or 78 per cent) see themselves graduating from peasant farming to commercial farming, it is difficult to see how this will be realised without adequate technological, financial and business support. The need for labour or manpower is central to increasing production for the farmers in the study area. Hence, the overwhelming number of smallholders (from all age groupings) indicated that a major challenge to increasing production is a lack of additional manpower.

3.3 Challenges and Risks

A form of empowering smallholder farmers would entail equipping them with robust coping mechanisms to withstand expected and unexpected risks that are common in agriculture. Like other farming groups, smallholders are not immune from such risks as pest and disease outbreaks, extreme weather events and market shocks. These risks threaten their household food and income security (Harvey et al. 2014).

Female smallholder interviewed highlighted weather (and therefore climate change) as, by far, the most crucial risk to agricultural activities, as did the male smallholders. But males also spoke more frequently about pests, market prices and erratic and costly agricultural inputs. The lack of contracts between these farmers and buyers (the state or private company) poses a huge risk. Farmers are therefore forced to sell their produce at far less than the prevailing market prices to avoid their produce from spoiling. This situation exposes farmers to both business and financial risks. B.H., a 43 year old who occasionally sells his produce to a private company, observed: 'Sometimes we borrow some money to increase the tillage so that we can make more money, but it just feels like a gamble because we have no contracts with these people'. Many of the agricultural challenges and risks are beyond what farmers are able to plan for or have the capacity to mitigate significantly, such as climate change, pests and diseases and fluctuating market prices.

Through local knowledge, the majority of smallholders in the study area indicated that they are engaged in mixed farming in order to mitigate the risk of failure in a major cash crop such as maize or cotton. They stated that they learnt this and other strategies over time through experience, as the agricultural landscape continues to change, so that the future is no longer predictable. For example, the majority (40 or 87 per cent) keep livestock as a cushion to protect them from the annual and seasonal risks they face.

Additionally, a good number of households have gone into charcoal burning to raise extra income in times when crops have failed or the market prices have plummeted. In fact, charcoal burning has turned out to be more lucrative than agricultural work, as the demand for charcoal keeps on increasing in urban centres. A.B., a 27 year male stated that 'I make a bit of money from selling charcoal [and more] than tilling my fields, and I have customers coming to pick up the charcoal from my homestead when it's ready'.

3.4 Institutional Arrangements and Support

Previous studies (Manda et al. 2020; Moonga and Mgemezulu 2005) show that institutional arrangements, such as vertical coordination (for example through contract farming) and horizontal coordination (through producer groups such as cooperatives), may aid small-scale farmers to overcome barriers of access to production, information, services and markets. They are numerous advantages for these farmers in belonging to organised cooperatives, including an increase in farmers' production and incomes through linkages with established businesses, markets, value chains, knowledge, technologies and agriculture inputs. Cooperatives are also seen as a means through which the government can implement its policies at the local level.

Though, as indicated, smallholders in the study area do not directly engage in contract farming, there are horizontal linkages existing. Results from the study show that about half (21 or 45 per cent) of local smallholders belong to cooperatives, which potentially enhances access to modern farming techniques and technologies and improvement in knowledge and skills in farming. Like in many other parts of the country, cooperatives are a conduit through which smallholder farmers access inputs either from state actors or their agents. Respondents also indicated that when new initiatives or programmes are introduced to the farmers in the village from outside, any resources or training schemes are usually channelled through registered farmer groups or agriculture cooperatives. Because of this, membership in cooperatives is seen as a positive to smallholders. However, as A.S. (a 34-year-old male) indicates, many smallholders prefer not to join cooperatives. This is because cooperatives that were previously funded and organised through the Ministry of Agriculture and cooperatives are cash strapped and are unable to inspire the confidence of smallholder farmers. Additionally, some smallholder farmers are not so keen on joining cooperatives because the benefits to cooperative members are mainly on new methods of agriculture that are linked to ultimately benefit private companies. In such cases, the training or information is only necessary for as long as the private company exists. Hence, the benefit to farmers is only short term, which is why certain cooperatives are not sustainable and offer very little value to farmers.

At the same time, belonging to cooperatives might facilitate access to some form of agricultural extension and training services. Although the state, through the Ministry of Agriculture, is tasked with the responsibility of agricultural extension in the country, many surveyed respondents were unable to remember if extension officers visited them in the last twelve months. These smallholders, typically not belonging to local cooperatives, in fact, do not receive such support. Some of the other farmers (generally affiliated with cooperatives) mentioned that they have participated in agricultural field days and agricultural training organised either by seed marketing companies or non-governmental organisations funded by international development partners.

Overall, the results from this study show that contact with extension officers occurs very irregularly, if at all. In addition, this implies that smallholder farmers in the area do not receive adequate training and support services to enable them to increase production as well as to become more resilient in the light of their multiple challenges and risks. In this regard, S.N. (a 28 year-old male) reported, 'we rarely receive extension officers in our village, and the only time we need them is when veterinarian services are required. And usually they cannot come through when required because they lack transportation to visit farmers'.

The respondents were asked to itemise what other form or type of support they receive from the state. The results showed that half of the respondents (23 or 50 per cent) received government support in the form of maize seed and fertiliser for maize (in various quantities) while the other half received no support. The latter farmers opt out of these subsidies, especially those farmers who have found other non-farm activities such as charcoal selling or selling land, where they are able to gain more than by cultivating maize. Despite the fact that the study area is ideal for the cultivation of other crops, the focus of the support is predominantly maize. As a limited form of contract farming, the government facilitates this kind of support and later offers to buy the maize after the harvest time. This is not a flawless process as there are usually delays in the delivery of seed and fertiliser, and even more delays when buying the harvested maize. These delays come at the expense of smallholder farmers who have to bear the cost of storing the maize as they wait for the government to collect it. There is adequate evidence that, in the process, there is significant wastage and spoilage of maize, without any insurance mechanisms for the affected smallholders. These losses defeat the purpose of the support given to the smallholder farmers.

3.5 Decision-Making in Terms of Pricing and Marketing

A critical factor in determining the level of empowerment among smallholder farmers relates to the decision-making process about the crops they grow and the market price for them. The study shows that the majority of respondents (39 or

85 per cent) cultivate maize and cotton for the market, and grow groundnuts, cowpeas and pumpkins for home consumption. This is consistent with farmers in most of the central and southern parts of Zambia.

As stated earlier, the number of smallholder farmers who are not affiliated with organised farming cooperatives (approximately 23 or 50 per cent) is significant in the study area, thereby leaving individual households to manage the production process as well as the marketing process. For the smallholder farmers that do belong to cooperatives, they do so in anticipation of benefits from the state, private-led initiatives or donor-funded projects. However, without collective marketing of their crops, smallholders are unable to gain access to bigger and more lucrative markets. Further, the decisions about what price households ought to sell their product do not lie with them. Rather, the decisions are influenced by the imperfect prevailing market conditions as well as the supply chain failures emanating either from the state or private companies, as typified by the comments of A.K. (a 54-year-old man) about the many marketing challenges they face: 'The price at which we can sell our crops, delays in the buyers or middlemen to pick up the harvest, our lack of transport to take the produce to people who need it in the city or millers, lack of proper storage which spoils the produce'.

Further, study participants were asked to state which crops they predominantly cultivated as cash crops (i.e. exclusively for the market). The overwhelming majority stated that cotton and soya beans are cultivated for this purpose. However, they indicated that they do not decide to grow crops based on the commodities that fetch good prices. Instead, they grow based on the availability of subsidised seed or fertiliser. This means that even if groundnuts are a high-value crop, as long as there are no subsidies for groundnuts, smallholders will continue cultivating maize or cotton. Additionally, the relative ease of selling a commodity is an important factor in choosing which crop to grow. For crops where state agencies or private entities come to collect the produce, more farmers are drawn to these crops. This decision, although not entirely advantageous for farmers, is an easier and more cost-effective option as lamented by T.H. (a 40-year-old female) who has previously tried to venture into non-traditional crops like groundnuts: 'We have heard of people who manage to take goats and eggs to Kasumbalesa, and you can become a millionaire in a short period of time, but you need a canter (light truck) or hire one which is very expensive. With a truck and a driver, you can take goats to [the Democratic Republic of] Congo'. Kasumbalesa is a border town between Zambia and the Democratic Republic of Congo. It is 479 kilometres from Shangala village, the study area. Kasumbalesa is one of the gateways to the massive Congolese market for numerous products, including agricultural produce.

Respondents were further prodded on what decision they make with respect to the livestock they rear. There was an overwhelming consensus that livestock is not ideally kept for resale but rather as a safety net. Livestock, especially cows, are sold to either fund capital projects such as replacing ploughs, upgrading a house or attend to urgent household needs. These household needs include paying school fees, taking patients to hospitals outside the district of Chibombo, paying dowry, settling family or inheritance conflicts.

Overall, there are a myriad of challenges that greatly impact how smallholder farmers are able to sell and market their produce. The majority of these challenges centre around a lack of transportation/bad feeder roads and unreliable middlemen. The first challenge speaks to the lack of infrastructure development in rural areas, which includes roads, storage facilities and training or research centres. This problem is the responsibility of large part of the government, but also partially the private sector. Secondly, while intermediaries or middlemen may be important in the value chain, farmers in this study feel manipulated by middlemen, who take advantage of the market failures or gaps to buy crops at their lowest prices from the farmers.

4 Empowerment and Neoliberalism

In what, if any sense, has neoliberalism's hold on agricultural policy in Zambia empowered smallholders? Overall, there is no unambiguous definition of the term empowerment. However, it is often understood as entailing the creation of conditions and opportunities for smallholder farmers to have the capacities to thrive, as per Amartya Sen's capability approach (Alkire 2005). At the same time, it is possible to speak about collective and individual empowerment. Collective empowerment happens through the joint alignment and action of smallholder farmers, including their ability to build and consolidate resources jointly. Individual empowerment refers to the ability of particular smallholders to access and manage capital-resources and to broaden their range of choices (Wortmannn-Kolundzija 2019). Eyben et al. (2008) define empowerment in the following way:

> Empowerment is fundamentally about power—about the power to redefine our possibilities and options and to act on them, the power within that enables people to have the courage to do things they never thought themselves to be capable of, and the power that comes from working alongside others to claim what is rightfully theirs.

In this respect, different scholars emphasise different aspects of power (including 'power to' and 'power with'). The phrase 'power with' stresses the need for collective action: empowerment entails generating collective action for reducing societal inequalities, securing more equitable access to labour, land and financial markets, and the development of more responsive and accountable state institutions. Individually or collectively, 'power to' refers to the self-activity of smallholders as they seek to broaden their opportunities and actions and expand their resources and capabilities (Eyben 2009; Eyben et al. 2008). Empowerment ought to improve the entrepreneurial skills of smallholders and enable their access to markets, research and development facilities, irrigation, technology transfer, extension services, and rural infrastructure (storage, roads, energy) (Bwalya and Deka 2016; Mason 2018; Ministry of Agriculture 2013). Overall, the basic premise behind any empowerment theory is the following desired outcomes: improved distribution and access to resources (capital, land, technology and labour) for smallholders; and smallholders' improved capacity to deal with, and counter, poverty and its consequences.

Neoliberal policies in Zambia have failed to empower smallholders. In fact, they are injurious to these farmers because of the latter's vulnerability to withstand the numerous financial, economic and climate change shocks. This is confounded by the fact that they already face immeasurable risks to their agricultural production, such as pest and disease outbreaks, extreme weather events and market shocks. The challenges have continued to undermine their household food and income security. Due to their reliance on agriculture, the lack of (or dismal support to) smallholder farmers has drastically affected their ability to improve their production capacity. This is evident in the ever-increasing poverty levels in the rural areas of the country despite the re-introduction of some agricultural subsidies (Harvey et al. 2014).

5 Conclusion

This chapter provides insights into the shortcomings of the current neoliberal policy and institutional landscape in Zambia with regard to empowering smallholder farmers. This landscape inhibits their capacity to withstand economic and climatic shocks, such as the ever-fluctuating price in agricultural commodities or droughts, respectively. Additionally, in the current uneven version of agricultural neoliberalism in Zambia, the government has adopted maize-centric subsidies (for seed and fertiliser) only, and this has stifled agricultural diversification, including into high-value crops. Smallholders in the country continue to experience a lack of financial support (for acquiring agricultural implements), as well as low levels of agricultural technology, research and development, and agricultural extension services. Ultimately, the state has a central role in enabling the empowerment of smallholder farmers (beyond merely providing agricultural inputs). Under neoliberalism, market forces are not levellers of agricultural social differentiation, and they do not facilitate significant poverty reduction amongst smallholders. Although not representative necessarily of rural Zambia, the case study of the Chibombo district is highly suggestive of this. Comprehensive studies of other districts are crucial to appreciate more fully the ways in which neoliberal policies affect the empowerment of smallholder farmers.

References

Adugna T, Heidhues F (2000) Determinants of farm households' access to informal credit in Lume district, Central Ethiopia. Afr Rev Money Financ Bank:27–45

Alkire S (2005) Why the capability approach? J Hum Dev 6(1):115–135. https://doi.org/10.1080/146498805200034275

Badiane O, Makombe T (2014) The theory and practice of agriculture, growth, and development in Africa. https://doi.org/10.35188/UNU-WIDER/2014/782-0

Benhammouche A, Skinner W (2016) President's report proposed loan and grant to the Republic of Zambia for the enhanced smallholder Agribusiness Promotion Programme (EB 2016/119/R.22/Rev.1). IFAD. https://webapps.ifad.org/members/eb/119/docs/EB-2016-119-R-22-Rev-1.pdf

Binswanger HP, Khandker SR (1995) The impact of formal finance on the rural economy of India. J Dev Stud 32(2):234–262

Bwalya M, Deka B (2016) Analysis of the second National Agricultural Policy 2016–2020. Policy Monitoring and Research Centre

Chapoto A, Haggblade S, Hichaambwa M (2012) Agricultural transformation in Zambia : alternative institutional models for accelerating agricultural productivity growth and commercialization by and David Tschirley agricultural transformation in Zambia : alternative institutional models for accelerating agricultural productivity, (June)

Chibomba K (2017) Investigating the effectiveness of Zambia's agriculture policy towards women empowerment

Chibwana C, Fisher M, Shively G (2012) Cropland allocation effects of agricultural input subsidies in Malawi. World Dev 40(1):124–133

Chikobola MM, Tembo G (2018) Gaps in the implementation of the e-voucher system in Zambia: implications for strategies to make the model efficient and effective. Afr J Agric Resour Econ 13(2):193–197

Collier P, Dercon S (2014) African agriculture in 50 years: smallholders in a rapidly changing world? World Dev 63:92–101

Dorward A, Kydd J, Poulton C, Stockbridge M, Cadot WJ, Chirwa E, Meganck M (2004) Agricultural liberalisation in Sub-Saharan Africa

Eyben R (2009) Collecting stories of empowerment, (March)

Eyben R, Kabeer N, Cornwall A, Malhotra A, Schuler SR, Boender C (2008) Conceptualising empowerment and the implications for pro poor growth A paper for the DAC Poverty Network. *World Bank.org*, (September), 71–88. http://books.google.com/books?hl=en&lr=&id=BzXyApyTGOYC&pgis=1

De La Torre Ugarte DG, Dellachiesa A (2006) Advancing the agricultural trade agenda: beyond subsidies. Geo Int Environ Law Rev 19:729

de la Fuente A, Rosales M, Jellema J (2017) Public economics for development 5–6. In *WIDER Development Conference*. https://www.wider.unu.edu/sites/default/files/Events/PDF/Papers/PubEconConf2017-de-la-Fuente.pdf, https://www.wider.unu.edu/sites/default/files/Events/PDF/Papers/PubEconConf2017-Giaccobasso.pdf

Habanyati EJ, Nyanga PH, Umar BB (2020) Factors contributing to disadoption of conservation agriculture among smallholder farmers in Petauke, Zambia. Kasetsart J Soc Sci 41(1):91–96

Harrison G (2019) Authoritarian neoliberalism and capitalist transformation in Africa: all pain, no gain. Globalizations 16(3):274–288

Harvey CA, Rakotobe ZL, Rao NS, Dave R, Razafimahatratra H, Rabarijohn RH, MacKinnon JL (2014) Extreme vulnerability of smallholder farmers to agricultural risks and climate change in Madagascar. Philos Trans R Soc B:Biol Sci 369(1639):20130089

Hazell P, Poulton C, Wiggins S, Dorward A (2010) The future of small farms: trajectories and policy priorities. World Dev 38(10):1349–1361. https://doi.org/10.1016/j.worlddev.2009.06.012

Heinemann E, Country A, Manager P, Ferreira C, Manager CP, Mcgrenra D, Officer GB (2011) Republic of Zambia Country strategic opportunities programme

IAPRI (2020) Zambia Agriculture Status Report 2020. http://www.iapri.org.zm/images/WorkingPapers/AgStatus_2017.pdf

Jayne TS, Chapoto A, Sitko N, Nkonde C, Muyanga M, Chamberlin J (2014) Is the scramble for land in Africa foreclosing a smallholder agricultural expansion strategy? J Int Affairs:35–53

Jayne TS, Mason NM, Burke WJ, Ariga J (2018) Taking stock of Africa's second-generation agricultural input subsidy programs. Food Policy 75:1–14

Jomo KS, Von Arnim R (2012) Economic liberalization and constraints to development in sub-Saharan Africa. Good growth and governance in Africa: rethinking development strategies https://doi.org/10.1093/acprof:oso/9780199698561.003.0017
Kamara A, Conteh A, Rhodes ER, Cooke RA (2019) The relevance of smallholder farming to african agricultural growth and development. Afr J Food Agric Nutr Dev 19(1):14043–14065. https://doi.org/10.18697/AJFAND.84.BLFB1010
Kherallah M, Delgado CL, Gabre-Madhin E, Minot N, Johnson M (2000) The road half traveled: agricultural market reform in Sub-Saharan Africa
Manda J, Khonje MG, Alene AD, Tufa AH, Abdoulaye T, Mutenje M, Setimela P, Manyong V (2020) Does cooperative membership increase and accelerate agricultural technology adoption? Empirical evidence from Zambia. Technol Forecast Soc Chang 158:120160
Marenya P, Nkonya E, Xiong W, Deustua J, Kato E (2012) Which policy would work better for improved soil fertility management in sub-Saharan Africa, fertilizer subsidies or carbon credits? Agric Syst 110:162–172
Mason NM (2018). Recent innovations to Zambia's Farmer Input Support Program & insights on short-run effects Zambia has had a targeted ISP since 2002/03. In: International Conference of Agricultural Economists
Mason NM, Jayne TS, Mofya-Mukuka R (2013) A review of Zambia's agricultural input subsidy programs : targeting, impacts, and the way forward by Nicole M. Mason, TS Jayne, Rhoda Mofya-Mukuka, Working Paper 77 August 2013 Indaba Agricultural Policy Research Institute (IAPRI), (August), 43
Mason NM, Jayne TS, Van De Walle N (2017) The political economy of fertilizer subsidy programs in Africa: evidence from Zambia. Am J Agric Econ 99(3):705–731. https://doi.org/10.1093/ajae/aaw090
Matenga CR (2017) Outgrowers and livelihoods : the case of Magobbo smallholder block farming in Mazabuka District in Zambia Magobbo smallholder block farming in Mazabuka District in Zambia. J South Afr Stud 43(3):551–566. https://doi.org/10.1080/03057070.2016.1211402
Ministry of Agriculture (2013) Republic Of Zambia National Agricultural Policy, December
Ministry of Agriculture and Co-operatives. National agricultural policy (2004–2015) (2004)
Minot N (2007) Contract fanning in developing countries : patterns, impact, and policy implications
Moonga PL, Mgemezulu O (2005) New challenges facing co-operatives and co-operative development in Eastern Province of Zambia. Republic of Zambia, Ministry of Finance and National Planning
Murisa T, Helliker K (2011) Chapter one contemporary rural realities in Southern Africa Tendai Murisa and Kirk Helliker. In: *Contemporary rural realities* (pp. 1–25)
Muyanga M, Jayne TS (2017) Can Smallholders Farm Themselves out of smallholder farming and poverty ? In: *Transforming agriculture for inclusive growth and sustainable livelihoods*
Otieno ZA (2007) Agricultural growth, rural poverty and hunger in Africa. In: *AAAE Conference Proceedings* (pp. 465–468)
Oya C (2007) Agricultural maladjustment in Africa: what have we learned after two decades of liberalisation? J Contemp Afr Stud 25(2):275–297
PMRC (2020) Policy monitoring and research Centre analysis of the second National Agricultural Policy 2016–2020
Phiri J, Malec K, Majune SK, Appiah-Kubi SNK, Gebeltová Z, Maitah M, Maitah K, Abdullahi KT (2020) Agriculture as a determinant of Zambian economic sustainability. Sustainability 12 (11):4559
Rakner L (2003) Political and economic liberalisation in Zambia 1991–2001. *Africa Today* (Vol. 52). https://doi.org/10.1353/at.2005.0064
Sebatta C, Mugisha J, Katungi E, Kashaaru A, Kyomugisha H (2014) Smallholder farmers' decision and level of participation in the potato market in Uganda. Mod Econ 2014
Sitko N (2006) The social life of maize: neoliberalism, food security, and non-market exchanges in southern Zambia. African Geographical Review 25(1):11–32

Sitko NJ, Jayne TS (2014) Structural transformation or elite land capture ? The growth of 'emergent' farmers in Zambia. Food Policy 48:194–202. https://doi.org/10.1016/j.foodpol.2014.05.006
Stringfellow R (1996) Smallholder outgrower schemes in Zambia
Swanepoel S, Davies F, Greenberg S (2015) Which way forward for Zambia's smallholder farmers: Green Revolution input subsidies or agro-ecology
Wedig K, Wiegratz J (2018) Neoliberalism and the revival of agricultural cooperatives: the case of the coffee sector in Uganda. J Agrar Chang, 18(2):348–369. ISSN 1471–0358
Wichern R, Chiwele DK (1999) *Impediments to agricultural growth in Zambia*
World Bank (2012) *Zambia Poverty Assessment* (Vol. 1)
Wortmannn-Kolundzija E (2019) *Empowering smallholder farmers through farmerorganizations: insights from Kenya and Burkina Faso*

Putting Agriculture Ahead? Some Reflections About the Early Years of Neoliberalism in Kenya

Fibian Lukalo

Abstract This article discusses the effects of the neoliberal agenda with reference to agricultural development, agricultural policies and land reform in Kenya. The centrality of the agricultural sector to rural livelihoods and to the economic development of Kenya and its linkages to land are intricately connected to the history of economic policy, politics and land reform. This chapter examines the background and policy context surrounding the agricultural debates in Kenya across two decades (the 1980s and 1990s), including how neoliberalisation had diverse and differentiated effects on the land reform agenda, the agricultural sector and the lives of the peasantry. In bringing to the fore three policy positions (Sessional Papers) as points of reference, the chapter presents an understanding of the historical, policy and discursive framework within which agriculture and land issues were debated and struggled over concerning the lives of rural Kenyans. Overall, it appears that neoliberalism, though not necessarily intentionally, further impoverished many Kenyans who relied on agriculture.

1 Introduction

On 22nd August 1978, the second President of Kenya (Daniel Moi) ascended to power and ruled for the next 24 years. It was during his tenure that Kenya went through various austerity measures or Structural Adjustment Programmes (SAPs), initially introduced during the 1980/1981 fiscal year. The conditional financial demands placed on Kenya by the World Bank and the International Monetary Fund (IMF) were broad and included trade liberalisation policies, domestic pricing policies, institutional reforms and investment policies. Over the next two decades (1980s and 1990s), the import-substitution policies that had been pursued since independence in Kenya were replaced by an open and liberalised trading regime (Rono 2002). Neoliberalisation of Kenya's economy was to have detrimental effects,

F. Lukalo (✉)
National Land Commission-Kenya, Nairobi, Kenya

F. Mazwi et al. (eds.), *Capital Penetration and the Peasantry in Southern and Eastern Africa*, Advances in African Economic, Social and Political Development, https://doi.org/10.1007/978-3-030-89824-3_8

including for smallholders in rural areas. To add to this, the coffee boom years of the late 1970s had ended, the East African Community trading block was weakening, and export markets were dipping. The presence of neoliberal measures depicted a national government that was not in control financially (vis-à-vis global forces) and did not seem willing to address the needs of the bulk of rural Kenyans or pursue pro-poor livelihoods, despite Moi's claims to the contrary.

There has been significant public debate and scholarly literature about the 'Moi regime-SAPs' nexus, and this deserves to be analysed further with specific reference to its impact on the lives and livelihoods of smallholders. This entails illuminating the effects of SAPs on Kenyan agriculture and their impact on relevant state agencies and land reform practices. To demonstrate the argument that the liberalisation policies had dire consequences on rural Kenyan livelihoods, reference will be made to three key Sessional Papers from the 1980s and how they moved the agenda for neoliberalisation in agriculture forward, while also linking this to the broader macro-political debates on land redistribution in Kenya. A variety of sources were consulted for this analysis of the effects of neoliberalisation in Kenya, including policy documents, national development plans, project documents and donor coordination reports. Drawing on archival data obtained from government documents and published land data sets on land settlement schemes, debates around land and agriculture are analysed in relation to *Sessional Paper No. 4 of 1980* on *Economic Prospects and Policies*, *Sessional Paper No. 4 of* 1981 (on *National Food Policy*), and *Sessional Paper No. 1 of 1986* (*Economic Management for Renewed Growth*).

In the ensuing examination of land, agriculture and neoliberalism in Kenya, I understand the 'major pillars of neoliberal policies' (Patnaik 2011: 8) as follows:

> The major pillars of neoliberal policies are: first, the imposition of deflationary cut-backs in state spending in nation states; second, openness of developing countries in particular to trade and capital flows through dismantling trade barriers; third, the dismantling, in developing countries only, of all price support mechanisms which existed earlier for stabilising prices for peasant producers, who constitute a large or major segment of the population; and fourth, a sustained attack on peasant-owned or -occupied land in the name of 'development' (Patnaik 2011: 8).

This entails a reduction of state intervention in the agrarian economy or at least a reconfiguration of the state's role.

This analysis of the effects of SAPs on rural livelihoods in Kenya proceeds as follows. I provide a brief overview of the economic and political context regarding agriculture, which in part contributed to the 1980s' economic hardships. I explain how certain factors, like the colonial agricultural policies and land resettlement agenda (after independence), when combined with the introduction of SAP austerity measures, pushed many farmers into economic dire-straits. As noted by Patnaik (2011: 8), 'history tells us that a deep financial and economic crisis has never occurred without a prior agrarian crisis'. I then explore how SAPs gave rise to gains and losses within the agricultural sector in the 1980s and 1990s. These two decades were marked by a rise in poverty levels and poverty-alleviation programmes (in the context of a pronounced development policy focusing on rural areas), alongside an increased number of rural people depending on farming. In this regard,

I situate the three government Sessional Papers within the framework of SAPs and discuss the implications of these policies and how, together with austerity measures more broadly, they impacted trade regimes of specific crops. Tied to this, the chapter focuses on government agencies linked to subsidies in farming and food and export crops.

2 White Highlands Agriculture and Land Resettlement Programmes Under Colonialism

Kenya's agricultural policy after independence pursued three main issues, namely, the land[1] resettlement programme, smallholder development, and the promotion of cash crops for smallholders, medium holders and large-scale farmers (Jabara 1985). This policy quest can be traced back to the 1910s through to the 1940s when the colonial authorities allocated scheduled[2] fertile agricultural land to white settlers (the White Highlands, approximately 7 million acres) through sales or 99–999 years' lease arrangements. From that time, Kenya became a primary producer of agricultural products for Britain, thus establishing unequal trade relations that were to endure until today. The colonial authorities established plantation estates where Africans were recruited and worked as cheap labour, while residing on small parcels of land adjacent to the large farms. Boone (2014) notes that by the 1930s there were approximately 580 European farmers with over 100,000 African workers providing cheap labour on these farms. However, the white settlers faced several challenges, which included underutilisation of land and a restive labour force, which was keen to return to its original (dispossessed) land.

The numerical growth of farms in the White Highlands from the 1920s to the 1940s was due to the availability of financial credit markets for settler farmers from 'British financial and mercantile capital . . . and the organisations of purchasing and marketing of export crops' (Berman 1990: 132). High-interest farming credit was often granted by commercial banks on the basis of the market value of the land. Small-scale white settler farmers entered into individual financial arrangements with merchant banks on a short-term basis, which was often pegged to future production as well as to the purchase and sale of crops from their farms. A combination of high speculative land prices, credit for farming, and holding of land far in excess of what was needed translated into a debt burden for many farmers (Van Zwanenberg 1975). Thus, farming for white settlers during this period was costly and unprofitable. To

[1]The programme was led by the Ministry of Lands Settlement and Water Development, which was established in April 1962. In December 1964 (after independence), it became the Ministry of Lands and Settlement.

[2]This term referred to the African 'Native lands' and the European 'White Highlands'. The White Highlands were areas that were 5000 feet above sea level and climatically suited for Europeans to live in and which they owned or managed. There was an exclusion of African rights holders in these lands.

overcome debts, settler farmers engaged in speculative behaviour by hoarding large land parcels, which they later subdivided and sold at a profit to the African petty bourgeoisie on a commercial basis (Berman 1990). Other white settlers continued holding on to their undeveloped land and lobbied the state to settle more farmers, a process which pushed land values upwards as they would be paid for 'the potential rather than current commercial value of their land' (Berman 1990: 410). By the 1930s, a free land market in the scheduled White Highlands was in existence, with land speculation becoming a problem for the colonial government (Okoth-Ogendo 1981). Wasserman (1974) notes that, at this time, plantation agriculture bolstered Kenya's economy, with sisal and coffee[3] accounting for over half of Kenya's exports.

Post-World War II, political and economic pressures began to change the course for white settler farmers in Kenya (Berman 1990). During the war, agricultural production was reoriented towards food grains to service the war effort. Funds meant for agriculture were also diverted to war-related activities. To avoid an agrarian catastrophe, the colonial government came up with a 'Recovery Phase' for agricultural policy from 1945 to 1950, a 1950–1955 'Planning Phase' and a 1955–1960 'Development Phase' (Berman 1990). The phases saw an increase in agricultural production, with agricultural exports rising from £4.7 million in 1945 to £14.8 million by 1950, and then £22.7 million in 1955 and £31.2 million in 1960. However, these figures were drawn mainly from Scheduled settler farming areas since statistics from African-held farms were not captured. Further, the government's agricultural programmes in these three phases in fact excluded African peasants except in areas where coffee and maize were grown. It was also during this period that land adjudication, consolidation and titling programmes began in rural Kenya for African farmers. This marked a shift from customary tenure to individualised and private ownership as per the British land tenure system (Okoth-Ogendo 1981). These three phases (including the opening of land markets and 'willing buyer-willing seller' land reform) had implications for agricultural activities and land tenure security post-independence.

Thus, as Kenya moved towards independence, the British Government started incorporating Africans into agricultural development by diminishing white settlers' position in farming and the economy in general.[4] This entailed a land transfer programme whereby land was returned to Africans at a cost—this has been called

[3]The Coffee Board was established in 1933 and, by 1935, coffee auctions were taking place in Kenya. Other early Boards or producer cooperatives included the Pyrethrum Board (1938), the Kenya Cooperative Creameries (1931) and the Kenya Farmers Association (1931).

[4]In 1954, three policy reports by the British government began to dismantle the barriers to African capital accumulation. First, *The East African Royal Commission* called for a free market in land. Second, *The Swynnerton Plan* advocated for the consolidation of all African holdings, enhanced security of tenure by individual title, and the rapid introduction of all suitable cash crops. Third, *The Carpenter Report* argued for a rise in cash wages to a family-based minimum level. Collectively, these reports impacted on agricultural development in Kenya (specifically, the *Swynnerton Plan* has had a lasting effect on land reforms).

the 'independence bargain'. The purpose of releasing blocks of land for purchase and redistribution[5] to Africans was fourfold: first, to reduce the political agitation that questioned continued unequal wealth and land ownership between whites and Africans; second, it was anticipated that the Africans who benefitted from the land through this programme would maintain the level of productivity already attained by the settler community; third, the transfers would create smallholder land parcels while maintaining high productivity levels; and, lastly, an economic dividend would arise regarding increased land tenure security, which would contribute to the commodification of land through sales, mortgage and land charges (Harbeson 1973; Hazlewood 1985).

From an economic perspective, an independent African government would look forward to inheriting a strong economy with a thriving agricultural sector. Nevertheless, the colonial land resettlement agenda did not focus on the rural Africans disinherited from their land. The resettlement programme emphasised the protection of the economic interests of those who already possessed land (Berman 1990). In 1962, the Government of Kenya purchased land through the 'Million Acre Settlement Scheme[6]', which targeted land owned by settlers of British origin. To purchase this land, loans and grants were provided by the British and West German governments, the Commonwealth Development Corporation and the International Bank for Reconstruction and Development (IBRD) (Shaffer 1967). The British Government provided 85 per cent of the finance (approximately £21 million), West German government 5 per cent (£1.2 million) and the IBRD 10 per cent (£2.4 million). The short-term objective of these land resettlement programmes (or settlement schemes) for Africans was 'to facilitate the transfer of power and to increase the chances of political stability after independence' (Harbeson 1973: 198). Cumulatively, in the 1961–1969 financial period, the land resettlement loans represented one-third of the foreign debt incurred by Kenya (Berman 1990). From 1963 to 1975, land transfers for smallholder settlements totalled 581,500 hectares, divided into 49,400 family-based holdings with an average size of 11.8 hectares (Leo 1981). In relation to the development of smallholder agriculture in Kenya, by 1979, out of an estimated 6.2 million hectares of farmland, two-thirds were operated by smallholder farmers owning an average farm size of two hectares or less (Livingstone 1981; Lukalo et al. 2019). But the settlement schemes also enabled African agrarian capital to facilitate and consolidate its position in farming. During the 1980s and 1990s, the settlement schemes continued with the hope of increasing food production.

These processes, though, favoured African elites who could hire-in labour, introduce and establish farm technology, and purchase inputs to maintain productivity. Hence, Africans who were well placed in (or connected to) government,

[5]Not all farm blocks were sold at this time. In Trans-Nzoia County, by 2019, there were two farms from the colonial era owned and farmed by the grandchildren of the original white settler. The Delamare Farm in Naivasha is also one such remaining land block from the colonial era.

[6]By 1971, 29,000 families had been settled on 'high density' plots and 5000 families on larger 'low density' plots.

Paramount Chiefs, elites and politicians (including their kin and communities) were the first groups to benefit from this programme, giving birth to an emergent agrarian class of rich to capitalist farmers which still exists in Kenya today. In some cases, the sons of Paramount Chiefs who benefitted from land became prominent politicians in Kenya. With respect to many settlement schemes in the Central, Rift Valley, Coastal and Western regions of Kenya, many politicians used their political and ethnic patronage to relocate their ethnic communities into key areas, leading to the genesis of many land conflicts around land and tenure insecurities. This explains why these areas are hubs for ethnic violence even today.

Further, in 1963, there were around 655 registered cooperative societies, which increased to 2652 by 1982. These cooperatives participated in the production, marketing and processing of agricultural products. Between 1963 and 1966, more than half of the registered cooperatives participated in the buying of large-scale European farms. But this was not for the purpose of farming; rather, they held the land for speculative purposes (see Zeleza 1990), thus inhibiting agricultural growth. This combination of the impact of the colonial legacy, European settler capital, industrialisation, and emerging African investments in property, land and production relations in large parts of rural Kenya, laid the grounds for the economic difficulties experienced in the next two decades.

3 Rise of Structural Adjustment

Like many African countries, Kenya began pursuing Structural Adjustment Programmes (SAPs) in 1980. Prior to liberalisation in the 1970s, the country was marked by reasonable levels of agricultural productivity, high budget allocations to agriculture (10 per cent of the national budget), and strong credit and marketing institutions that supported agriculture (Gitu 2006). For many (large and small) farmers, the Agriculture Finance Corporation[7] and Kenya Farmers Association provided credit and farm inputs. For harvesting, marketing and food storage, the National Cereals Produce Board (NCPB—maize, wheat and other cereals), Kenya Meat Commission (meat and hides), Kenya Cooperative Creameries (KCC—milk, butter, cheese), Kenya Sugar Authority (KSA), Kenya Tea Development Authority (KTDA) (smallholder tea) and Kenya Planters Cooperatives Union (KPCU—coffee) provided output markets and set producer prices. Government agricultural extension workers and technical staff offered and monitored maintenance of agricultural quality and high standards (Gitu 2006). Passed on from the colonial regime were statutory marketing institutions and state boards (for instance, Sisal Board, Sugar

[7]The Agricultural Finance Corporation (AFC) was established in 1963, initially as a subsidiary of the Land and Agriculture Bank and then reconstructed in March 1969 by an Act of Parliament. The main function of the Corporation was to assist in the development of Agriculture and Agricultural Industries. This it would achieve by making loans to farmers, Cooperative Societies, Public Bodies, Local Authorities and other Persons engaging in agriculture or agricultural industries.

Board, Kenya Dairy Board), which regulated the production and marketing of important agricultural commodities. These marketing boards initially seemed to have been effective, and some like the KTDA recorded success stories (Lamb and Muller 1982). Inflation in the 1970s, though led to low output prices for farmers even under state-controlled marketing boards.

More broadly, by the early 1980s, the country was experiencing reduced investor confidence after the failed 1982 political coup, the 1983–1984 prolonged drought,[8] rises in global oil prices, domestic inflation[9] and the adverse effects of the global recession. Due to exogenous developments related to the 1980–1981 world recession, the Kenyan shilling was devalued, a high level of debt was experienced, and the shortage of foreign currency became significant (Atambo 1987). Atambo (1987: 5) notes that 'debt in 1984 was US$ 3062 million [...] 53.3 per cent of the Gross National Product'.

In 1983, the government's monopoly in the pricing and marketing of fertilisers ceased with the introduction of significant changes to the fertiliser policy, which included (i) liberalizing import procedures to allow private importers and distributors, (ii) setting distribution margins to remote areas, and (iii) packaging fertiliser in smaller quantities for smallholder farmers. These measures coupled with increased fertiliser aid, resulted in an upward use of fertiliser—but mainly in large-scale farms. Hence, there was an increase from 136,000 tons in 1980/1981–1982/1983 to 227,000 tons in 1984/1985–1986/1987 (Gugerty and Cook 2008). However, the 1983–1984 drought across all farming regions watered down the agriculture-based production gains of this policy. Many elite Africans (government officials and politicians) continued to have a strong interest in agriculture. These elite Africans owned large farms (and demanded fertiliser) and were able to consolidate their interests through the formation of lobby groups like the Kenya National Farmers Union and thereby dictate the direction of government support. During this time, smallholder farmers faced massive crop failures and severe food stress, and this led to the staple food (maize) being imported on a large scale. Specifically, at the farm level, smallholder families were unable to feed themselves, while consumer goods were expensive, fertilisers became unaffordable and paid farm work was not guaranteed. The national maize production was below 50 per cent of requirements, which necessitated 425,000 tons of food aid imports in 1984–1985; as well, wheat and potato production were 70 per cent below normal (Cohen and Lewis 1987).

Agricultural production faced enduring challenges. Notably, agriculture continued to rely heavily on the erratic availability and patterns of rain, with the little drive towards different crops (diversification), irrigation and new technologies. Furthermore, the focus was still on primary farm products with a narrow range of

[8]The droughts of 1974–1975, 1979–1980, and 1983–1984 significantly affected agricultural production and led to massive food imports especially of maize, beans, rice and milk.

[9]The Kenyan shilling was devalued by 5 per cent in February 1981 and 15 per cent in September 1981. A further devaluation of 14 per cent was pushed for by the IMF and implemented in December 1981, in time for another IMF standby arrangement.

agriculturally-based manufactured products. Given the droughts of the 1970s and early 1980s, Kenya soon became food deficient, and some regions were declared 'food aid' regions, implying that 70 per cent of the population living in these areas was in distress (Shisanya 1990). As this was happening, more and more people bought land and settled within the settlement schemes. The culmination of these developments was rapid land fragmentation and economic hardships for ordinary Kenyans, especially those living in rural areas. The overall trajectory-entailed neoliberalisation, including rolling back of the state in the provision of agricultural support, only leading to a further crisis in agriculture for smallholders. Overall, this entailed increased social inequalities, deepening rural poverty, and political and economic downturns.

4 Structural Adjustment and Its Effects

As elsewhere, the key ingredient of the SAPs in Kenya was an economic model of private ownership, competitive markets and an outward-oriented development strategy (Rono 2002). What was initially touted as economic relief programmes, gradually shifted into the political domain by advocating for popular participation in decision-making; decentralisation of power structures (with a rural focus); special measures to alleviate poverty; protection of the vulnerable; accountability; and the reduced role of the government in the economy (Rono 2002). Sender and Smith (1984) highlight that 'getting prices right' became an essential part of the neoliberal agenda in agriculture in developing countries. For example, with the liberalisation agenda, the dominant role of the National Cereals and Produce Board in purchasing, marketing and setting of prices for maize and wheat was severely curtailed. It was expected that the elimination of price distortions would unleash the productive potential of undervalued, exploited and heavily taxed peasants.

The government's commitment to neoliberalisation was enunciated initially in specific policy regimes, namely, in the *Sessional Paper No. 4 of 1980* on *Economic Prospects and Policies* (Republic of Kenya 1980), followed by *Sessional Paper No. 4 of* 1981 (on National Food Policy). From the 1980s onwards, there thus arose the erosion of facilities like agricultural extension, credit to farmers and social services, all of which had a negative impact on the lives of vulnerable rural dwellers. The neoliberal agricultural programme, by deregulation of markets and withdrawal of the government from direct support to farmers, undercut the lives and livelihoods of smallholders or at least contributed to this.

One key challenge facing agriculture in Kenya and other developing nations was related to global commodity shocks, which are often associated with the production and export of primary commodities (Patnaik 2011; Moyo and Yeros 2005). During the late 1970s, there was increased agricultural productivity, marked by land improvements, development of the plantation system (tea, coffee, sugar cane, pineapples, sisal), uptake of machinery use and improved road transportation in some agricultural regions. For example, in the period 1976–1978, the use of tractors for farming increased by 7.9 per cent, fertilisers by 5.9 per cent and pesticides by 5.8 per cent. Increased use of tractors was not wholly targeted at smallholder farms. However, the budgetary allocation to agriculture was high and, in 1976–1977,[10] the boom in coffee and tea exports was accompanied by a general improvement in rural lives (Ongile 1999). Nonetheless, when the coffee[11] boom subsided, it contributed to an appreciation of the exchange rate and expansion of domestic credit and money supply, which then had a negative ripple effect on agriculture in the 1980s (Bevan et al. 1989). The policy shift of focusing on export commodities, which is often linked to neoliberalism, was disastrous for most rural households (Lofchie 1994).

Indeed, after a decade of SAPs, the *African Development Bank Report* (1994) flagged certain concerns, including the decrease in Kenyans' daily calorie consumption per capita (from 2241 in 1980 to 2109 in 1991). In per capita terms, food consumption grew at an annual rate of 6.2 per cent in the 1984–1988 period and fell to 2.6 per cent in the 1988–1992 period. From 1984 to 1988, the average annual growth of food production was 7.7 per cent, and this growth dropped to −0.1 per cent between 1988 and 1992. Thus, trends in food production were reflected in calorific and food consumption. A study conducted during this time in Embu District in Central Kenya noted a decline in household energy intake, especially the prevalence of protein energy malnutrition amongst children (Neumann et al. 1989).

5 Full-Scale Liberalisation: Sessional Paper No 1. of 1986

Neoliberalisation in Kenya received a further push forward in 1986, when the *Sessional Paper: Economic Management for Renewed Growth* was published. This 115-page document spelt out, in very clear terms, Kenya's long-term approach to economic woes. It emphasised the importance of unfettered (free) private sector-led economic development and reiterated the dominant role of agriculture in economic growth and job creation (Republic of Kenya 1986). In this Sessional Paper, agriculture was to serve several purposes until the year 2000, namely:

i. Provide food security for the population of almost 35 million.
ii. Generate farm family incomes that would grow by at least 5 per cent per year.
iii. Absorb new farmworkers at the rate of over 3 per cent a year and increase farm productivity.
iv. Supply export crops sufficient for a 150 per cent increase in agricultural export earnings by 2000, and.
v. Stimulate the growth of productive off-farm activities in rural areas in order that the off-farm jobs would grow at a rate of 3.5 per cent to 5 per cent per year (Republic of Kenya 1986).

[10] The East African Community broke down in 1977, and this adversely affected Kenya's non-traditional exports as well as local domestic border trade mainly in food.

[11] Coffee production had declined by more than 50 per cent between 1988 and 1998.

As alluded to earlier, the 1980s were marked by greater food insecurity, and hence the Sessional Paper sought to reduce this deficit. As one of the key pillars of the Paper, decentralisation was designed to facilitate this. The District Focus for Rural Development put great emphasis on service delivery at the district level, including in relation to planning and implementing.

The 1986 Sessional Paper sought to pursue the following issues more fully, as per a strident neoliberalism: liberalisation of prices and marketing systems; financial sector policy reforms; international trade regulation reforms; government budgetary rationalisation; divestiture and privatisation of parastatals; and civil service reforms (Central Bureau of Statistics 1997). Thus, this policy document was mainly driven by an emphasis on privatisation and the gradual weakening of the role of government intervention in the agricultural sector (and indirectly the land sector). This was to be brought about by the implementation of appropriate policies, particularly those that alleviated saving, fiscal and foreign exchange constraints. The Sessional Paper explicitly identified resource gaps as a key for enhanced economic growth (Rono 2002). For example, the agricultural policy was to pursue self-sufficiency in food commodities like maize, wheat, rice, milk and meat. Gitu (2006) notes that self-sufficiency in food was only met in the 1970s (prior to neoliberalisation), thereby emphasising Kenya's ongoing vulnerability to exogenous shocks resulting from an export driven economy vulnerable to commodity fluctuations and prices controlled on the global market.

While the volume of exports stagnated after 1985, the volume and cost of imports increased, which caused a serious deterioration in trade and necessitated large capital inflows (Mose 2007) Because of this, this period in Kenya's history was characterised by a serious balance of payment problems. By 1986, the overall goal of the Kenyan government had shifted from overall food sufficiency to a strategy that targeted seven commodities that informed the food and agricultural policy. These were maize, wheat, milk and horticultural crops for home consumption and export. Coffee and tea were encouraged for purposes of raising farm income and earning foreign exchange. Because land is a critical factor when addressing food sufficiency, the 1986 Sessional Paper highlighted the role of land in the following ways:

> 5.78. In this situation, private owners have a social obligation to put their land to its best use [. . .] First despite growing population pressure on land there must be limits to the subdivision of small farms. Subdivision should be prevented beyond the point where total returns to land begin to diminish. Second, Kenya cannot feed itself [. . .] if land is allowed to lie idle or underutilised in large land holdings. [. . .] Government recognises the sensitivity of land issues.
>
> 5.79. There has not been a major review of land policy since independence [. . .;] to correct this situation, the Government will appoint a high-level commission to review the land tenure laws and practices of the country and to recommend legislation that will bring the laws and practices of the country into conformity with Kenya's development needs (Republic of Kenya 1986: 88).

The question of land is important in food production, but it was until 2009 that the first National Land Policy was passed in Kenya. Prior to that, Land Acts and other statutory guidelines governed the land sector.

Almost 85 per cent of maize is grown and produced on smallholder farms, and most of it is consumed at the farm level. The process of liberalising the maize market was initiated in 1988 under the Cereals Sector Reform Programme, which focused on the rules governing maize trading and movement, reduction in costs of maize purchased at the National Cereals and Produce Board, and monitoring of the pricing policy (Republic of Kenya 1991). The main motive was to encourage the private sector in becoming involved in maize marketing. The study by Wangia et al. (2002) on maize notes that 1989–1995 was identified as a period of gradual liberalisation and 1995–1999 as full liberalisation for the maize sector. Prices were decontrolled in 1988, and interest rates deregulated in 1991 (Swamy 1994). Maize continued to be the staple crop of Kenya (grown on smallholder farms), with the total land area under maize estimated to be at 1.5 million hectares with an annual production estimated at 3.0 million metric tons. However, even to date, the country is unable to produce enough maize for its citizens' requirements and this can be traced to the liberalisation of the sector.

The marketing of maize in the pre-liberalisation period consisted of informal systems operating side by side with the formal system. The formal maize system, as noted, was regulated and managed by the National Cereals and Produce Board (NCPB). The colonial government had formed the Maize Marketing and Produce Board and Control Board (MMPB) in 1939 to regulate the operations of the regional marketing boards. The NCPB was formed in 1979 by merging the maize board with the wheat board in order to streamline the handling, marketing and management of all grains grown in Kenya. For many years, state marketing boards had regulated prices of agricultural produce and exercised the right to veto all private bulk sales of maize between maize regions (Mose 2007). In their study on the impact of the NCPB on maize farming, Jayne et al. (2005) note that in the 1989–1994 period, political dynamics greatly shaped and influenced the growing areas for maize and maize prices. During this period, the NCPB's buying price from farmers indirectly lowered the price of maize in key wholesale markets by 20 per cent (Poulton and Kanyinga 2013). The complete liberalisation of the production and marketing of maize was only realised in the mid-1990s. The intention was to broaden the role of market signals and align relative prices more closely to those of the world markets, so as to improve agricultural terms of trade for increased agricultural production and economic performance (Nyantigo and Okello 1998).

From 1995, after full market liberalisation, the buying price of NCPB served to raise maize prices by around 20 per cent in key wholesale markets, yet NCPB had never exceeded 27 per cent in the purchase of the total production of maize. The beneficiaries of this purchase were the large maize growing areas in Nakuru, Uasin-Gishu and Trans-Nzoia. The hardest hit by these inflated prices were the smallholder farmers and consumers of maize who sold their produce to informal markets with low purchase prices. The supply and demand of the market (prices) were not necessarily divorced completely from the control of the state. Whereas the maize farmers were at liberty to sell their products to any buyer, the NCPB, with heavy funding from the government, indirectly controlled the maize prices. During the harvesting season, middlemen would rush to buy the dried maize at a throwaway farm price and sell it to NCPB in bulk at a higher price. This became the era for the emergence of the 'exploitative' middleman.

Admittedly, Argwings-Kodhek (1991, 1998) reports that 59 per cent of Kenyan households reported better availability of maize in the liberalisation era and 31 per cent in the pre-liberalisation one. In terms of the convenience of selling maize, 88 per cent preferred the liberalisation period and 7 per cent the pre-liberalisation one. However, the liberalisation of the economy did not increase the production of most agricultural crops (as promised by neoliberalism), which continued to be on a decline. Declining maize (and coffee) production took place as producer incentives weakened during this agricultural marketing liberalisation. Between the years 1990 to 2000, Kenya's average annual agricultural growth slowed down to 1.1 per cent, and the agricultural variety of crops did not diversify during these years (Jayne et al. 2005). As well, in the end, the liberalisation of agricultural commodity marketing had devastating effects for both producers and consumers (Jayne et al. 2005) as, in large part, the system became differentiated and disjointed (Zeleza 1990).

Overall, the period of liberalisation was fraught with patchy, intermittent and unstable development, especially in rural areas with the government being slow to make changes in many sectors. For this, Nyantigo and Okello (1998) note that liberalisation did not have the intended results due to several factors, which include poor sequencing and timing of policies that were not in line with the institutional capacities (for example, Ministry of Agriculture) to implement the changes. This is despite the fact that the arrangement of government services changed from supply oriented to demand driven, with the beneficiaries of research and extension services required to support activities through levies or 'cost-sharing'. In addition, instability and lack of coordination in policy implementation affected investors' confidence in the markets and did not allow the private sector to take up the activities once controlled by the government. Presupposing a total liberalisation of the markets would entail relinquishing the role of government in policy making, policy implementation, and regulation. For instance, in the agricultural sector, the government, through Kenya Seed Company, continued to control the quality and standards of hybrid seeds for maize. Government control remained evident since not all markets or the private sector functioned effectively, and they needed to be monitored and oversight provided. In this regard, Nyantigo and Okello (1998) argue that the government's implementation of its liberalisation policies negatively affected the development of the agricultural sector and food security environment for years.

6 Conclusion

From a historical perspective, the distribution of farmland in Kenya, and the flow of capital in and out of agriculture, perpetuated the marginalisation of smallholder farmers in rural areas. Invariably, this maintains an unproductive agricultural system that lags behind in technological advancements and contributes minimally to growth. This chapter has shown how the 1980s through to the 1990s marked a pivotal moment in the economic and agrarian history of Kenya, including in relation to differentiated effects when it comes to agricultural productivity (in some cases, rising, in others declining). The overall impact of policy reforms (as articulated in three Sessional Papers), in the context of neoliberalism, on the long-term (inclusive) development of agriculture has been negative. These policies of liberalisation, together with climatic changes, the aftermath of a political coup, and a problematic rural development agenda, created an uncertain environment for smallholder farmers to enjoy the benefits from agriculture. There were no meaningful measures in the 1980s and 1990s to ensure continued agricultural state support and service delivery for small-scale rural farmers in the short, medium and long term. The agricultural system for smallholder farmers faced imminent collapse when the agencies responsible for supporting production, marketing, and extension services were reduced drastically, and, regrettably, the effects of this are still felt today. For instance, government-led extension services to farmers remain non-existent in many parts of rural Kenya.

References

African Development Bank (1994) Selected statistics on regional member countries, Abidjan

Argwings-Kodhek G (1991) Policy issues facing the maize sector in the North Rift. Tegemeo Institute of Egerton University

Argwings-Kodhek G (1998) Contemporary issues determining the future of Kenyan agriculture: an agenda for policy research. Tegemeo Institute of Egerton University

Atambo CPG (1987) National security implications of the 1884 drought in Kenya, Unpublished Research Report submitted to Maxwell Air Force base Alabama

Berman B (1990) Control and crisis in colonial Kenya: the dialectic of domination. James Currey, London

Bevan D, Collier P, Gunning JW (1989) Fiscal response to a temporary trade shock: the aftermath of the Kenyan coffee boom. World Bank Econ Rev 3(3):359–378

Boone C (2014) Property and political order in Africa: land rights and the structure of politics. Cambridge University Press, New York

Central Bureau of Statistics (1997) Economic survey. Nairobi, Government Printer

Cohen JM, Lewis DB (1987) Role of government in combating food shortages: lessons from Kenya 1984–1985. In: Glantz MH (ed) Drought and hunger in Africa. Cambridge University Press, Cambridge, pp 269–296

Gitu KW (2006) Agriculture development and food security in sub-Saharan Africa (SSA). FAO, sub-regional office for East & Southern Africa, Rome; Italy

Gugerty MK, Cook J (2008) Political economy of fertilizer policy in Kenya (Brief). Evans School of Policy Analysis and Research, University of Washington, Seattle

Harbeson JW (1973) Nation-building in Kenya. North Western University Press, Evanston

Hazlewood A (1985) Kenyan land-transfer programmes and their relevance to Zimbabwe. J Mod Afr Stud 23(3):445–461

Jabara CL (1985) Agricultural pricing policy in Kenya. World Dev 13(5):611–626

Jayne TS, Myers RL, Nyoro J (2005) The effects of government Maize marketing and trading policies on Maize market prices in Kenya, WP Series. Tegemeo Institute of Agricultural Policy and Development, Nairobi

Lamb G, Muller L (1982) Control accountability and incentives in a successful development institution: the Kenya Tea Development Authority. Staff Working Paper, No. 550, Washington, DC: World Bank

Leo C (1981) Who benefitted from the million-acre scheme? toward a class analysis of Kenya's transition to independence. Can J Afr Stud 15(2):201–222

Livingstone I (1981) Rural development and incomes in Kenya. ILO, Addis Ababa

Lofchie M (1994) The politics of agricultural policy. In: Barkan J (ed) Beyond capitalism vs socialism in Kenya and Tanzania. Lynne Rienner, Boulder, Colorado, pp 129–173

Lukalo F, Boone C, Joireman S (2019) Mapping settlement schemes in Kenya. National Land Commission, Nairobi

Mose LO (2007) Who gains, who loses? the impact of market liberalisation on rural households in Northwestern Kenya. Unpublished PhD Thesis, Wageningen University

Moyo S, Yeros P (eds) (2005) Reclaiming the Land: the resurgence of rural movements in Africa. Zed Books, Asia; Latin America; London

Neumann C, Trostle R, Baksh M, Ngare D, Bwibo N (1989) Household response to the impact of drought in Kenya. Food Nutr Bull 11(2):1–15

Nyantigo H, Okello J (1998) Kenya's agricultural policy and sector performance: 1964 to 1996. Occasional paper, OP/04/98. Institute of Policy Analysis and Research

Okoth-Ogendo HWO (1981) Land ownership and land distribution in Kenya's large-farm areas. In: Killick T (ed) Papers on the Kenyan economy: performance, problems and policies. Heinemann, Nairobi, pp 329–338

Ongile GA (1999) Gender and agricultural supply responses to structural adjustment programmes: a case study of smallholder tea producers in Kericho, Kenya. The Nordic African Institute, Uppsala

Patnaik U (2011) The agrarian question in the neoliberal era. In: Patnaik U, Moyo S (eds) The Agrarian question in the neo-liberal era: primitive accumulation and the peasantry. Pambazuka Press, Dar es Salaam

Poulton C, Kanyinga K (2013) The politics of revitalising agriculture in Kenya. Policy Brief 059, Future Agricultures Consortium, Brighton

Republic of Kenya (1980) Sessional paper No. 4 of 1980 economic prospects and policies. Government Printers, Nairobi, p 35

Republic of Kenya (1981) Sessional paper No. 4 of 1981 on national food policy. Government Printers, Nairobi, p 52

Republic of Kenya (1986) Sessional paper No. 1 of 1986 economic management for renewed growth. Government Printer, Nairobi, p 115

Republic of Kenya (1991) Economic survey. Government Printers, Nairobi

Rono JK (2002) The impact of the structural adjustment programmes on Kenyan Society. J Soc Dev Afr 17(1):81–98

Sender J, Smith S (1984) What is right with the Berg Report and what's left of its critics? IDS Discussion Paper 192, Sussex

Shaffer N (1967) Land resettlement in Kenya. Yearb Assoc Pac Coast Geogr 29:121–139

Shisanya C (1990) The 1983–1984 drought in Kenya. J East Afr Res Dev 20:127–148

Swamy G (1994) Kenya: patchy, intermittent commitment. In: Husain I, Faruqee R (eds) Adjustment in Africa: lessons from country case studies, World Bank Regional Study. World Bank, Washington DC, pp 193–237

Swynnerton RJM (1954) A plan to intensify the development of African agriculture in Kenya. Government Printer, Nairobi

Van Zwanenberg P (1975) Kenya's primitive colonial capitalism: the economic weakness of Kenya's settlers up to 1940. Can J Afr Stud 9(2):277–292

Wangia C, Wangia S, De-Groote H (2002) Review of Maize marketing in Kenya: Implementation and impact of liberalization, 1989–1999. Paper presented at the 7th Eastern and Southern Africa Regional Maize Conference, Nairobi, Kenya

Wasserman G (1974) European settlers and Kenya colony: thoughts on a conflicted affair. Afr Stud Rev 17(2):425–434

Zeleza T (1990) The development of the cooperative movement in Kenya since independence. J East Afr Res Dev 20:68–94

Part IV
Neoliberalism, Extroverted Production and Implications for the Peasantry

Neoliberal Agrarian Policies and Terms of Incorporation in Rural Mozambique

Natacha Bruna

Abstract The current scramble for resources in Africa has become a major driver of social exclusion and ensuing negative implications for rural livelihoods, albeit in differentiated ways. Pre-existing structures and inequalities that resulted from historical colonial paths and specific economic, traditional and legal contexts conditioned the heterogeneity of rural populations; and, consequently, how differently they experience and react to current processes of land grabbing. This chapter aims to understand the differentiated outcomes, implications and reactions of each segment of the rural population in the context of Mozambique specifically, building on Shivji's concept of the working people. Presently, most large-scale investments in rural areas in Mozambique involve ways of integrating the affected smallholders into the dynamics of rural development. A critical examination of such policies and approaches is presented by looking particularly at processes of smallholder integration, as materialised through corporate social development plans. This entails analysing the terms of incorporation of the different segments of the rural population, including wage workers, poorer peasants, women and local elites. Empirical findings show that most of the smallholders end up adversely incorporated into investment-led rural development projects, ultimately resulting in the inclusion of the few and the exclusion of the majority.

1 Introduction

In the midst of the current scramble for resources in Africa, land grabbing has become a major driver of social exclusion, and it augmented negative implications for rural livelihoods (Amanor 2012; Hall et al. 2015; Moyo et al. 2012). In this context of this neoliberal restructuring, large-scale land acquisitions are conducted through different processes and models of land acquisition. The various outcomes of the current global resource rush include expulsion of people through direct land

N. Bruna (✉)
Erasmus University Rotterdam, Rotterdam, The Netherlands

F. Mazwi et al. (eds.), *Capital Penetration and the Peasantry in Southern and Eastern Africa*, Advances in African Economic, Social and Political Development, https://doi.org/10.1007/978-3-030-89824-3_9

expropriation, the transfer of land control, for instance, through contract farming, resettlement of people that results in the unfair reallocation of fertile/resource-rich land, and other mechanisms of adverse incorporation, and social and gendered exclusions (Borras and Franco 2012; Hall et al. 2015; Hickey and Du Toit 2013; Tsikata and Yaro 2014).

Prevailing public discourses systematically use claims of employment creation and livelihood generation to impose and enforce such neoliberal economic policies, involving the promotion of foreign direct investment to explore and regularly extract natural resources. However, the quality of employment and livelihoods is questionable. In the end, local conditions play a critical role regarding the outcomes of such investments, particularly as related to land tenure, labour regimes, livelihoods and local economies (Ali and Stevano 2019; Hall et al. 2017).

In Mozambique, where the land is owned by the state, foreign investments in rural areas are expected to entail ways of integrating the affected smallholders in an inclusive process of socio-economic development. The right to use land in Mozambique (legitimised by a legal document called *Direito de Uso e Aproveitamento da Terra*—DUAT) is conditioned by a set of factors, including mandatory consultation with (and consent of) local residents (rural households) and possibly resettling them to other areas and/or compensation (monetary and/or non-monetary). Lately, large-scale land-based investments in the country have involved differentiated mechanisms of integration and implementation of development projects. Some forms are becoming very common, including out-grower schemes, corporate social responsibility projects, social development plans and so on, aiming to provide alternative livelihood strategies and income generation, or even an optimistic long-term plan of employment creation.

It is in this context that Portucel Moçambique, a forest plantation company, acquired an area of 350,000 hectares where thousands of rural households reside. The company plans to develop an eucalyptus plantation on two thirds of the acquired land. In this regard, the company would negotiate with the households for a transfer of a share of their land—the requirement was that each household would keep at least 2.9 hectares of land for its subsistence. Rather than the resettlement of people whose landholdings had been taken in full (i.e. complete land alienation), the company and the government agreed that a Social Development Plan should be implemented. As a result, and before even consulting the affected households, the company received a 50-year DUAT approved by Mozambique's Council of Ministers. Currently operating on around 13,500 hectares of eucalyptus, the company plans to integrate the local population in development processes based mainly on employment creation and providing agricultural inputs and technical assistance.

The degree to which rural people become meaningfully incorporated into these foreign investments is conditioned by the mechanisms of compensation which vary from project to project. In this light, this study analyses the character of integration and incorporation of the rural population in the face of neoliberal agricultural intensification with specific reference to the case of Portucel Moçambique. It takes a careful look at the strategies that claim to 'compensate' for (for example) the loss of land incurred by rural populations with the implementation of land-based projects, particularly forest plantations. Further, the role of local elites, class dynamics and gender within the rural population are important with regards to benefit distribution, social differentiation and exclusion. Overall, the chapter attempts to answer the following question in relation to the case study: What are the differentiated implications of capital penetration in rural areas, how are different segments of rural working people integrated, and how do they react to it?

2 Methodology and Research Design

In order to answer the above research question, the study was conducted using a Marxist Agrarian Political Economy lens. The research itself is based on a predominantly qualitative approach both for data collection methods and the data analysis process. Primary data on perceptions and characteristics of the main actors were collected, including the following actors: peasants and heads of rural households, peasant women, workers (casual and permanent), and local elites (community leaders, government officials and others). Qualitative data was collected using both existing documentation and primary data collection methods in the study sites. The research focuses on the District of Ile.

Ile district is located in Zambézia province (6633 km^2 and 318,383 inhabitants), with around 56.2 inhabitants per km^2 (INE 2012). In the district, most households built their houses using 'precarious' materials (adobe or sticks), and 97% covered their houses using grass/palm tree leaves. Less than 1 per cent of the population has access to piped water and electricity (INE 2012). The households are mostly subsistence producers with some market integration, and the production techniques are rain-fed and labour intensive. Households provide their own labour force and use simple tools such as hoes and barely have access to fertilisers. They produce mostly maize, peanuts, beans and cassava. Cassava represents the most produced crop in the district (more than 30 per cent of the planted area on average and more than 50 per cent of total production) (INE 2012).

Documentary analysis regarding governmental policies and company reports were very useful in understanding the economic and environmental public policies directed to each study site and nationally. These documents included: national strategies, programmes and policies for the agricultural sector, the national strategy for climate change mitigation and adaptation strategies, yearly district (District of Ile) strategic plans including economic and social reports, Portucel's yearly reports, Portucel's social development plan and other relevant reports on the company's activities and Ile district-related economic and social policies.

Primary data gathering was done during fieldwork that consisted of five field visits made intermittently between 2015 to 2019. The data collection methods included in-depth interviews that followed a purposive sampling process that consisted in selecting a particular subset of interviewees whose experiences could directly inform the research question. This included those whose lives were directly affected by the process of land acquisition (such as heads of households and women who went through expropriation by the company, and people that were employed by the company) and those who participated in the process of land acquisition (local elites, local government officials and so on). The selection method followed the snowball technique, in which interviewees were asked to indicate/nominate, through their networks, other informants that could potentially contribute to the study. This was done, until data collection reached saturation point, where no new or contradictory information was provided by the informants.

Data collection also included focus groups discussions where informants were segregated into small groups (around six to eight individuals with similar experiences—either workers or expropriated individuals) to together discuss specific issues regarding their perceptions of the process of land acquisition by the company (including questions around participation, justice and negotiation) and the implications for their livelihoods (income, food production and other general household needs). Lastly, the researcher engaged in participant observation, including multiple visits to the study sites and spending time in the districts, 'localities' and villages in the district.

The data analysis process was conducted using process tracing (Bennett and George 2005), aiming to keep track of and trace the links between possible causes and observed outcomes. This entails aiming to identify causal inferences with a temporal dimension of events. Consequently, validation was guaranteed by using the Constant Comparison Method based on comparing pieces of data, and coded data were driven by trends of similarities and differences between perceptions of all groups of interviewees, following Boeije's (2002) insights with respect to conducting a purposeful approach of constant comparison.

3 'New Scramble' for Africa and Terms of Incorporation

3.1 Trajectories of Agrarian Change and Capital Penetration: Terms of Incorporation and Pre-Existing Inequalities

The implications of land grabbing on the ground have been studied significantly in the last decades. Overall, there are differentiated implications of and reactions to land grabbing (Amanor, 2012; Borras and Franco 2013; Chambati et al. 2018; Hall et al. 2015; Li 2011; Shivji 2019). Analysis of forms of integration as an outcome of land grabbing leads to debates around adverse incorporation, which happens when rural populations that go through processes of expropriation are incorporated (through different exploitative mechanisms) into the practices of corporations, markets and value chains, but simultaneously being excluded from the benefits of accumulation processes (Hall et al. 2015; Hickey and Du Toit 2013). These mechanisms can include precarious jobs offered by the corporation, unfair contract farming framings, high risks market integration and so on.

Labour dynamics is an issue that is also debated, especially in cases where land is needed, and labour is not, and people end up landless (Li 2011). When labour is not proportionally needed, some rural people become employed while others join the army of a relative surplus population. There are even cases where land is not expropriated but landholders lose control of land (Peluso and Lund 2011).

A range of diverse reactions (resistance and adaptation) from rural populations are considered in the literature (Amanor 2012; Edelman et al. 2013; Hall et al. 2015; Moyo et al. 2012; Shivji 2017; White et al. 2012; Zoomers 2010). Hall et al. (2015) examined the diversity of political reactions from below in the context of dispossession, oppression and social differentiation in the countryside in the midst of the resource rush. These included the dual front of 'struggle against dispossession' and 'struggle against exploitation' and the diverse range of political reactions that went beyond explicit and overt 'resistance', including seeking integration into land deals (Hall et al. 2015).

More recently, the work of pan-Africanist scholars (Amanor 2019; Jha and Yeros 2019; Mazwi et al. 2019) call attention to Global Value Systems (GVSs) as the main feature of contemporary capitalism, where production, processing, distribution and consumption of a single commodity happens in different parts of the globe. By applying this to global agriculture, they put forward the notion of Global Agricultural Value Systems (GAVSs) to further understand processes of global production and consumption, and agrarian change, in the global South, particularly land acquisition and integration schemes (such as contract farming) and their implications for rural populations' survival strategies. By examining USA imperialism and integration of smallholders into agricultural markets and agribusinesses, Amanor (2019) argues that integration schemes lead 'to increasing extraction of surplus by agribusiness and increasing cost of production for the farmer' (Amanor 2019: 30–31).

Shivji (2017) in fact analyses the process of surplus extraction by capital and shows how it is done at the cost of rural working people's necessary consumption. He refers as 'Working people' to the different segments of the rural population which go through exploitation processes, thereby feeding accumulation; thus it is a class against capital, including formal workers, informal workers, peasants, women, rural poor, etc. In this context, the specific positionality of different segments of the working people in rural areas in the context of land grabbing will lead to differentiated positions, reactions and outcomes for rural households. In turn, this is shaped by the specific mechanism of compensation implemented by a particular investment project, including efforts aimed at local community development and corporate social responsibility.

3.2 Segments of the Working People and Terms of Incorporation: Labour, Diversification of Livelihoods, and Gender

Land grabbing entails the separation of people from their means of production as put forward by Marx (1889), who underlined the role of industrialisation in absorbing the so-called 'relative surplus population' that was constituted by peasants 'free' of land and 'free' to sell their labour. Current dynamics of expropriation show very complex contextual and historical specificities regarding the interrelation of labour dynamics, on- and off-farm activities, and gendered (and other identity-based) inequalities in shaping rural livelihood strategies.

Shivji (1987) explains that capital maximises its rate of exploitation by letting peasants retain their means of production and retain control over the labour process so that the costs of peasant reproduction are carried out by the peasants themselves. Additionally, he (Shivji 2017) points out cases where men become semi-proletarianised by working in plantations and women remain 'peasantised', with both subsidising capital as both live 'sub-human' lives 'while exerting super-human labour'.

A very specific feature of some African countries, conditioned by the model of colonisation, is the diversification of rural livelihoods. Bryceson (1990) claims that 'rural income diversification' entails the 'expansion of rural dwellers' income sources away from own farm labour' (Bryceson 1990: 172). Referring to the agrarian class structure, scholars speak about the changing division of labour based on diversification of rural livelihoods, with proletarianisation being of significance (O'Laughlin 1996; Wuyts 2001). As highlighted by Moyo et al. (2012), 'multi-occupational' livelihoods and 'semi-proletarianisation' have deepened over a number of decades, with smallholders practicing more than just subsistence production.

In the context of wage employment, Gyapong (2020) studied the implications of the global land rush on wage labour, examining the 'job creation rhetoric under a laissez-faire investment environment' (Gyapong 2020: 4). She confirmed that policy frameworks that emphasise the employment potentials of large-scale agricultural investments usually go hand in hand with legislation that facilitates capital accumulation. As a result, 'non-inclusive' or 'inadequate' labour regulations do not provide a basis for creating long-term employment benefits, at least in the case of large-scale agricultural land investment.

Overall, diversification of rural livelihoods calls for attention to the gendered division of labour within the household. Gender relations strongly shape the outcomes of land grabbing at local levels. Many cases show that men usually become gainfully incorporated through employment and other mechanisms, while women are further excluded from these processes and gender inequalities are intensified (Gyapong 2020; Hall et al. 2015; Julia and White 2012; Levien 2017; Tsikata and Yaro 2014). Tsikata (2016) looks specifically at how gendered land tenure systems have contributed to the disadvantages of rural women's livelihoods. She points out the importance of recognising the importance of the gendered division of labour in reproduction and in the control of resources, as this affects how women experience processes of land grabbing, implying higher levels of exploitation for this segment of the working people. Additional exploitation of women often takes place in the process of subsidising capital (Shivji, 2017).

As well, Tsikata and Yaro (2014) underline how pre-existing gender inequalities and gender biases embedded in the investment projects are implicated in post-project livelihood activities. They argue that even projects that seemingly include mechanisms of community inclusion might fall short of protecting women's livelihoods or even limit female access to opportunities if these pre-existing inequalities are not addressed. In the context of incorporation of smallholder farmers into global circuits of accumulation, Torvikey et al. (2016) bring to the fore how men and women are positioned differentially in terms of out-grower value chain employment benefits, as men occupy higher earning positions on permanent contracts, whereas women as disposable casual workers.

Beyond the labour needs specific to each investment or process of dispossession and the class and gender/identity dynamics prevailing, it is important to understand the institutional context in which land grabbing happens. The role of the state, property relations, customary rights and legislation shape land grabbing processes, outcomes, implications and reactions from below.

4 Neoliberal Agrarian Policies and Forest Plantations in Mozambique: The Case of Portucel

4.1 Brief Historical Background, Rural Settings and Rural Livelihoods

There are five main characteristics of colonial exploitation in Mozambique (Serra 2000): (1) export of labour force; (2) production and export of low-processed agricultural commodities such as sugar, tea, sisal, copra, cotton and others in a not substantive amount; (3) imposition of taxes; (4) use of seasonal labour; and, (5) preservation of small-scale family production for subsistence. Labour force exploitation was one of the main strategies of colonial Portugal and of foreign capital concessions in colonial Mozambique—which shaped dynamics of semi-proletarianisation among the peasantry. In the period from 1930 to 1970, Portuguese colonialism intensified the integration of peasants into the global capitalist economy, including transforming native Mozambicans from the southern parts into a labour reserve for South African mining capital. Meanwhile, the centre and north of the country were turned into a plantation economy and family sector as producers of food and cash crops for the external market (Serra 2000).

The first scramble for Africa shaped agrarian societies into what they look like today. Historical processes of agrarian transformation as a result of colonialism and imperialism are still present, at least implicitly, particularly with regards to rural livelihoods, land distribution and vulnerabilities. In the specific case of Mozambique, the imposition of taxes on the native population alongside labour exploitation and taxes and dividends from the concession of land to foreign investors through the plantation economy were the main features of Portuguese colonialism in Mozambique. Semi-proletarianisation started right after the intensification of gold demand from the Portuguese crown when peasants would divide their time between the gold mines and their farms for subsistence. This historical path set the stage for multiple changes in rural livelihoods in the country. In this light, current market integration and diversification of rural livelihoods while maintaining smallholders' link to the land in order to provide them with a level of subsistence is a clear continuity of colonialism. Maintaining smallholders' farming of land for food and, simultaneously, exploiting their labour, was and is a strategy of the capitalist classes to subsidise and smoothen their own activities and capital accumulation.

Two aspects of the colonial economic structure are worth underlining: (1) dependency of South African capitalism on Mozambique in relation to transit transport services (ports and railways) and the supply of migrant labour, and (2) colonial Mozambique's production of primary commodities destined for exports (cashew, cotton, sugar, copra and tea) (Bowen 2000: 27–28). These constitute the base for the emergence of the current extractivist model of development existing in Mozambique, which shapes households' local economies and rural development trajectories. According to Wuyts, these features resulted in three main clusters of livelihood strategies for the peasantry, namely: (i) selling crops to the market, (ii) selling labour (to plantations in the North and Centre regions, and as a labour reserve for South African mining), and (iii) practicing agriculture for own consumption.

After independence, peasants engaged even further in diversified strategies of livelihoods, which, from the perspective of O'Laughlin (2002), expresses the peasantry's agency in resisting and creating their own paths of livelihoods and survival. Forced labour and forced cropping, as well as resistance to both of these forms of coercion, as well as ongoing processes of commodification and proletarianisation, hence go some way in explaining the current complexities of multiple livelihoods in rural Mozambique.

With the adoption of the Bretton Woods institutions' structural adjustment programmes, the Mozambican economy took a neoliberal turn which only intensified after the 2000s. High levels of foreign direct investment (FDI), engaged in extract-and-export schemes, directed both to the extractive industry and the agricultural sector, made Mozambique one of the main targets of land grabbing in the last decade (Land Matrix[1]). Rural development and livelihoods are being highly shaped by these dynamics, as evidenced by the foreign investments of Portucel Moçambique and the implications of its land acquisition model and social development plan for the district of Ile.

[1] https://landmatrix.org/map/

4.2 *Portucel Moçambique, Land Acquisition Model and Social Development Plan*

Forest plantations were introduced in the country around the 1920s as part of colonial economic policy. In the post-colonial socialist period, plantations were part of the agrarian policy, but this intensified recently with the emphasis on neoliberal policies that now guide the Mozambican Government. As well, forest plantations were included in the narratives of climate change mitigation and were introduced as part of the national strategy to mitigate climate change, specifically the REDD+ (MITADER 2016).

In this context, Portucel Moçambique (with 20 per cent of its shares belonging to the World Bank's International Finance Corporation) initiated one of the largest megaprojects in Mozambique and the largest in the agricultural sector, not only in terms of the size of the land occupation but also in terms of volume of investment (around 2.5 billion USD). The Navigator Company (formerly Portucel Soporcel group) is currently one of the world's largest producers of bleached eucalyptus pulp (BEKP) and the first European producer of uncoated fine printing and writing paper (UWF). It began its activities in 2009, grabbing, with the support of the State, over 350,000 hectares of land in the Zambézia and Manica provinces. In Zambézia, the company focused on two districts, Ile and Namarroi (a total of 173,327 hectares), predicting a plantation of approximately 120,000 hectares of eucalyptus trees.

The company was authorised to acquire 356,000 hectares of land in Mozambique for 50 renewable years (i.e. this can be renewed and extended if the company complies with its proposed exploration plan) and to plant approximately two-thirds of the area. According to the company's plan, the first phase of the investment includes the plantation of a forest base of about 40,000 hectares alongside the supply of a eucalyptus wood chip production unit (to be built) which will guarantee the export of around one million tons per year. The second phase would comprise the expansion of the forest base to 160,000 hectares and the construction of an industrial pulp production unit.[2]

As an estimate, around 25,000 families were resident on those 356,000 hectares. Up to 2019, around 3500 families have had shares of their land 'transferred' to Portucel (but with exceptional cases of total land transferred). Portucel has managed to plant only 13,500 hectares of eucalyptus in both provinces, but most of Portucel's activities are concentrated in Zambezia province. It is in Zambezia that the company installed its nursery, one of the biggest in Africa, that feeds the plantations of both provinces and occupies an area of 7.5 hectares (with an annual installed production capacity of more than 12 million clonal eucalyptus plants).

Contrary to the Mozambican Land Law, Portucel's land occupation model does not involve resettlement. It negotiated with the Ministers' Council that, in exchange for the land, it would offer employment and implement a Social Development

[2]http://www.portucelmocambique.com/Portucel-Mocambique

Plan—the Portucel Social Development Plan (PSDP)—for the communities residing in both provinces. The plan aims to invest US$40 million to improve the living conditions of approximately 25,000 families residing in the company's areas.

The main objective of the PSDP, from the company's perspective, is to create and share value and prosperity with local communities through forest plantation investments and by way of (1) training on farming techniques (Climate Smart Agriculture); (2) distribution of livestock and seeds; (3) construction of barns; (4) water holes; and (5) construction and rehabilitation of roads and bridges. The company claims that about 5800 families and 115 communities in the Provinces of Manica and Zambézia have already benefitted from the PSDP, which has been implemented since 2015.

Besides not resettling the households whose land has been 'transferred' to the company, one very important process that was not fully respected by the company is the legal requirement of 'community consultation'. The Land Law and its statutes state that any household that is about to transfer land to another individual or company should be properly consulted, present and state their consent, and accept the compensation for the loss of land (either new areas to reside or other types of compensation).

This procedure was not met. The company and the government organised consultations after granting the land to the company. These consultations did not involve negotiating the transfer of land. Rather, what was negotiated was how much land each household would be willing to transfer in exchange for being incorporated into the PSDP or to gain employment. Additionally, not all households were consulted, such that some went through the expropriation of land without ever being informed about the conditions of the transfer. In the main, community leaders and local rural elites were present in such meetings and not ordinary smallholders.

Overall, two main deviations from the law were apparent during the process of land acquisition. The first was the decision about 'no resettlement policy' for the local smallholders, and the second was the non-inclusive and non-participatory nature of the consultation process (entailing limited or no negotiation and consent). The process was a top-down one with high levels of imposition.

5 Implications and Reactions of the Working People

5.1 *Neoliberal Authoritarianism and Marginalisation of Local Needs*

The historical path of imposing agricultural policies with no regard to existing peasant economies and the overall agrarian question of the country is systematically marginalising rural households. Data from interviews confirmed that the land occupation process undertaken by Portucel did not follow the Land Law (and its recognition of customary rights) and that the project was implemented in an authoritarian and undemocratic way—as most of the households were not consulted and some did not even give consent to 'transfer' the land. As indicated, the Mozambican Land Law states that the transfer of land rights first requires public consultation with current landholders. Multiple heads of households claim that not only were they not consulted but that, even if they disagreed or protested the land acquisition by the company, they were still going to lose the land. Also, the repressive character of the government itself regarding any negative reactions on the part of smallholder farmers was a consistent issue during the land acquisition process. As one peasant women said:

> We were not consulted at all. We would just see machines coming and cleaning our land for their own ends. If you wanted to complain the leader would come and would tell you that the land is not ours, the land belonged to the Government and God. And they would come in, cutting down everything... Even if you protest, they wouldn't accept. (Expropriated peasant woman, Ile, 2019)

During the interviews, a concurrent question asked of those who had been disposed of land related to their feelings towards the investment being implemented in their areas. A consistent answer was that eucalyptus does not constitute a priority, as the priority would be to produce food instead (as '*eucalyptus does not kill hunger*', in the words of one smallholder). Clearly, this was not taken into account when the decision was made by the Mozambican government to agree to Portucel's project. The plantation investment privileges external investors' will to accumulate and international market demand for primary commodities. Certainly, local needs and priorities do not constitute the central agenda of this project, as smallholders were actually marginalised and their aspirations ignored.

One might argue that it would be through incorporation into the PSDP that the local population would benefit from food production, income-generating projects and other projects that aim to bring about social and community development. However, again, the design, planning and implementation of the PSDP were insensitive to smallholder viewpoints and the livelihood concerns of affected households. The PDSP was designed in a top-down manner without fully considering the priorities and aspirations of the local population. One example of this was the introduction of new crops by distributing new seeds that were not a part of the local households' diet or that did not grow properly in their soils such that, consequently, food production was undermined. During one interview, a head of household claimed that locals wanted an orange agro-processing unit since the region produces significant volumes of oranges that end up rotting. However, no development assistance in this regard has been forthcoming.

5.2 *Inefficient and Insufficient Compensation for the Loss of Livelihoods*

The PSDP constituted a set of projects to be implemented in order to compensate for the loss of land and forest resources incurred by rural households. These projects were expected to provide agricultural inputs and technical assistance. Multiple promises were used to 'convince' households to transfer their land, at least for those few who were actually consulted (and not regarding the implementation of the project itself, but merely regarding the transfer of land). A consistent feature emerging from the interviews with all segments of the working people was that Portucel had failed to keep its promises, such as employment, distribution of seeds and improvement of overall livelihoods conditions. To quote one local:

> They promised us a lot of benefits... for 50 years! So, I thought even when I die and my grandchildren will still benefit from this. And we started to "give" our land... But we don't see all of those things they promised; ... even they said they would bring seeds, but we have been receiving only 1 or 2 kilogrammes per household per year. They also promised us goats, pots and other things. These promises are yet to be fulfilled. (Expropriated peasant man, Ile, 2019)

Although some rural households acknowledge that they have been receiving seeds and technical assistance, they complain that the seeds were insufficient for the needs of each household, were distributed late in the season and/or they were not appropriate for the edapho-climatic conditions of the region:

> Yes, they distributed seeds including beans and maize. But because the soil is not compatible, they have to change to other seeds that are compatible here;... most of us are asking for seeds that are compatible to our land. For example, peanuts, beans [would be better], because maize does not grow here, maybe with manure. (Community Leader, Ile, 2019)

Most of the households interviewed claimed that one of the reasons why they did not protest and thereby allowed their land to be 'transferred' to Portucel, was because they believed that the company would provide permanent employment for at least one person in each household, which would allow them to have a fixed monthly income that could compensate losing part of their land. Nevertheless, most of the households (around 80 per cent) only had access to casual work or did not have access to work at all. Most of the interviewees who had access to casual work said that it did not compensate at all for the loss of land as they would work on average one to two months, earning 170 Meticais a day (around 2 to 3 USD):

> Yes, I worked there, maybe for a month or so. With the money I bought salt and food. I couldn't even buy a bicycle, because the money was so little... Life got worse;... before we were able to produce in our farms, even to sell produce. After Portucel came, everything stopped, [I] can't even produce cassava, can't get any money, nothing. Before I could even buy clothes for my children, buckets, plates, pots.... (Expropriated Peasant woman, Ile, 2019)

Besides having lost their land with insufficient compensation for their losses, households went through a loss of access to forest resources as a result of the company's deforestation. Those forest resources such as mushrooms and small animals highly contributed to meeting their dietary needs, firewood to cook or even grass to build their houses—all central to local livelihoods and social reproduction. The implementation of the project thus seriously curtailed access to such resources. However, not all rural households were affected in the same way, so the next section focusses on differentiated implications and responses by distinct segments of the working people.

6 Differentiated Reactions and Implications for Differentiated Segments of the Working People

Overall, as discussed, the process of land expropriation provided unfair and insufficient compensation for rural households in a context where their voices were not heard. With exception of local elites, there was a convergence among the interviewees that the PSDP and the employment opportunities provided by the company were insufficient to cover their losses. The process of land acquisition was negatively perceived by most households and is believed to have intensified localised poverty.

The affected rural households did not constitute a homogeneous class. On the contrary, factors such as class, gender, kinship, and age differentiated the working people into distinct groups that went through differentiated experiences, terms of incorporation and outcomes with reference to the process of land grabbing. More broadly, regarding global processes, pre-existing inequalities within rural societies shape the dynamics of incorporation and condition the experiences of each segment of the working people. At the same time, the segments of working people are not clearly delimited and segregated. The categories present grey boundaries, and households may migrate from one segment to another or even belong to multiple segments.

The key distinctions were made in relation to similarities and differences in terms of experiences and outcomes vis-à-vis the neoliberal land grabbing process. I thus identified the following four segments of the working people and discussed their specific experiences and terms of incorporation: (1) wage workers; (2) poorer peasants; (3) women; and (4) local elites.

Wage workers are a significant segment of the working people because the company was able to provide employment for rural households with permanent jobs mostly as guards, nursery workers, and '*agentes de ligação*' (i.e. men that liaise between community and the company) as well as seasonal workers for the plantations. Gender inequalities are very clear and culturally present in this particular area and, because women usually undergo multiple forms of marginalisation within and outside the community, it is indeed relevant to underline their experiences.

Local elites, who are influential members of the rural population, are likely to constitute the better off segment of the working people, retaining power nowadays as a result of localised historical dynamics. This group of individuals is a product of pre-colonial, colonial and post-independence rural structures and traditional native leadership, and they have access to conditions for accumulating from below based on owning large plots of land or by advantageously taking over colonial investments in the post-independent period after the Portuguese flee the country or even via links to the revolutionary force—Frelimo (the party in power since independence).

6.1 Permanent Wage Workers: More Land, More Benefits

Most of the households employed by the company were casual workers, who only worked once or twice to prepare and clean plots of land before planting and did not work for the company again. This labour relation did not have a significant impact on their livelihoods. The story about permanent workers, whether with or without a formal contract, is somewhat different. These are usually men who had relatively large plots of land (prior to Portucel) that were not in use or used as fallows in preparation for subsequent seasons or to distribute among the next generation.

Because they owned more land than relatively poorer peasants, they were able to transfer relatively larger plots of land to the company and remain with relatively enough smaller plots for their own subsistence. They tended to be the first to be called and offered a permanent job. Being employed means that they get a fixed monthly income that is partially invested in their farmland (inputs and labour), and they are able to produce enough food and cash crops to sell in the markets. They began to hire-in labour (approximately 5 to 8 people, usually women and poorer peasants) plus making use of the labour of their wives, for their farms. Beyond this, they receive seeds and usually technical assistance for their farms as part of the PSDP, which poorer peasants do not (the more land you give, the more you are prioritised in the PDSP activities as well).

However, accumulation from below and significant life improvements were not confirmed during the interviews with these permanent workers. These wage workers would acknowledge the benefits of a monthly salary but would complain about the burden of work versus the amount of money they receive. A permanent worker—a guard—oversees 48 blocks of eucalyptus and controls fires. These workers need a cellphone and a bicycle to do the work, but they have to buy these themselves. Some are able to, and some are not, and they have to walk long distances to take care of distant blocks of eucalyptus. One guard highlighted:

> My life has gotten better. Now I can buy things for my children that I wasn't able to buy before, like radio, bicycle… Before I was working with no formal contract, until 2018. But I receive the same salary since 2018: 4200 Meticais [around USD 62] per month. They say the salary depends on the Government; [my salary would improve] if the Government raises the salary [official minimum wage]. But as my wife works in the farm [his land] with some people we hired, we manage to get produce to sell in the market. (Portucel Guard, Ile, 2019)

Although they have access to more money, the overall household expenses are still not fully met. They have to compensate with overexploitation of their own labour, including the wives' agricultural labour and the latter's contribution to social reproduction. So, they end up subsidising capital via self-exploitation:

> Since I started working in the company my life improved, not totally, but at least the minimum. But the negative part is the working time [the load of work]. We can't add our value to the community and have businesses that help the community grow… I was working in the field and lost my phone. It costs 600 Meticais and I receive 500 or 400 Meticais. I am not going to be able to buy a new one. We want a salary that enables us to grow. It is hard to wake up and go to my farm at 4 am to 7 am and then go work the rest of the day for the company. (Portucel Worker, Ile, 2019)

Although many permanent wage workers have connections to local elites by kinship, most of them do not own enough means of production to accumulate from below as the local elites do easily. They might be better off than many other segments (such as poorer peasants and women), but they still struggle to fulfill their livelihoods and social reproduction needs. They do this by further self-exploitation. They claim that they want better terms of incorporation, but their current economic status inhibits any struggle on their part against dispossession or protests against Portucel.

6.2 *Poorer Peasants: Intensified Drudgery and Self-Exploitation*

This segment is constituted by smallholders who always owned relatively less land and did not have links with local elites. Before the company arrived, most of them practised subsistence agriculture and maybe eventually would sell any surplus (if there were any) in the market. Because of the PSDP promises (including about employment) that were made by the company, most transferred their land to the company (for some, they were forcedly expropriated), ending up with not enough land to survive or even with no land at all. For those who were 'lucky' to be called for casual work, they also experienced labour exploitation:

> They want us to work from dawn to dusk. It is very hard work, and the pay is low, does not compensate and we are not happy with that, the money is so little. They hire us to work only a few days and then try to make [through severe labour demands] the most of our work during each day from dawn to dusk. (Expropriated peasant man, Ile, 2019)

Nowadays, this segment of the working people is experiencing intensified poverty and food insecurity and has had to adopt other livelihood strategies for survival. The most common strategies include: (1) selling labour to better off households (permanent wage workers or rural elites); (2) borrowing or renting land from family or other members of the community; (3) engaging in migrant work; and (4) migrating permanently.

In going through the dispossession of most of their land (or all of it), poorer peasants are encountering significant difficulties in securing food. This is exacerbated by the rupture of access to forest resources to meet their food needs (including hunting small animals and collecting mushrooms), which was a key livelihoods strategy before the deforestation undertaken by Portucel. Additionally, the smaller plots of land that were left are surrounded by eucalyptus plantations and do not register the same levels of productivity as before—particularly given the current competition for water and destruction of ecosystems and soil nutrients as a result of land intensification from the forest plantation.

6.3 *Women: Exclusion and Sub-Human Lives*

Although women and poorer peasants present many similarities in terms of implications of the process of expropriation, and many unmarried or widowed women are part of the poorer peasant segment, there are very relevant specificities that should be underlined. More so than men, women interviewed claimed that they were not consulted before the company occupied their lands. This may be explained with respect to the gender inequalities in rural Mozambique, as traditional and customary cultural habits usually exclude women from decision-making processes. This involves excluding women from meetings with outsiders and the government in deciding the future of the community. Usually men, mostly elite men, are present in such meetings and in contributing to the decision-making process. Even in ensuring that women (in one particular community) were interviewed for this study, men (particularly the community leader) had to be present.

In relation to labour dynamics, many women interviewed were employed by the company as casual workers rather than long-term, permanently or formally. Also, they were badly paid, as one women noted: '*I worked for less than a month. With the money I bought salt and food. Didn't even buy a bicycle. The money just wasn't enough*'. Usually, members of their families (husband, sons, nephews, sons-in-law) were employed instead of them, who owned the land in the first place. A community leader in Ile explained that, in his view, (usually older) women that transferred their land should transfer their casual job opportunity ('offered' by the company as an exchange for her land) to young and capable men, who in the end, will share the remuneration with her in half. On a woman's behalf, he explains this situation as follows:

> She [previous land owner] and her daughter gave their land [to Portucel]. But because they are women, they can't handle this type of job, only men can handle [it]. After the men got the job [casual employment], they shared the income in half. One half for them [women land owner] as land owners and the other half for the men that worked... For the other one [another woman that was present at the meeting] as well, because they don't have sons, don't have men in their families, it was the same process. (Community Leader, Ile, 2019)

Noticeably, though, many women in other communities were able to access casual employment at Portucel. This shows how opportunities may be grabbed from women by men due to localised systems of gender inequality.

As noted, one of the strategies of poorer (male) peasants was to migrate or move to peri-urban areas to look for employment; meanwhile, their wives stayed on the land and became fully responsible for both household social reproduction and farm work. For example, before Portucel expropriated their land, Dona Deolinda and her husband would work on the farm with the help of people who would get paid for their labour in exchange for food (from the farm). After Portucel and the loss of land, her husband went to the city looking for jobs in construction while she stayed at home farming on borrowed land and offering and hiring out her labour to better off households from the village. Seemingly living under sub-human conditions, Dona

Deolinda and other women experience significant burdens and a very precarious existence, and she lamented:

> It's bad. I don't have anything. Not cassava, anything. I don't understand why cassava and beans do not grow next to the eucalyptus; it absorbs all the water. My husband had to move to the city to work in construction and he sends me a little money that is not enough. I have to work in other people's farms to get some money. (Expropriated Peasant Woman, Ile, 2019)

As a kind of ecological rupture, women spoke of their small plots and gardens right next to the eucalyptus plantation and how this remaining small plot of land did not produce food for subsistence because of the absence of water. Another ecological rupture, as noted, was the lack of access to forest resources, including mushrooms and other edibles. Overall, these women, instead of struggling for better terms of incorporation, would much rather have their land back. As Dona Zita claims: '*I would rather have my land back. They took over our land in vain*'*!*

6.4 Local Elites: Intensification of Social Differentiation by Accumulation from Below

Community leaders (by lineage and kinship) and their relatives, richer/better off peasants (have larger plots of land and livestock), and local government officials constitute rural local elites in the study area. They are usually very influential within the community and are at the forefront of decision-making and negotiation processes with external actors. This puts them in an advantageous position in terms of access to information and eligibility regarding external programmes, and enhances their opportunity of receiving any benefits deriving from such progammes. A clear example of this is the process through which the PSDP was implemented, including the beneficiary selection process.

For the implementation of the PSDP, smallholders were aggregated into groups, and the group leader would benefit from a demonstration plot—a portion of land to implement new farming techniques so that others would follow. For that reason, the group leader would receive seeds and other inputs and any technical assistance necessary to maintain the demonstration plot as an example of improved productivity, thereby facilitating learning by other smallholders. Information from the field confirmed that the most influential members of the community were chosen—they were the ones that met the criteria, including having an ID card and enough land alongside experience with the commercialisation of surplus and a firmly established market network. By interviewing one of the elected leaders, who previously owned the community mill, certain advantages were identified:

> I didn't get employed. My benefit is to be the group leader. With the income I managed to buy a motor pump to irrigate my farms using a solar panel. I thank Portucel for these improvements... What I didn't like is that they didn't keep all promises. Myself, I am fine, but others are sad. If at least they build a hospital, improve schools, build a secondary school for our children .... [it would be better]. (Demonstration Plots Leader, Ile, 2019)

Besides having the privilege of accessing inputs and technical assistance, they have the capacity to hire-in labour to work on their other farmland, where they may also apply these new agricultural practices. Labour availability is crucial in applying these techniques (practices) because they require more work than traditional techniques, and the rest of the smallholders do not have the money to pay for extra hired labour. As one demonstration plot leader highlighted:

> I was chosen to be responsible for a group of 24 farmers. I am responsible for taking care of the demonstration field by introducing new farming techniques. They taught me how to farm using these new techniques. The other 24 hardly make it. Maybe they can apply these new techniques in smaller areas. Because it is hard work [comparing with traditional techniques]. To do half a hectare or one hectare of that is really hard work. I have at least 6 to 8 people working for me and I pay 50 meticais per day. (Demonstration Plot Leader, Ile, 2019)

The efficiency of these demonstration plots has been questioned because most smallholders are not even able to reproduce the new techniques. Also, it is clear how unevenly distributed these 'benefits' from PSDP are on the ground. In certain cases, some local elites have benefitted both by being employed and at the same time holding a demonstration plot, which will further allow accumulation from below. Because of this uneven distribution of benefits, the company is able to form alliances and ensure that the local elites are on their side. In a way, this unfair incorporation of local elites into the process facilitates the company's modus operandi and undercuts resistance from within the community.

7 Reactions and Resistance from Below

Differentiated reactions from different segments of the working people were observed. There was a mix of struggles, from improved incorporation into the Portucel process to struggles against dispossession caused by Portucel. With the exception of local elites, it is clear that a significant share of households is not satisfied and is to some extent frustrated with the process of land expropriation and the ensuing compensation, including in relation to the implications arising from the implementation of this project—economic, social and environmental implications. So, some unorganised, covert and unstructured forms of resistance are unfolding, resembling Scott's (1989) everyday forms of resistance.

Complaints and badmouthing are very common when people refer to the company and the company's practices, even in conversations with 'outsiders'. Further than that, the guards registered multiple cases of people quietly cutting down eucalyptus trees as a form of protest. There is also evidence of starting fires deliberately in order to destroy large hectarages of eucalyptus plantations in different parts of the region, either because the smallholders did not receive compensation or because they wanted their land back. One woman expressed her frustration and anger in the following way:

> Nothing got better. We are here crying. We want our land back to farm because we see nothing now. They fooled us and brought nothing that they had promised. They said they would bring zinc plates for our homes, that we would benefit from this company for 50 years and so on. Nothing was done. That is why we are crying. Even the seeds they promised, they don't bring them anymore. And then I think "why did I accept this transfer of land in the first place?". (Expropriated Peasant Woman, Ile, 2019)

Some smallholders feel that they still need to be compensated or at least compensated more fully. But others, mainly women, would rather have their land back so that they are able to farm again and get their food and life back. A sense of injustice is shared among most of the households, even the ones that got some benefits out of the programme, because they are all able to grasp that the community is only receiving a small share of the pie. Hence, they feel they deserve more:

> Why doesn't the company hire us from the community to do the jobs that their technicians and their contractors [outsourcing of planting eucalyptus] do? The money they pay these out-comers they could be paying us. Why do we, land owners, have to suffer in order to gain something? The contractors receive 40,000 or even 50,000 meticais and community members work and receive only 700 meticais. This creates adversity in the community. We already transferred our land, where our children would be producing. But now, someone else is making profit out of it. We feel very sad. When we work there [casual work] they come and abuse us, insult us, offend our people working there. We already complained to the company and called them out in order for them to change this situation. The community is crying, is still crying. It is sad. If we transferred the land it is because we were afflicted, we needed help. We are not against the company, we are against seeing other people benefitting from this project, not us. (Portucel Worker "Agente de ligação", Ile, 2019)

8 Conclusion

The current global resource rush under neoliberal policies is reshaping rural settings and livelihoods, claiming to be promoting rural employment and social development. However, many studies reveal patterns of dispossession, exclusion and intensification of poverty in rural areas. Corporations (such as Portucel) have been implementing social development plans in order to incorporate rural households into the process of development and thereby improve their livelihoods, though without always taking into account pre-existing rural structures and dynamics. Trends indicate that such mechanisms of incorporation are not improving the rural livelihoods of smallholders as they rather constitute a consolidated mechanism for the legitimation of capital accumulation and land gabs. Moreover, most smallholders end up adversely incorporated into foreign investment-led rural development, ultimately resulting in the inclusion of the few and the exclusion of the majority.

The findings for this study of Mozambique showed that different segments of the rural population experienced Portucel's social development plans differently, conditioned by the pre-existing rural structures and inequalities. In this way, intra-community relations and inequalities exacerbate the implications of dispossession and expropriation. Local elites were able to be incorporated insofar as they showed signs of accumulation from below. Workers, poorer peasants and women underwent exploitation of their labour to feed the accumulation of the company and the local elites. The weight and costs of social reproduction were further transferred and carried ultimately by women, who were excluded the most from the process.

Because of differentiated experiences and outcomes regarding the process of land grabbing and the mechanism of incorporation, different reactions and struggles arose. A mix of struggles against dispossession (and wanting their land back) and struggles for better terms of incorporation appear in the different segments of the working people. Struggles against dispossession prevailed in particular amongst the most marginalised segments, whereas struggles for better terms of incorporation were identified in better off segments.

Overall, it is important to underline that both pre-existing structures and inequalities and the mechanism of incorporation heavily condition the outcomes of land grabbing and the reactions from below. This is because they determine both the level of exclusion that each segment experiences as well as the compensation for their losses resulting from expropriation. This chapter demonstrates and strengthens the argument that the working people are not a homogenous class in rural spaces. The struggles of different segments of this class may diverge, converge and overlap and they may differ in reactions and implications.

References

Ali R, Stevano S (2019) Work in the agro-industry, livelihoods and social reproduction in mozambique: beyond job creation. In: *IDeIAS* (No. 121)

Amanor KS (2012) Global resource grabs, agribusiness concentration and the smallholder: two west African case studies. J Peasant Stud 39(3–4):731–749. https://doi.org/10.1080/03066150.2012.676543

Amanor KS (2019) Global value chains and agribusiness in Africa: upgrading or capturing smallholder production? Agrar South J Pol Econ 8(1–2):30–63. https://doi.org/10.1177/2277976019838144

Bennett A, George AL (2005) Case studies and theory development in the social sciences. MIT Press, Cambridge, MA

Boeije H (2002) A purposeful approach to the constant comparative method in the analysis of qualitative interviews. Qual Quant 36(4):391–409. https://doi.org/10.1023/A:1020909529486

Borras SM, Franco JC (2012) Global land grabbing and trajectories of Agrarian change: a preliminary analysis. J Agrar Chang 12(1):34–59. https://doi.org/10.1111/j.1471-0366.2011.00339.x

Borras SM, Franco JC (2013) Global land grabbing and political reactions "from below". Third World Q 34(9):1723–1747. https://doi.org/10.1080/01436597.2013.843845

Bowen ML (2000) The state against the peasantry: rural struggles in colonial and postcolonial Mozambique. University Press of Virginia, London

Bryceson D (1990) Food insecurity and the social division of labour in Tanzania, 1919–1985. Springer, Cham

Chambati W, Mazwi F, Mberi S (2018) Agrarian accumulation and peasant resistance in Africa. In: inclusive development in Africa: transformation of global relations. African Institute for South Africa & CODESRIA, Dakar/Pretoria. https://doi.org/10.1080/03056244.2015.1049520

Edelman M, Oya C, Borras SM (2013) Global land grabs: historical processes, theoretical and methodological implications and current trajectories. Third World Q 34(9):1517–1531. https://doi.org/10.1080/01436597.2013.850190

Gyapong AY (2020) Political dynamics of global land grabs: exploring the land-labour nexus on Ghana's eastern corridor. Erasmus University Rotterdam, The Hague

Hall R, Edelman M, Borras SM, Scoones I, White B, Wolford W (2015) Resistance, acquiescence or incorporation? An introduction to land grabbing and political reactions 'from below'. J Peasant Stud 42(3–4):467–488. https://doi.org/10.1080/03066150.2015.1036746

Hall R, Scoones I, Tsikata D (2017) Plantations, outgrowers and commercial farming in Africa: agricultural commercialisation and implications for agrarian change. J Peasant Stud 44(3):515–537. https://doi.org/10.1080/03066150.2016.1263187

Hickey S, Du Toit A (2013) Adverse incorporation, social exclusion, and chronic poverty. CPRC Working paper 81. Chronic Poverty Research Centre. Manchester University

INE (2012) Estatisticas do Distrito de ille. Novembro, 2013. www.ine.gov.mz

Jha P, Yeros P (2019) Global agricultural value systems and the south: some critical issues at the current juncture. Agrar South J Pol Econ 8(1):14–29. https://doi.org/10.1177/2277976019851929

Julia, White B (2012) Gendered experiences of dispossession: oil palm expansion in a Dayak Hibun community in West Kalimantan. J Peasant Stud 39(3–4):995–1016. https://doi.org/10.1080/03066150.2012.676544

Levien M (2017) Gender and land dispossession: a comparative analysis. J Peasant Stud 44(6):1113–1136. https://doi.org/10.1080/03066150.2017.1367291

Li TM (2011) Centering labor in the land grab debate. J Peasant Stud 38(2):281–298. https://doi.org/10.1080/03066150.2011.559009

Marx K (1889) Capital: a critical analysis of capitalist production, London

Mazwi F, Chemura A, Mudimu G, Chambati W (2019) Political economy of command agriculture: a state-led contract farming model. Agrar South J Pol Econ 8:232–257. https://doi.org/10.1177/2277976019856742

MITADER Forest Investment Plan (FIP) for Mozambique (2016) Second draft. UT-REDD. Ministry of Land, Environment and Rural Development (MITADER). Available at http://www.redd.org.mz/uploads/SaibaMais/ConsultasPublicas/Proposta%20do%20Plano%20de%20Investimento%20do%20FIP.pdf. Accessed 1 Sep 2019

Moyo S, Yeros P, Jha P (2012) Imperialism and primitive accumulation: notes on the new scramble for Africa. Agrar South J Pol Econ 1(2):181–203. https://doi.org/10.1177/227797601200100203

O'Laughlin B (1996) Through a divided glass: dualism, class and the agrarian question in Mozambique. J Peasant Stud 23(4):1–39. https://doi.org/10.1080/03066159608438618

O'Laughlin B (2002) Proletarianisation, agency and changing rural livelihoods: forced labour and resistance in colonial Mozambique. J South Afr Stud 28(3):511–530

Peluso NL, Lund C (2011) New frontiers of land control: introduction. J Peasant Stud 38(4):667–681. https://doi.org/10.1080/03066150.2011.607692

Scott JC (1989) Everyday forms of resistance. Copenhagen J Asian Stud 4:33–62

Serra C (2000) Historia de Mocambique. Univesidade Eduardo Mondlane. Unpublished PhD Thesis

Shivji IG (1987) The roots of the agrarian crisis in Tanzania: a theoretical perspective. East Afr Soc Sci Res Rev III(1):111–133

Shivji IG (2017) The concept of 'working people'. Agrar South J Pol Econ 6(1):1–13. https://doi.org/10.1177/2277976017721318

Shivji IG (2019) Sam Moyo and Samir Amin on the peasant question. Agrar South J Pol Econ 8 (1–2):287–302. https://doi.org/10.1177/2277976019845737

Torvikey GD, Yaro JA, Teye JK (2016) Farm to factory gendered employment: the case of blue skies outgrower scheme in Ghana. Agrar South J Pol Econ 5(1):77–97. https://doi.org/10.1177/2277976016669188

Tsikata D (2016) Gender, land tenure and agrarian production Systems in sub-Saharan Africa. Agrar South J Pol Econ 5(1):1–19. https://doi.org/10.1177/2277976016658738

Tsikata D, Yaro JA (2014) When a good business model is not enough: land transactions and gendered livelihood prospects in rural Ghana. Fem Econ 20(1):202–226. https://doi.org/10.1080/13545701.2013.866261

White B, Borras SM, Hall R, Scoones I, Wolford W (2012) The new enclosures: critical perspectives on corporate land deals. J Peasant Stud 39(3–4):619–647. https://doi.org/10.1080/03066150.2012.691879

Wuyts M (2001) The agrarian question in Mozambique's transition and reconstruction. WIDER Discussion Paper, No. 2001/14. https://www.econstor.eu/bitstream/10419/52819/1/333286502.pdf. Accessed 10 May 2020

Zoomers A (2010) Globalisation and the foreignisation of space: seven processes driving the current global land grab. J Peasant Stud 37(2):429–447. https://doi.org/10.1080/03066151003595325

Socio-Economic Effects of Neoliberal Transformation on Irrigated Agriculture in Eswatini: A Case of Sugarcane Farmers' Groups in the Komati Downstream Development Project

Nicollete Mhlanga-Ndlovu

Abstract Since the early 2000s, the Government of the Kingdom of Eswatini has been implementing neoliberal transformations in the agricultural sector, with the aim of primarily promoting the production of cash crops (mainly sugarcane) through the conversion of subsistence farming into commercial agriculture. The main drivers behind this paradigm shift have been poverty eradication and promotion of food security as well as income generation for livelihoods improvement. Despite the intensification of irrigated agriculture since the 1990s, food security has deteriorated, with many rural communities within Eswatini remaining dependent on food aid as the local cereal production has suffered a massive decline. This has largely been caused by an increased focus on export-oriented strategies compared to food grain production. Based on interviews conducted at the Komati Downstream Development Project, the study shows that neoliberal reforms in Eswatini did not improve food security for the great majority of smallholder producers and that the reforms have exacerbated challenges faced in the sugar industry. The chapter concludes by recommending the strengthening of capacities of farmers' associations for an improvement in sugarcane yields.

1 Introduction

In the Kingdom of Eswatini, agricultural development and policy have evolved over the years resulting in the expansion of the agricultural sector and observable growth in labour productivity. It is critical to conduct an analysis and assessment of recent trends in agricultural development and especially smallholder irrigation agriculture in the country. Such an analysis would enable us to track policy direction, highlight emerging challenges, and identify opportunities for agricultural development innovation. Since the early 2000s, the government of the Kingdom of Eswatini has been

N. Mhlanga-Ndlovu (✉)
Independent Researcher, Manzini, Eswatini

F. Mazwi et al. (eds.), *Capital Penetration and the Peasantry in Southern and Eastern Africa*, Advances in African Economic, Social and Political Development, https://doi.org/10.1007/978-3-030-89824-3_10

implementing neoliberal transformations in the agricultural sector, with the aim of primarily promoting the production of cash crops (mainly sugarcane) through the conversion of subsistence farming into commercial agriculture. The main drivers behind this paradigm shift have been poverty eradication, food security and income generation for the improvement of livelihoods (Terry and Ryder 2007; UNCTAD 2000).

Despite the intensification of irrigated agriculture in the country since the 1990s, food security has deteriorated, with many communities within Eswatini remaining dependent upon food aid, as local cereal production has been dwindling. The sustained focus on export-oriented strategies compared to producing food for local consumption likely contributed to this. The shift from subsistence farming has resulted in major changes in the policy domain, not only in relation to agricultural policies but also to water policies. Although the Kingdom of Eswatini has been hailed as a success story with regards to smallholder irrigated agriculture, its food security status falls short of what is necessary.

This chapter is based on a combination of evidence gleaned from a review of the relevant literature and from interviews held with key informants representing local Farmers' Associations. After discussing, briefly, the neoliberalisation of agriculture in Eswatini in the ensuing section, the chapter offers a review of the sugar industry in Eswatini. This is followed by an examination of neoliberal transformation of agricultural policy pertaining to the production of sugar and, then, an analysis of smallholder sugarcane irrigation schemes and the food insecurity dynamics involved. The chapter concludes by considering the way forward on the issue of out-grower schemes and their influence, especially regarding food security.

2 Sugarcane Production in Eswatini

The Kingdom of Eswatini is a landlocked country located in Southern Africa bordered by South Africa on all but the east, where it borders with Mozambique. With a population of 1.1 million and a Gross Domestic Product (GDP) per capita of US$4146 in 2019, Eswatini is classified as a lower middle-income country (World Bank 2019). The current National Development Strategy expresses the ambition of the country, namely, to be considered amongst the countries with a first-world status by the year 2022. However, progress towards the realisation of this goal has been hampered by sluggish implementation, the 2015/16 El Niño-induced drought as well as volatile transfers from the Southern African Customs Union (SACU) (CIA 2021). In 2018, Eswatini ranked 144 of 189 countries in the Human Development Index (HDI), placing the country in the bottom quintile of the medium human development category (UNDP 2020).

The Eswatini economy and agricultural sector in particular have undergone radical changes since the late 1990s. As a country in transition, several development initiatives encouraging smallholder diversification towards commercial agriculture have been a key feature in Eswatini, and large-scale sugarcane production is a major agricultural activity resulting from these development initiatives (FAO 2015). In the years prior to the 1999 National Development Strategy (NDS), the agricultural policy in Eswatini focused on achieving food security through promoting the cultivation of the national staple crop (maize) as well as increasing export earnings, mainly through sugarcane (AfDB 2002). The implementation strategies at the time included price controls for maize produce, subsidies for agricultural enterprises, free water for sugar cane irrigation, levies on agricultural imports and centralised support for the delivery of agricultural programmes. This meant that the private sector had minimal input into the outcomes of the sector. This was seen as increasingly problematic, and therefore the NDS promoted the transformation of rain-fed subsistence maize farms into irrigated, commercial sugarcane production spaces (Terry and Ryder 2007; FAO 2008).

Sugar is the country's key export commodity, and accounts for over half of Eswatini's agricultural output and contributes about US$285million to the country's GDP (SSA 2018). The industry also absorbs 35 per cent of private-sector wage employment and 11 per cent of national wage employment. At a national level, the crop is now produced on 70,000 hectares (all irrigated), with 6 million tons of sugar produced annually (SSA 2020). The volume of sugar has increased by at least 65 per cent in the last 20 years, largely attributed to governments' expansionist programmes for sugarcane production in the smallholder sector (Eswatini Sugar Association 2020). This expansion is driven by a combination of state and international capital, drawing influence from the World Bank and the International Monetary Fund (IMF), which encouraged the production of export-oriented crops, arguing that this stimulated economic growth (Dubb et al. 2017). The overall sugar production trends are partially climate-related. For instance, the impact of drought conditions in 2015/2016 led to a significant reduction in sugarcane production.

In Eswatini, the significant development of the sugar sub-sector has for many years been stimulated by the preferential access quotas of the European Union (EU) market (Richardson 2012). To take advantage of the preferential access and the competitive prices (two to three times the world market price) offered by this market, the Eswatini government-supported sugarcane production expansion efforts through out-grower production schemes. The first out-grower scheme was established in 1962, but the number of small sugarcane farmers only increased dramatically from the late 1990s to the early 2000s. This was facilitated by the fact that sugar mills were looking to increase their cane output but were restricted by the unavailability of Title Deed Land (Terry and Ogg 2017).

Therefore, thousands of smallholder farmers (who previously relied on rain-fed agriculture on Swazi National Land) were integrated into commercial sugarcane production as part of the government's plans to improve food security through the commercialisation of smallholder agriculture by generating income for smallholder households. Because of this expansion, Eswatini has over the years become the region's largest producer of sugarcane outside South Africa, with sugar accounting for 43 per cent of the country's exports and 50 per cent of the country's foreign exchange (Dubb et al. 2017).

Undoubtedly, smallholder agriculture is the backbone of rural livelihoods in Eswatini, with over 70 per cent of the country's population relying on subsistence farming (WFP 2019). However, the incorporation of smallholders into the sugar industry means that individual households within a chiefdom have had to let go of their family fields in order to join a Farmers' Association (FA). This is land upon which they had been growing maize for household consumption and perhaps a limited cash crop such as cotton for the market. Joining the FA meant that the individual fields were consolidated into a sugar cane farm run by the FA under the guidance of Eswatini Water and Agricultural Development Enterprise (ESWADE), one of the major sugar millers/corporations.

Smallholder growers in Eswatini currently contribute 28 per cent to sugarcane production after miller-owned estates, who contribute 49 per cent (USDA 2019). They have more than tripled their share of sugar production in the last 20 years, with this growth fuelled by commercial investments supported by the government and donors as a means of bringing employment and essential skills into a modernising agricultural and industrial sector. Moreover, this has taken place due to the availability of loans and grants provided by the millers and financial institutions, hence playing a significant role in offering finance to smallholders.

3 Neoliberalisation of Agriculture

Positive effects of sugarcane out-grower schemes on household incomes have been identified elsewhere in sub-Saharan Africa (Herrmann and Grote 2015; Shumba et al. 2011), indirectly addressing food security. However, other studies have reported that cash cropping undermines food and livelihood security as well as nutritional diets, especially for smallholders (Shivji 1992; Moyo 2011; Patnaik 2011; Chambati et al. 2018). Critics of such extroverted production have gone further to argue that it is very labour intensive and places women and children in precarious situations (Mazwi et al. 2020; Shivji 1992).

The dominant narrative paints the sugar industry as a critical component of the Kingdom's agricultural and economic development strategy, demonstrated by the contribution of sugar to infrastructural development, job creation and the balance of payments. Thus, sugar is central to Eswatini's political economy, crucial for government revenue and job creation, and core to attracting foreign investment into the agricultural sector. In fact, the expansion of sugarcane production was implemented on this premise, namely, that it would improve the country's foreign exchange through export earnings and be instrumental in alleviating rural poverty by increasing smallholders' incomes, especially in the Lowveld part of Eswatini.

Neoliberal changes within the agricultural sector of Eswatini have been carried out with the aim of primarily promoting the production of cash crops (mainly sugarcane) through the conversion of subsistence farming into commercial agriculture, thereby reducing and facilitating income generation (Terry and Ryder 2007; UNCTAD 2000). This has been coupled with the need for institutional reforms within the agricultural and water sectors, with decentralisation central to this. Institutional reforms have included the formation of Farmers' Associations, Water Users' Associations, Irrigation Districts, River Basin Authorities and the National Water Authority. Several policies and pieces of legislation had to be reviewed, such as the Irrigation Policy, the Water Act, the Water Policy, Water Pricing Regulations, among others. The main aim has been to allow poor rural communities improved and greater access to public services through what is known as demand-driven development.

Sugarcane was the government's preferred crop in pursuing economic development as it allowed poor farmers to access the credit necessary to venture into commercial (sugarcane) production, ensuring that sugarcane surpassed maize as the main crop grown in rural Eswatini (Terry and Ryder 2007). The ESWADE was then created to enable smallholders to develop a sugarcane farm enterprise as well as cope with the business of budget management, input procurement and irrigation maintenance (Terry and Ryder 2007). Under ESWADE, two major irrigation development projects were developed by the government: the Komati Downstream Development Project (KDDP) and the Lower Usutu Smallholder Irrigation Project (LUSIP). The KDDP and the LUSIP were established to provide technical capacity for the FAs and support them to realise the intended objectives of poverty alleviation, food security and livelihoods' improvement through income generation. More specifically, ESWADE offered an extension and agronomic support to the individual farmers' associations to help them establish and operate these new small-scale commercial sugar cane farms. There are three sugar corporations/mills that grow a substantial portion of Eswatini's sugar cane, and they are supplemented by the increasing acreage managed by smallholder schemes.

Much of the sugarcane growing takes place in deep rural areas where, historically, significant poverty exists, and food security is precarious. Households in these rural communities have pooled their land resources together in forming farmers' associations. Once a FA has been formed, the entity is formally registered as a company where each member is entitled to a shareholding and dividends. They also elect a management committee that directs and steers the affairs of the FA and often times hires a Farm Manager to deal with the technical affairs of the farm. The FAs are considered full legal entities or companies able to bear financial risk. In facilitating the shift from subsistence agriculture to commercial farming in rural areas, the government, through international development agencies, availed capital loans for the establishment of these smallholder sugarcane schemes as well as capacity building initiatives and other incentive mechanisms.

Therefore, the credit funds availed, by in particular the African Development Bank (AfDB) through the government of Eswatini, were disbursed directly to the associations via loans obtained at local financial institutions that were part of the implementation arrangement. The farmers' associations used these funds to carry out the agricultural and infrastructural development necessary to establish commercial sugarcane farms. Furthermore, the associations are required to obtain a sugar quota from the National Sugar Association and then enter into a formal agreement with a sugar mill that has the role of marketing that FA's produce. Additionally, the sugar mill and farmers' association have a stop-order payment arrangement whereby the sugar mill withholds the association's loan repayments from the proceeds from processed sugar that would be due to the farmers' association. Loans to farmers' associations were stipulated to be repaid within five years, but some take up to 13 years to repay their loan. The proceeds from processed sugar that the sugar mill pays to the farmers' association are divided amongst the association's members equally regardless of land contribution.

4 Food Security

Eswatini has made considerable progress with regards to the incidence of poverty, currently standing at 58.9 per cent, following a decline from 69 per cent in 2001 (World Bank 2019). However, poverty is still rife in the rural areas and especially in the Lubombo and Lowveld areas of the country. More specifically, the proportion of people living below the poverty line is most pronounced in the Lubombo region, at 67.3 per cent (MEPD 2019), and thus these people are more vulnerable to food insecurity. Addressing ongoing poverty is critical for socio-economic development, especially in a developing country like Eswatini. This raises crucial questions about the contribution and effectiveness of sugar cane out-grower schemes for poverty reduction and food security initiatives in the country.

According to the 2019 Vulnerability Assessment and Analysis Report (VAAR), there was a marked increase in the population facing severe and acute food insecurity in the 2018/2019 review period, while there was a doubling of the proportion of those in a crisis situation. The main causes of vulnerability are said to be prolonged droughts, significant unemployment and high food prices, not to mention the constant burden of the high prevalence of HIV and AIDS amongst the adult population (Eswatini VAC 2019). The Zero Hunger Strategic Review 2018, completed with the aid of the United Nations World Food Programme, Food and Agriculture Organisation and United Nations Development Programme, confirmed that the country is food insecure and unable to meet the national minimum nutritional requirement for grain or protein sources (Eswatini ZHSR 2018).

As this chapter seeks to show, food insecurity in Eswatini has deepened in recent years because of a turn to neoliberalism in agriculture, and specifically with reference to sugarcane production. The neoliberal economic policy reforms promoted and implemented in the country for over 25 years have not met the intended objectives of poverty eradication and food security. The household-based subsistence farms converted into sugarcane production units have not led to meaningful change in this respect.

Over a number of years now, Eswatini has not been able to meet its cereal requirements, thereby escalating the country's overreliance on South Africa for imports. As was evidenced during the El Niño drought of 2015/16, the country suffered greatly from fluctuating world market prices for agricultural commodities, especially the country's staple, maize (SEPARC 2017). Studies conducted on the impacts of sugarcane production on the natural environment in Eswatini also reveal the replacement of biodiverse agroecosystems with monocultural practices that erode biological diversity, promote pest and disease infestation, deplete soil fertility, and pollute the soil and water through the application of harmful agrochemicals (Mhlanga-Ndlovu and Nhamo 2017).

In this context, the final report of the World Food Summit (1996) states that food security exists when all people at all times have physical and economic access to sufficient, safe and nutritious food to meet their dietary needs and food preferences for an active and healthy life. Understanding the food security outcomes of Eswatini's smallholder sugar arrangements can be a daunting task considering the multiple mechanisms linking smallholder production to food security. This is further complicated by the fact that food security is defined across four pillars (availability, access, utilisation and stability), implying that sufficient quantities of appropriate foods should be consistently available. Availability is the most commonly addressed in studies exploring the influence of out-grower schemes' expansion on food security since the availability of food is expected to decline as land, labour and other resources are diverted from food crops to cash crops. The reduction of land for food crops is of grave concern, as producing additional food for a growing population, while combating poverty and hunger as well as coping with the impacts of climate change is the major challenge facing agriculture in Africa in the coming decades (FAO 2017). This places out-grower schemes/contract farming at the centre of debates on key and appropriate paradigms of food security in most of sub-Saharan Africa.

Therefore, the assumption made by the Eswatini government that engaging smallholder farmers in commercial and irrigated agriculture will help the country achieve food security without addressing the availability aspects of food is a critical oversight. The smallholder sugar cane schemes have been promoted as the vessels for poverty reduction, enhanced food security and diversified rural livelihoods, yet there is little evidence on the ground supporting this bold claim. Instead, food security and livelihoods have shown limited if any improvement.

5 Threats to the Sugar Industry

Although Eswatini's sugar industry is one of the world's leading cost-competitive producers of high-quality sugar, increases in production costs are negatively affecting this competitiveness and are projected to slow down profitability and dampen the industry's sustainability. Sugarcane farmers are facing huge costs of production, especially from electricity costs which come as a result of irrigation. Despite the contribution that has been made by the out-grower schemes of providing market access and other essential services for smallholders, the neoliberal policy underpinning the out-grower schemes has failed to holistically resolve a number of issues, including unemployment, poverty, hunger and social inequality.

The sustainability of the sugar industry is also threatened by changes in the EU's sugar policy, which has resulted in a decline in exports to the EU market, one of Eswatini's main export markets (Richardson 2015). The reforms in the EU's sugar policies include the removal of restrictions for domestic sugar beet production and ending preferential access for sugar imports from least developing countries. The initial implementation of the EU sugar reform between 2006 and 2010 resulted in a 36 per cent reduction in the EU reference price for sugar (Richardson 2012), hitting Eswatini harder than any of the other countries in the region. With the decline in EU exports, Eswatini has become more dependent on regional markets, yet regional markets tend to be highly volatile. Currently, SACU (the regional customs union) serves as the primary market for Eswatini sugar, absorbing 59 per cent in 2019 (SSA 2020).

Further, the sugar industry faces severe threats emanating from climate change effects. Compromised water availability has been cited as a negative factor in the short and medium term for the sugarcane industry due to lowered water availability and rationed irrigation for sugar cane producers. As the frequency and intensity of extreme weather events increases, thereby altering temperatures and rainfall patterns, the sugar cane industry faces long-run sustainability threats with regards to profitability (Mhlanga-Ndlovu and Nhamo 2017). The complex relationship between changing weather patterns and profitability of sugarcane production poses severe challenges for the Eswatini sugar industry and the significant percentage of smallholders who rely on the sugar industry for their livelihoods, especially considering that most sugarcane producers work small farms, at less than 50 hectares.

6 The Case of the Komati Downstream Development Project

This section discusses at a more empirical level the socio-economic impacts of sugarcane production expansion in Eswatini, thereby contributing to the growing literature on the consequences of diverting large-scale subsistence farmland to the production of cash crops. In showing the socio-economic effects of neoliberalism on smallholders, the specific focus is on the Komati Downstream Development Project (KDDP). The project area is located in the lower reaches of the Komati River Basin, stretching from the Nyonyane Sisa Ranch near Madlangempisi to the Mananga border in the northeast corner of the country. This area is characterised by high rates of poverty which are partly due to prolonged and frequent droughts, while the majority of households relied historically on subsistence agriculture for their livelihoods.

The KDDP was conceptualised with the aid of the AfDB in 2001, with the goal of lifting 20,000 people out of poverty by means of commercialising their agricultural activity. The land developed under the KDDP was directly connected to 1800 households. These households were trained and organised into initially 27 farmers' associations by the Swaziland Komati Project Enterprise (SKPE), now known as ESWADE, which was the implementing agency for the government. It aimed to develop and convert 4200 hectares of farmland from rain-fed subsistence agriculture to irrigated, commercial sugarcane farms. This was done in part by providing capital loans and capacity building for agricultural and infrastructural development as well as project management skills to the beneficiaries, thereby intensifying and diversifying their crop production. The stated overall objective was to reduce poverty and transform subsistence farmers into small-scale commercial entrepreneurs with increased household income (AfDB 2002).

In conducting the study of KDDP, the author was able to reach out to five FAs in the month of January 2021 and conducted interviews through the phone and email using a questionnaire administered to farm managers. The names of the FAs interviewed are Calamuva Farmers' Association, Mpofu Farmers' Association, Ayandza Emadvodza Farmers' Association, Bambanani Farmers' Association, and Mangweni Tingonini Famers' Association. In addition, the Emandla Ekuphila Irrigation District Manager responsible for water use monitoring and reporting within the Komati Basin was interviewed. The five FAs interviewed represent about 361 individual members and a corresponding number of individual households which had given up their subsistence farms. The farmed area totals 878.2 hectares of land. The oldest of these associations was established in 1997 and the most recent one in 2013, thus representing about 24 years of experience in the sugarcane industry.

The interviewees all indicated that once a household joins an FA, it is not allowed to withdraw membership. Moreover, there are no mechanisms in place to resolve any social conflicts which might arise within a FA. The respondents indicated that the government terminated the services rendered by ESWADE in the year 2017 due to financial constraints. However, the FA members (i.e. the farmers) and FAs were not ready to operate on their own. The Royal Eswatini Sugar Corporation took over from ESWADE, but its services exclude 'social support' such as addressing any land and membership disputes.

Prior to the formation of the FAs, most members of associations used their land to grow maize, cotton and groundnuts. After joining the farmers' association and converting their land for sugarcane production, households were expected to grow food crops elsewhere or in their backyards and supplement this by purchasing foodstuffs from retail shops in the area (as well as in neighbouring South Africa where prices are cheaper than in Eswatini). As one farmer association put it:

> Although the introduction of sugar production was a welcome development for most farmers in the areas because it enhanced their incomes, the major challenges faced by farmers is that most of their land is now under sugar production leaving them with little or no land to grow crops such as maize. This threatens their food security (Interview with Farmers' Association, January 2021).

An AfDB appraisal document for this project states that some of the farmland (up to 1000 hectares of the 4200 hectares) would be used to grow maize, vegetables and bananas for household consumption with surplus produce sold on the national and regional markets. However, none of the respondents alluded to this provision. On the claim that, as the main cash crop, sugarcane production facilitates income generation at the household level, the respondents indicated that over the years, the income received has not been able to match the high food prices. Additionally, during droughts, food accessibility and availability has been a big challenge, as indicated in the following quotation:

> The over-emphasis and focus on sugarcane has deprived us of growing our own food. As such, we suffer from drought impacts like all other people in the country; yet, we have irrigation infrastructure and water within reach (Interview with Farmers' Association, January 2021).

Available evidence indicates that Eswatini has experienced, for some time now, a severe decline in the output of food crops as the support rendered by the government towards food crop production has diminished (World Bank 2011). The total area under food crops has declined as more farmers are shifting to the cultivation of sugarcane. In particular, the area under maize production has severely declined, while the area under sugarcane production has continued to rise, since the late 1990s. From around 2011, Eswatini's maize production averaged 90,000 tons and, at best, only met approximately 45 per cent of its domestic requirement of 245,000 tons (Mohammed and Dlamini 2018).

The food security concerns are furthermore relevant in light of the severe drought experienced by the entire southern African region in 2015/2016, such that 350,069 people were in need of urgent food assistance (WFP/FAO 2016). The 2015/2016 El Nino-induced drought exacerbated the situation resulting in a 67 per cent drop in maize production in Eswatini, forcing the country to import over 30,000 tons of maize from South Africa and to depend on food aid to supplement the shortfall. It also led to an escalation in the price of maize and other essential food commodities. Moreover, due to drought, sugarcane growers suffered severe losses because of a 15.6 per cent drop in cane production (SEPARC 2017). This reduced smallholder households' incomes accordingly, and, crucially, no compensation was provided for losses incurred due to this extreme weather event. As shown by a number of studies in Tanzania, Kenya and Zimbabwe, the sugar industry is characterised by asymmetrical relations whereby agrarian capital does not compensate farmers during seasons of natural disasters (Martiniello 2016, 2017; Mazwi et al. 2020).

Undoubtedly, frequent droughts, inadequate farming technologies and low investments in agricultural inputs contribute to the decline of production in (largely, rain-fed) maize in Eswatini. However, this decline is also a consequence of the shift of smallholder farmers to supposedly profitable sugarcane production. The country is now a net importer of its major staple, maize, to cover for the massive shortfall of nearly 50 per cent of domestic demand on average. Eswatini's import dependence exposes the country to exogenous food market shocks detrimental to domestic food security. This has generated great concerns about the realisation of food security, also considering that the prices of food staples are on the rise. This reliance on imports imposes a burden on the (already vulnerable) Eswatini government struggling to provide social services to its population. In the current era of the COVID-19 pandemic, growing maize imports also hamper the purchase of life-saving vaccines from pharmaceutical countries producing them. This reflects the far-reaching consequences of failure to invest in domestic food production.

In an analysis of the transition from subsistence to communally managed cash cropping, Terry and Ryder (2007) report that poor smallholders in Eswatini were (by the mid-2000s) unable to meet their food requirements after converting all their land to sugarcane production. The situation today under KDDP is very similar. High production costs and the lengthy maturity period associated with sugarcane farming compromise community livelihoods as well as threaten food security, as these factors negatively influence household income—which corroborates results of studies from other countries such as Uganda and Tanzania (Martiniello and Azambuja 2019). Most smallholders have become reliant on the market to meet their food requirements. For these out-grower households, a decline in income implies a decline in the quality and quantity of food consumed as well as exposure to escalating food prices, which compromises the food access and utilisation pillars of food security. This confirms assertions by critics of out-grower production that extroverted crop production has an effect of undermining the dietary and nutritional requirements of out-grower producers (Shivji 1992; Mazwi 2020).

One of the FA interviewees indicated that a key incentive promised to smallholders for sugar cane conversion was that of job creation during the initial land clearing and infrastructural development on the converting farmland, as well as seasonal work involved with planting and harvesting the sugar cane crop. However,

> What turned out was that the very few who were employed were poorly remunerated. Working on one's field was more rewarding than the so-called employment which was generated. Incomes for a single labourer could not sustain a household of two people for the whole month (Interview with Farmers' Association, January 2021).

What also eventually happened in most cases was that the FA made use of contractors for the initial land development and irrigation infrastructure installation. These contractors often came in with their own labour and, as a result, overlooked the hopeful locals who ended up only receiving the seasonal low-paying work of planting and harvesting sugar cane.

All five FAs indicated that smallholder members of FAs are not allowed to withdraw from the schemes. Therefore, becoming a membership of a farmers' association is obtained by giving up family-owned subsistence farmland on a permanent basis. When asked if there is ever any resistance to this appropriation, one FA representative noted that:

> A majority of households are always in favour of forming the Farmers' Association and the minority are left with no choice and no voice; . . . we have not had a case of any physical resistance to the appropriation (Interview with Farmer Association, January 2021).

To be sure, in Eswatini generally, there is no documented resistance to participation in sugarcane farmers' associations by individual households nor any organised movements in opposition to the appropriation of farmland from households—as has been the case in other parts of the world (Vergara-Camus and Kay 2017). This is reminiscent of the appropriation of land from the Swazi nation during the late 1800s when King Mbandzeni granted massive land-use rights to Boers for mining and grazing, an event that had far-reaching effects on land tenure in Eswatini (Rose 1987). In the case of today's sugarcane farming, smallholders are led to believe that they stand to benefit by increased household incomes and enhanced buying power as part of meaningful land-use reform.

Further exacerbating food insecurity in the KDDP project is that none of the sugarcane farms (at least of those forming part of the study) engaged in intercropping with food crops, though some farmers' associations may set the boundary of the farm to allow members to grow food crops as desired. At the same time, some smallholders resort to illegal crop production along riverbanks, a practice that undermines the ecological stability and health of water resources and hampers adequate environmental management.

Farmers' association representatives also confirmed the (earlier-mentioned) challenges faced by the sugarcane industry, which threaten sustainability, including increased tariffs on electricity (with irrigation methods requiring electricity), as well as the shortage of skilled managers to adequately run the farming business. Drought and climate change were cited as additional problems affecting crop yield, as farmers experienced an increased frequency of dry spells associated with heatwaves and disastrous floods from time to time. Further exacerbating the situation is inadequate infrastructure to make good use of the wet weather when it occurs. Indeed, rainwater-harvesting mechanisms would be valuable in cushioning the industry during droughts as well as providing opportunities for diversification into food crop production and other income-generating activities. Another issue raised is the decrease in the price of sugar while taxes remain high and have in fact increased.

All these challenges faced by the sugarcane industry as a whole are, in turn, experienced by the smallholders at the household level and undermine efforts to achieve food security. For instance, the farmers' associations, which are legally registered as companies, are now receiving reduced dividends (at the end of the year), and this makes it extremely difficult for the associations to pay off debts incurred for the farm inputs. Elsewhere in Africa, sugar out-grower producers are shown to be perpetually indebted to the plantation estate and private commercial banks (Martiniello 2016; Mazwi 2020). As indicated by a leader of one farmers' association:

> Some FAs have not been able to pay off their initial capital loan due to challenges faced as a result of low yields and high interest rates (Interview with Farmers' Association, January 2021).

The reduced income must then be shared amongst as many as over 100 smallholder members per association, and this gives rise to disputes between shareholders and fuels power struggles resulting in significant discord within associations. Dividends are said to range from a minimum of 5000 Emalangeni (US$350) to 40,000 Emalangeni (US$2800) per shareholder, which is insufficient to cover a family's subsistence if not supplemented.

Admittedly, some sugarcane smallholders in Eswatini had achieved meaningful increases in income when comparing the situation before the out-grower schemes were introduced (Terry and Ogg 2017), which leads to validations of the strategy of extending sugarcane production to the smallholder sector. On this note, some FA respondents spoke about sugarcane farming enabling income generation for purchasing cars, connecting to the electricity grid, and building proper houses. As well, the existing irrigation and electricity infrastructure could be diverted or used for food crop production to increase food security if threats to the viability of the sugar industry become insurmountable (Terry and Ogg 2017).

These seeming improvements in rural livelihoods are, however, still inadequate. For instance, not all members are progressing, and food security remains an almost insurmountable challenge (Interview of Chairman of a Farmer Association, January 2021). Higher gross incomes do not always translate into enhanced food security, especially as the income received from sugarcane comes as one lump sum once a year. This means that, for the rest of the year, there is no constant income received. The implication, therefore, is that poor households with no or limited livelihood alternatives remain trapped in poverty and hunger, and even the slightest shock is highly likely to worsen the situation deeply.

In the end, addressing the food concerns among smallholder households in Eswatini calls for a significant increase in the productivity of food crop subsistence agriculture to ensure long-term food security. This requires the allocation of more irrigated land for food crops as well as the promotion of crop diversification and other techniques to improve food security and prevent soil degradation.

7 Conclusion

This chapter examined the criticism that neoliberal policy reforms in Eswatini have undermined food crop production through the expansion of out-grower schemes. Undoubtedly, based on the evidence, diverting large land tracts from subsistence farming to commercial sugarcane production has compromised food security in the country, especially the food availability pillar. The production of staple food crops has severely declined over the years, while the area under sugarcane production has increased. Considering though the ongoing differential views with regards to the food security impact of out-grower schemes, this has to be explored further by integrating all the pillars of food security, including availability, access, utilisation and stability. This will provide a comprehensive and robust assessment of the influence of neoliberal policy reforms on food security. This evidence is largely lacking in the literature in the context of Eswatini, yet it is pivotal in supporting food security and development policy.

While acknowledging the serious environmental implications of sugarcane plantation expansion, including the livelihood consequences of this, future expansion is probably inevitable, especially with the potential of biofuel production and the creation of additional markets (notably, the African Continental Free Trade Area). Meanwhile, sugarcane production is extremely vulnerable to the effects of a changing climate, making the availability of water for irrigation a critical constraint on sugarcane expansion and other future large-scale agricultural developments reliant on irrigation. Thus, it is important that necessary strategies are put in place to allow sustainable sugarcane production to maximise its development benefits towards the achievement of Sustainable Development Goals (SDGs), at the same time minimising the negative social and environmental impacts. This would include improving water storage below the Maguga Dam (along the Komati River) and improving access to potable water for surrounding communities to reduce incidences of illegal water connections, as well as improving water use efficiency by adopting available technologies such as drip irrigation rather than sprinkler systems. These mechanisms would greatly improve water availability issues.

The foregoing demonstrates that prime farmland suitable for the production of food crops to alleviate poverty and improve food security was given up in favour of cash crop production, but not necessarily as a first choice to small-scale landowners. It is noteworthy therefore, that the majority interviewed stated that, given the opportunity to acquire more land, smallholders would diversify and grow food crops or venture into livestock farming rather than expand their sugarcane farms. The high poverty levels pose a major threat to household food security since income is a critical determinant of a household's ability to access food. These interviews confirmed that neoliberalism in Eswatini, as far as the sugarcane industry goes, has not led to significant improvements to food security for the great majority and that the industry faces challenges that threaten future productivity.

The various environmental, economic and social impacts associated with sugarcane out-grower schemes presents an important research opportunity to better understand how these vehicles of development can deliver more sustainable and equitable growth to the Eswatini economy and livelihoods. This is important from a policy perspective, taking into consideration the pivotal role of the sugar industry in Eswatini's economy and livelihoods. The formation of farmers' associations has been beneficial for enhancing farming efficiencies through resource pooling, and some farms are able to employ qualified specialists into management positions. It would be important to strengthen capacity building for farmers' associations to help them improve their sugarcane yields so that the objective of poverty alleviation and enhanced livelihoods is realised. It is also paramount that food production is prioritised, especially given that there is irrigation infrastructure already in place to allow for the year-round growing of various crops for both home consumption and income generation.

References

AfDB (2002) African Development Bank Kingdom of Swaziland country strategy paper operations department

Central Intelligence Agency (2021) Africa: Eswatini, Website: https://www.cia.gov/library/publications/the-world-factbook/geos/wz.html. Accessed Apr 2021

Chambati W, Mazwi F, Mberi S (2018) Agrarian Accumulation and peasant resistance in Africa. In: Inclusive development in Africa: transformation of global relations. African Institute for South Africa & CODESRIA. https://doi.org/10.1080/03056244.2015.1049520

Dubb A, Scoones I, Woodhouse P (2017) The political economy of sugar in Southern Africa—introduction. J South Afr Stud 43(3):447–470. https://doi.org/10.1080/03057070.2016.1214020
Eswatini G (2019) of Kingdom of Eswatini Vunerability Assessment and Analysis Report, July
Eswatini Sugar Association (2020) Integrated Annual Report 2020/2021. http://www.esa.co.sz/wp-content/uploads/ESA_Integrated_Report_2021.pdf
FAO (2008) National Forest Monitoring and Assessment – NFMA. http://www.fao.org/forestry/47655/en/
FAO (2015) The economic lives of smallholder farmers: an analysis based on household data from nine countries
FAO (2017) The future of food and agriculture: trends and challenges. Food and Agriculture Organisation of the United Nations, Rome. http://www.fao.org/3/i6583e/i6583e.pdf
Felgenhauer K, Wolter D (2009) Outgrower schemes: why big multinationals link up with African smallholders. OECD, p 3
Herrmann R, Grote U (2015) Large-scale Agro-Industrial Investments and Rural Poverty: evidence from Sugarcane in Malawi. J Afr Econ 24(5):645–676. https://doi.org/10.1093/jae/ejv015
Martiniello G (2016) "Don't stop the mill": South African capital and agrarian change in Tanzania. Third World Thematic: A TWQ J 1(5):633–652
Martiniello G (2017) Bitter sugarification: agro-extractivism, outgrower schemes and social differentiation in Busoga, Uganda. Paper presented at 5th International Conference of the BRICS Initiative for Critical Agrarian Studies. October 13–16. RANEPA. Moscow
Martiniello G, Azambuja R (2019) Contracting Sugarcane farming in global agricultural value chains in Eastern Africa: debates, dynamics, and struggles. Agrarian South: J Polit Econ 8(1–2):208–231
Mazwi F (2020) Sugar production dynamics in Zimbabwe: an analysis of contract farming at Hippo Valley. Rev Afr Polit Econ 47(166):568–584
Mazwi F, Chambati W, Mudimu. (2020) Tobacco contract farming in Zimbabwe: power dynamics, accumulation trajectories, land use patterns and livelihoods. J Contemp Afr Stud 38(1):55–71. https://doi.org/10.1080/02589001.2020.1746752
Mhlanga-Ndlovu BFN, Nhamo G (2017) Am assessment of Swaziland sugarcane farmers association vulnerability to climate change. J Integr Environ Sci 14:39–57. https://doi.org/10.1080/1943815X.20171335329
Ministry of Economic Planning and Development (2019) The kingdom of Eswatini Voluntary National Review 2019 Report. https://sustainabledevelopment.un.org/content/documents/24651Eswatini_VNR_Final_Report.pdf
Mohammed M, Dlamini T (2018) Predictors of food insecurity in Eswatini: lessons from the 2015/16 El Niño induced drought. Afr Rev Econ Fin 10(2):69–96
Moyo S (2011) Primitive accumulation and the destruction of African peasantries. In: Patnaik U, Moyo S (eds) The agrarian question in the neoliberal era: primitive accumulation and the peasantry. Pambazuka Press, Cape Town, pp 61–86
Patnaik U (2011) The agrarian question in the neoliberal era. In: Patnaik U, Moyo S (eds) The agrarian question in the neoliberal era: primitive accumulation and the peasantry. Pambazuka Press, Cape Town, pp 8–57
Richardson B (2012) Trade, aid and rural development: EU sugar policy and the experience of Swaziland. European Centre for Development Policy Management, Discussion Paper 133. https://ecdpm.org/wp-content/uploads/2013/10/DP-133-Trade-Aid-Rural-Development-EU-Sugar-Policy-Swaziland-2012.pdf
Richardson B (2015) Sugar. Polity Press, Cambridge
Rose L (1987) Customary land dispute management in Swaziland. A report prepared for the Ministry of Agriculture and Cooperatives Mbabane, Swaziland and the Land Tenure Center, University of Wisconsin-Madison
SEPARC (2017) The socio-economic impacts of the 2015/16 EL Niño induced drought in Swaziland. Prepared for the National Disaster, Management Agency. https://media.africaportal.org/documents/Drought-Study-Report.pdf

Shivji IG (1992) The roots of an agrarian crisis in Tanzania: a theoretical perspective. University of Dar es Salaam

Shumba E, Roberntz P, Kuona (2011) Assessment of sugarcane outgrower schemes for bio-fuel production in Zambia and Zimbabwe. WWF-World Wide Fund, Harare

Swaziland Sugar Association (2018) Integrated Annual Report. http://www.esa.co.sz/wp-content/uploads/ESA_Intergrated_Report_2018.pdf

Swaziland Sugar Association (2020) Integrated Annual Report. http://www.esa.co.sz/wp-content/uploads/ESA_Intergrated_Report_2020.pdf

Terry A, Ogg M (2017) Restructuring the Swazi sugar industry: the changing role and political significance of smallholders. J South Afr Stud 43(3):585–603

Terry A, Ryder M (2007) Improving food security in Swaziland: the transition from subsistence to communally managed cash cropping. Nat Resour Forum 31(4):263–272

UNCTAD (2000) Policies for small scale sugarcane growing in Swaziland. Report Prepared for United Nations Conference on Trade and Development (UNCTAD) under project SWA/99/A06

UNDP (2020) The next frontier: human development and the anthropocene briefing note for countries on the 2020 Human Development Report

USDA (2019) Sugar annual: rapid expansion of the eswatini sugar industry continues. https://apps.fas.usda.gov/newgainapi/api/report/downloadreportbyfilename?filename=Sugar%20Annual_Pretoria_Swaziland_4-15-2019.pdf

Vergara-Camus L, Kay C (2017) Agribusiness, peasants, left-wing governments, and the state in Latin America: an overview and theoretical reflections. J Agrar Chang 17:239–257. https://doi.org/10.1111/joac.12215

WFP/FAO (2016) 2015–2016 El Niño: WFP and FAO Overview

World Bank (2011) Swaziland rural sector review: priorities for the development of smallholder agriculture in Swaziland. Agricultural and Rural Development Unit (AFTAR) Country Department AFCSI African Region. Document of the World Bank. Report No. 70200-SZ. June 27, 2011

World Bank (2019) The World Bank in Eswatini. https://www.worldbank.org/en/country/eswatini/overview. Accessed 12 Jan 2020

World Food Programme (2019) Draft Eswatini country strategic plan (2020–2024)

World Food Summit (1996) Rome declaration on world food security and world food summit plan of action. World Food Summit, 13–17 November 1996, Rome, Italy

Meeting Global Capital in a Village: The Expansion of Tobacco Contract Farming in Zimbabwe

Yumi Sakata

Abstract Foreign interests in Africa's resources and markets have been rising in recent years. Various studies have described the flow as a 'new scramble' that intensified in the twenty-first century. While the continent has been depicted as being in crisis, suffering from a limited inflow of foreign investment, it is now receiving more global investment than at any time in the previous five decades. This chapter argues, however, that capital penetration often leaves farmers in precarious conditions and fosters the 'scramble' for Africa even more, without safeguarding smallholder farmers. This is demonstrated through a case study of tobacco contract farming in contemporary Zimbabwe. As shown in a series of works by the Sam Moyo African Institute of Agrarian Studies based in Harare, Fast Track Land Reform Programme (FTLRP) reconfigured the agrarian structure of Zimbabwe, including through repeasantisation as reflected in the tobacco sub-sector. The chapter presents case study based results of the socio-economic impacts of tobacco contract farming on smallholder farmers and argues that, while contract farming resuscitated the tobacco industry post-FTLRP, it also exposed smallholder farmers to the viscidities of global markets.

This chapter is based on a paper presented at the Sam Moyo African Institute of Agrarian Studies in 2018, titled 'International Companies and Contract Farmers after Fast Track Land Reform Programme in Zimbabwe'.

This chapter does not reflect the views of my current institutional affiliation. The research for this chapter was conducted while the author was a research associate of the Sam Moyo African Institute of Agrarian Studies and Centre for Applied Social Sciences at the University of Zimbabwe.

Y. Sakata (✉)
Sam Moyo African Institute of Agrarian Studies (SMAIAS), Harare, Zimbabwe

F. Mazwi et al. (eds.), *Capital Penetration and the Peasantry in Southern and Eastern Africa*, Advances in African Economic, Social and Political Development, https://doi.org/10.1007/978-3-030-89824-3_11

1 Introduction

The Fast Track Land Reform Programme (FTLRP), initiated in 2000, sought to redress the racially skewed land tenure and inequalities developed during the era of 'settler-colonial agrarian capitalism' (Moyo and Nyoni 2013: 195). Through the FTLRP, the land was redistributed to over 150,000 peasant households and over 20,000 small- to middle-capitalists, thus resulting in the reconfiguration of the agrarian structure in Zimbabwe from bi-modal to tri-modal (Binswanger-Mkhize and Moyo 2012; Moyo 2011a). The FTLRP encompassed a shift from the bi-modal structure comprised of the unequal distribution of land between predominantly large-scale farmers and the marginal peasantry to the tri-modal structure consisting of the peasantry, medium- to large-scale capitalist farms, and estates (Moyo et al. 2009; Moyo and Chambati 2013; Moyo and Yeros 2013).

The FTLRP received criticism from academia, media and civil society groups, based on the claim that the Programme violated 'human rights' through the attacks on (now former) white commercial farmers and the replacement of freehold title with promissory land tenure (Hammar 2001; Richardson 2005). Western countries such as the European Union (EU), United States of America (USA), Canada, and Australia imposed sanctions on Zimbabwe because of the 'violent character' of FTLRP and disrespect for property rights (Mamdani 2008; Moyo and Chambati 2013). This was soon followed by the suspension of finance lending to the country by international financial institutions such as the International Monetary Fund (IMF) and the World Bank (IMF 2000).

As Zimbabwe became increasingly isolated both politically and economically post-2000, her foreign currency earnings declined, import capacity fell, and inflation rates escalated (Moyo and Nyoni 2013). The period from 2000 to 2008 was characterised by heterodox state-interventionist policies regarding the broader national economy and more particularly the state sought to revive the economy through the agricultural sector. This approach was a departure from the laissez-faire stance adopted during the Structural Adjustment Programme (SAP) of the 1990s (Mazwi et al. 2019).

Externally, the state adopted a 'Look East Policy' to attract Chinese and Indian capital, which became instrumental in financing specific export-oriented crop commodities through contract farming arrangements, from about 2004 (Mazwi et al. 2019; Moyo and Nyoni 2013; Mukwereza 2015; Sachikonye 2016). In this respect, the financial capacity of the government became depleted post-2000, but the expanded number of smallholders (peasants) brought about by FTLRP increasingly looked for state support. In this context, government's agricultural input subsidy programmes such as 'Command Agriculture' were introduced (Mazwi et al. 2019).

A number of studies have shown how agricultural production declined significantly post-FTLRP (Moyo et al. 2009; Moyo and Nyoni 2013; Scoones et al. 2011). Among other agricultural commodities, tobacco was severely impacted by the FTLRP, resulting in massive declines in crop output. While previously tobacco had been grown by large-scale white capitalist farmers for exports under the bi-modal agrarian structure, the FTLRP democratised the tobacco industry and brought in thousands of black smallholder farmers who had traditionally been excluded from the production and marketing of this commodity (Moyo and Nyoni 2013). These smallholders were drawn from the newly-established resettlement areas, and long-established communal areas, and they began producing the crop despite its demand for intensive capital and labour (Sakata 2018). The smallholders became the dominant drivers of the tobacco industry resulting in the recovery of the sector. In the 2018/2019 season, as much as 90 per cent of the country's tobacco was produced by smallholders or peasants (TIMB 2020).

The resurgence of the tobacco sector was driven by two factors, namely, the de-racialisation of the sector and the reinsertion of capital. By redistributing land to the marginal peasants through FTLRP, the state de-racialised the tobacco sector and expanded the participation of black peasants in the production process. The reinsertion of capital through the introduction of tobacco contract farming arrangements in 2004 reconfigured the tobacco commodity market by connecting peasant tobacco growers directly to the capital. Contract farming had the effect of liberalising the sector. Prior to contract farming, the state regulated the marketing and pricing of the crop, with marketing restricted to three auction floors (Moyo and Nyoni 2013). The Tobacco Marketing Board (TMB), a state marketing board, had a central role in the production and marketing of the commodity. The establishment of contract farming brought in new players and restructured the marketing of the crop. Among the tobacco companies providing finance to farmers through contract arrangements are those from both the West and the East, including the United Kingdom (UK), China and Japan (Sakata 2018; Mazwi et al. 2020).

Several works have described the current inflow of foreign capital into Africa as a 'new scramble' for African resources (Carmody 2011; Melber and Southall 2010; Moyo et al. 2012). With the continent has been depicted as undergoing a perpetual crisis for many years due to limited economic growth and minimal foreign capital inflows (Arrighi 2002), Africa has in recent years received more global investment than at any time over the past five decades (Melber and Southall 2010). Although the new scramble for Africa is typically discussed in the context of land grabs, scramble for mineral resources, or remilitarisation, this chapter discusses the inflow of foreign capital through contract farming arrangements. It examines whether this creates conditions for, and forms part of, a new scramble in rural Zimbabwe, and it identifies the specific benefits and losses for smallholder farmers under tobacco contract farming.

The chapter proceeds as follows. The first section briefly details the reconfiguration of the agrarian structure through the FTLRP. Secondly, the chapter examines the evolution of the tobacco industry after the FTLRP. Based on our empirical studies, it then discusses how smallholders are engaged in contract farming arrangements. Lastly, the chapter offers an analysis of the benefits and losses for smallholders under tobacco contract farming in rural Zimbabwe.

2 Reconfiguration of Zimbabwe's Agrarian Structure

Zimbabwe's FTLRP implemented from the year 2000 to 2003 has been extensively documented and debated. The works by Sam Moyo and his colleagues at the Sam Moyo African Institute of Agrarian Studies (SMAIAS) in Harare show that FTLRP reconfigured the agrarian structure from a bi-modal to a tri-modal agrarian structure (Chambati 2013; Moyo 2011a, 2013; Moyo and Nyoni 2013; Moyo and Yeros 2013).

The bi-modal structure was characterised by agricultural dualism, which emerged from white settler-colonial land dispossession, largely divided into 4500 large-scale capitalist white farmers on the one hand and close to a million black smallholder farmers who had access to small pieces of land in the former Reserves or Tribal Trust Lands (now communal areas), on the other (Moyo 2013; Chambati 2013). The new tri-modal agrarian structure, composed of smallholder farmers, middle- to large-sized capitalist farms, and estates, is unique in the sense that it is based on clear demarcations in state policy (Chambati 2013; Moyo and Nyoni 2013; Moyo and Yeros 2013). A number of factors differentiate the various modes within the agrarian structure, such as landholding sizes, forms of land tenure, social status of land-holders, and dominant forms of labour used (Moyo and Nyoni 2013; Moyo and Yeros 2013; Moyo 2011a). The smallholder farmers are dominant in terms of the absolute number of farms in the country, comprised of communal, old resettlement, and A1 farms.[1] Farmers in this category hold usufruct permits over their agricultural land and depend on family labour and own finances for social reproduction (Moyo and Nyoni 2013; Moyo and Yeros 2013; Mazwi et al. 2021). The second grouping under the tri-modal agrarian structure is medium- to large-scale capitalist farms incorporating small-scale commercial farms (SSCF), A2 farms, and large-scale commercial farms (LSCF). The farmers in this category hold 99-year non-tradable leases over their land and depend more on hired labour than family labour (Moyo and Nyoni 2013; Moyo and Yeros 2013). The third grouping comprises agro-estates (both state- and privately-owned), conservancies, and institutional estates. The agro-estates hire large numbers of permanent and seasonal labours and contracted out-growers (Moyo 2011a; Moyo and Nyoni 2013).

Under the emergent tri-modal agrarian structure, the smallholder and medium-based capitalist farmer base have been substantially enlarged, while the presence of the (largely, white) LSCF sector has been diminished (Moyo 2011b). As well, there has been the addition of thousands of black A2 farmers operating middle-sized and large-sized farms (Moyo 2011b). Although agro-estates retained hold of about 5 per

[1] The FTLRP redistributed lands through small-scale (A1) farms and medium-scale commercial (A2) farm schemes. The size of A1 farms varies depending on the condition and the environment of the agricultural lands. However, Moyo (2013) shows that the average size of an A1 farm was 20 hectares, including access to common grazing areas, and the average size of an A2 farm was 142 hectares. The reform had produced about 145,800 A1 farms and 23,000 A2 farms by 2010 (Moyo 2013: 43). Communal areas account for 42 per cent of land in the country, and 74.2 per cent of these areas are located in the poorest rainfall zones (Moyo 1992: 9).

cent of the entire agricultural land, actors involved in their businesses (such as out-growers and shareholders) are now more diversified in terms of race, nationality and class (Moyo and Nyoni 2013: 203).

3 Evolution of the Tobacco Industry

3.1 De-racialisation of the Industry

The tobacco industry steadily aligned with the overall agricultural class transformation undertaken through the FTLRP. The presence of small to middle-sized tobacco growers was enhanced, and the structure of the tobacco industry was 'de-racialised' as a result of the fast track. A century earlier, after the arrival of the British South African Company column in 1890, white settlers soon turned to agriculture on land dispossessed from the indigenous population. Settlers from Europe and South Africa started growing tobacco in the early 1920s and, by 1945, the crop surpassed gold in Southern Rhodesia's generation of exports and foreign exchange value (Rubert 1998). In specific relation to the tobacco sector, the bi-modal agrarian structure strictly speaking did not exist, as tobacco growing was insignificant amongst the peasantry. An agrarian dualism did exist, however, between white settler capitalists on the one hand and blacks as highly-exploited wage-workers on the other.

Table 1 shows the areas planted of tobacco and tobacco yields by several classes in 1995, 2000, and 2012.[2] It demonstrates how the presence of small- and middle-class tobacco growers was enlarged on a massive scale over this period and that tobacco growing increasingly took on a tri-modal form. In respect of tobacco production in 1995, before the FTLRP, large-scale capitalist farmers dominated by producing 98 per cent of the tobacco crop, and they accounted for 94 per cent of the land under tobacco nationally. Stimulating tobacco production in the 1990s was the neoliberal Economic Structural Adjustment Programme (ESAP) which deliberately promoted the production of export commodities, resulting in Zimbabwe emerging as a powerhouse in the global production of tobacco (Moyo 2000). By 2012, the production of tobacco and the contribution by the LSCF sector had decreased dramatically to 21 per cent, while middle-scale farms' contribution to overall national production had increased to 26 per cent. More importantly, small-scale farms emerged as the largest class of tobacco farmers by producing 53 per cent of the total national tobacco production. In respect of the area occupied by tobacco for 2012, as shown in Table 1, small- and medium- farms occupied more than 85 per cent of the entire tobacco-growing area (62.9 per cent and 23.4 per cent,

[2] This data does not consider the estates growing tobacco, since neither the Central Statistical Office nor Tobacco Industry and Marketing Board (TIMB) provide statistics on the estates growing tobacco.

Table 1 Tobacco growers by class (1995–2012)

Year	1995				2000				2012			
	Production		Area		Production		Area		Production		Area	
	Tons	%	Ha	%	Tons	%	Ha	%	Tons	%	Ha	%
Small scale	3598	2	3760	5.2	9258	4.8	11,204	14.6	73,656	53	58,317	62.9
Medium scale	326	0.2	427	0.6	1051	0.6	834	1.1	36,449	26	21,670	23.4
Large scale	174,728	97.8	68,273	94.2	179,333	94.6	64,448	84.3	29,074	21	12,718	13.7
TOTAL	178,652	100	139,170	100	190,242	100	76,486	100	139,170	100	92,705	100

Source: Compiled by the author from Zimstat (2012b) data Ha = Hectares

respectively). Hence, fast track led to a more inclusive tobacco production structure in relation to both its class and racial composition.

3.2 *Look East Policy: Reliberalisation of Tobacco Industry and Penetration of Capital*

Tobacco production for white commercial farmers was spurred on by state subsidies during the colonial era and into the first decade of independence through the Agricultural Finance Bank of Zimbabwe, a state-owned bank. Neoliberal policies of the 1990s saw the state rolling back from financing the agricultural sector and the increased role of private commercial banks in financing tobacco (Moyo 2000). However, the active participation of private commercial banks was short-lived as the capital flight was witnessed soon after the implementation of FTLRP. Private commercial bank support declined significantly from the year 2000, and the state departed from neoliberal policies and introduced heterodox economic policies (Moyo and Nyoni 2013). But after a few years, through the 'Look East Policy' and partial reliberalisation, which entailed the retention of foreign exchange reserves for agrarian capital, there was a reinsertion of capital into the agricultural sector (Moyo and Nyoni 2013). With this reinsertion of capital, the tobacco industry (and the amount of tobacco produced) managed to take off again after a temporary decline in the volume of agricultural finance from 2000 to 2004 (Moyo 2011a).

The tobacco contract scheme commenced in 2004. Before then, all the tobacco produced in the country was sold at the three licensed auction floors. Since the introduction of the contract farming scheme, tobacco growers can now choose whether to market their crop at the auction floors or through the contract farming arrangement. Irrespective of the marketing arrangements, the number of tobacco growers, the overall area of tobacco planted, and the volume of tobacco sales all increased in the context of contract farming.

The expansion of small- to medium-sized farms under the FTLRP and the introduction of contract farming made tobacco farming increasingly popular and possible among farmers. For instance, while the number of tobacco growers at independence in 1980 was 1547, in 2014, 87,166 farmers were registered as tobacco growers (TIMB 2015). Among this total, about 36 per cent (31,487) were A1 farmers, and about 45 per cent (39,094) were communal farmers (TIMB 2014). Thus, the peasantry now dominates the industry by constituting more than 80 per cent of tobacco growers. Despite this, the overall benefits of tobacco production for smallholder farmers remain a subject of contestation (Mazwi et al. 2020; Sachikonye 2016; Sakata 2018). The area planted for tobacco also increased, and even more remarkably so. During the 2014 agricultural season, the land size of the tobacco crop planted in the country reached the largest ever since 1980.

Additionally, the volume of tobacco sold through contract arrangements and the tobacco auction floors has significantly increased since the introduction of tobacco contract farming in 2004. In 2008, when the volume of tobacco sales was at its lowest for several decades, some 49 million kilogrammes were transacted: 18 million kilogrammes through auction floors and 31 million kilogrammes through contract sales (TIMB 2014). Tobacco sales increased exponentially to 216 million kilogrammes in the 2014 season (TIMB 2014). In the 2018 agricultural season, the volume of tobacco sales then increased to some 253 million kilogrammes (36 million kilogrammes sold through the auction floors and 217 million kilogrammes through contract sales) (TIMB 2018). While the entire volume of tobacco sales increased on a major scale (by more than fivefold from 2008 to 2020), tobacco sales through contract arrangement increased nearly sevenfold during the same period. Tobacco sales at the auction floors also increased, but the level is insignificant compared to contract marketing arrangements. In summary, for 2018, 86 per cent of tobacco was sold through contract arrangements and 14 per cent sold through the auction floors (TIMB 2018). Clearly, the introduction of the contract farming arrangement increased the volume of tobacco production at the national level.

The contract farming arrangement is open to all farming classes, from LSCF to smallholders. Interestingly, 'donors and think tanks assume that the FTLRP land beneficiaries are inherently incapable of producing (agricultural commodities) commercially and promote privatising land tenure, ostensibly to improve access to credit' (Moyo and Nyoni 2013: 198). However, international tobacco corporations have adopted a different stance, expanding their operations towards the resettlement areas and also communal areas after the FTLRP. Among the 145,725 registered tobacco growers in 2018, about 87 per cent were smallholders, made up of 50 per cent as communal area farmers and 37 per cent as A1 farmers (TIMB 2018). In the 2019/2020 season, the predominance of smallholders further increased to 90 per cent (out of a total of 185,920 farmers registered as tobacco growers) (TIMB 2020).

The dominance of smallholder farmers in contract-based tobacco production is partly explained by the state-driven reconfiguration of the agrarian structure, which has left agrarian capital with no choice but to engage smallholders as they constitute the majority. Moyo (2011a: 957) observes that some contractors also prefer peasants and middle-scale producers because they are perceived to be 'less able to resist lower price margins compared to larger-scale producers, who generally have a higher social standing and fare better in procuring inputs using their own income, credit and subsidies'. The effects of contract farming on small-scale famers are discussed later by way of empirical research, but it is noticeable that—along with the FTLRP—it has brought about positive impacts for the tobacco industry at the national level. The following section discusses the players in the contract farming tobacco industry in Zimbabwe.

3.3 Contract Farming and the Players in the Industry

According to the World Investment Report (WIR) from 2009 (UNCTAD 2009: xvii), 'contract farming activities by TNCs [Transnational Corporations], are spread worldwide, covering over 110 developing and transitional economies, spanning a wide-range of commodities and, in some cases, accounting for a high share of output'. The World Bank sees contract farming as an institutional innovation that reduces the transactional costs and risks for smallholder farmers (World Bank 2007: 237). In identifying some of the key players in contract farming, Watts (1994: 9) studied the early development and characteristics of contract farming in sub-Saharan Africa, and defined contract farming as 'a form of vertical integration between agricultural producers and buyers (exporters, agro-processing companies or retailers at the end of the value chain)'.

Contract farming is not new in Zimbabwe as it has been practised through tea, sugar, and cotton production since the mid-1950s (Jackson and Cheater 1994; Sachikonye 2016). After independence, the Zimbabwean government at times supported contract farming where possible, in seeking to undercut the dualistic dimension of the agrarian economy and in an attempt to integrate black farmers into global value chains. The government became a major lender of loans to black farmers as a means of stimulating contract farming arrangements with estates under out-grower schemes (Moyo 2013; Sachikonye 1989).

In the case of tobacco, and subsequent to the FTLRP, the government introduced the contract farming arrangement aimed at filling the existing gap in financing given the expanded smallholder under the tri-modal agrarian structure and the persistent economic challenges (Mazwi et al. 2020; Moyo and Nyoni 2013; Sachikonye 2016). Mazwi et al. (2020) describe Zimbabwe's tobacco contract farming as a centralised model. Tobacco companies, via their extension workers, engage farmers through contracts that are signed on an annual basis. These private companies supply agricultural inputs, or even cash for labour costs, to producers, with these input expenses being deducted at the marketing stage by contract firms. The package of inputs usually consists of fertiliser, chemicals, baling material, and coal or firewood for curing. There is no intermediary between capital and smallholders since the latter are directly tied to private firms.

Under the contract arrangement, the contracting firms solely determine the price of tobacco brought by contracted farmers under the supervision of the Tobacco Industry and Marketing Board (TIMB), the statutory body which regulates the Zimbabwean tobacco industry. In the 2018/2019 season, the average price of tobacco was US$2.33 per kilogramme compared to US$1.74 per kilogramme offered by buyers at the auction floors (TIMB 2020). Although each private company determines the tobacco price for their growers' tobacco (without bidding), the contracted tobacco price has been higher than the price at the auction floors since 2009. An interview conducted with a TIMB official found that contracting firms offer higher prices as a strategy to keep farmers under their contracts.[3] More than 30 contracting firms were registered officially during the 2018/2019 agricultural season. Among these 30 firms, Tian-Ze, a Chinese state-owned company from the Yunnan province, was the biggest buyer and the biggest contractor in terms of production volumes. Its number of contracted farmers remains small though because it contracts exclusively with middle- and large-scale farmers. The company buys tobacco both from contracted farmers and the auction floors. Tian-Ze played a 'pivotal' role in resuscitating the tobacco industry in Zimbabwe and was instrumental in the success of the 'Look East Policy' within the tobacco sector (Mukwereza 2015). It was founded following the visit of a high-level Chinese government delegation at the invitation of the government of Zimbabwe in 2004. Since then, Tian-ze has invested heavily in the Zimbabwean tobacco sector. As Mukwereza (2015: 10) highlights, the company 'brought capital, competition, confidence, and improved prices' to Zimbabwe.

Other than Tian-Ze, there were about 19 purely local contracting firms, while another 10 companies are 'officially' international or 'have a foreign flavour'.[4] Out of 10 international or 'foreign-flavoured' companies, three are from China, and they mainly enter into contracts with A2 or commercial farmers. Three other companies are apparently connected to the USA, two companies are working with (or for) Japan, and one company is part of a British group, while still another one has connections with the United Arab Emirates.[5] While there is no doubt that Chinese companies have played a leading role in boosting the tobacco industry since the mid-2000s, there are clearly other companies (from other nations) operating in the industry, which significantly impacted the growth of the sector. Other than the international companies, there are several local companies engaged in the contract farming tobacco arrangement. However, what is often understated as having contributed to the penetration of capital post-2004 was the reliberalisation of the economy in general and the agricultural sector in particular by the government of Zimbabwe, by introducing a policy that allowed for the retention of a certain percentage of foreign exchange from export sales (Moyo and Nyoni 2013).

[3]Interview with a TIMB official on 10 May 2015.

[4]Interview with an anonymous informant on 20 May 2015. The issue of company share in Zimbabwe tends to be sensitive. Foreign companies operating in Zimbabwe need to meet the requirements of the Indigenisation and Economic Empowerment Act enacted in 2008, which requires all companies operating in the country to transfer 51 per cent of their company shares to local African companies. Several tobacco companies are registered as 'local' but they still appear to have a pronounced international dimension.

[5]The companies' origins are based on the interview with an anonymous informant on 20 May 2015.

4 Small-Scale Tobacco Growers in Marondera District

I now examine the benefits of contract farming for contracted smallholder tobacco farmers in the context of capital penetration by analysing the cost of production as well as returns in comparison to independent producers. This is based on a field study conducted with small-scale A1 farmers.

4.1 Methodology

The study interviewed 42 A1 farm owners using questionnaires in June and July 2015. I also interviewed to Chief, a councillor, village heads, war veterans, and Agritex[6] officers of the research area to understand the historical and agricultural backgrounds. The study took a comparative approach to contract farming in order to assess its differential impact on smallholders. The study was undertaken at two broad levels. The first level is contracted tobacco farmers, and the second level is independent (non-contract) tobacco farmers. 42 tobacco smallholders were interviewed; 36 contracted smallholders and 6 non-contracted smallholders. As well, the study divided the contracted farmers into several groups according to the contracting firm.

4.2 The Research Area

To understand the performance of contracted smallholders, Ward 7 of Marondera District in Mashonaland East Province was chosen as a field site. The population of Ward 7 is 5417 people and the number of households is 1346 (Zimstat 2012a). The ward has 32 villages, and each village has its own village head. The ward is situated about 40 kilometres south of Marondera town, the capital of the province, and about 100 kilometres southeast of Harare. The area falls into agricultural region IIb[7] and was a significant large-scale tobacco-growing area under colonialism. The ward was also one of the first areas where land occupations were carried out in the late 1990s, before the government officially launched the FTLRP (*The Herald* 1998a, b). Until the arrival of white settlers, the area was governed by Chief Svosve, and, in the late 1940s, the Svosve people were forced to move to a rocky, less fertile area, now

[6]'Agritex is a department within the Ministry of Agriculture, Mechanisation and Irrigation Development. Its main mission is to provide administrative, technical and advisory support to farmers' (Zamchiya 2011: 1095).

[7]Zimbabwe is divided into five agro-ecological regions, from region I to region V, known as natural regions on the basis of the rainfall regime, soil quality, and vegetation among other factors. Region II, where annual rainfall is between 750 to 1000 millimetres, is divided into IIa and IIb according to the level of probability of rainfall of more than 500 millimetres between October and April and the length of the growing period (see FAO 2006).

called Svosve communal land.[8] From then, the whole ward became occupied by LSCFs, until the dawn of land occupations led by war veterans and the Svosve people in the late 1990s and into the year 2000. The area is now redistributed amongst A1 and A2 farmers.

The survey found four different contracting firms operating in the area. All four contracting firms do not disclose their company profiles on websites. But an interview with a TIMB official[9] revealed that, among the four, two are local companies, and another two are international firms. The two international contracting firms trace their origins to the USA, and one local contracting company is apparently producing tobacco for a Japanese related tobacco company.[10] Of the 36 interviewed contracted A1 farmers, 12 fell under contracting firm A (international), 7 farmers under contracting firm B (international), 10 farmers under firm C (local), and 7 farmers under firm D (local, Japanese).

4.3 Characteristics of A1 Farmers in the Research Area

All the farmers interviewed owned (or at least possessed) six hectares of arable land, a separate 1 hectare for the homestead, and communal grazing land. More than half the interviewees, 25 of them, resettled into the area between the year 2000 and 2005 and had engaged in farming for more than 10 years when the study was conducted. Another 13 interviewees resettled between 2006 and 2010, and another 2 interviewees after 2011. This means that a substantial number of farmers now had a wealth of experience in tobacco production, which is essential in enhancing productivity.

All 42 interviews were conducted by farm owners except for one case, which involved an interview with the wife of the landowner. The data shows the tobacco production is male dominated.[11] In terms of household sizes, more than half the households (24 farmers) had 5 to 7 family members (including the interviewee). The size of households has been shown to be important for tobacco and contract farming in general since production is labour intensive for the tobacco production process with specific reference to contract farming (Sachikonye 1989; Mazwi et al. 2020).

Apart from tobacco, the farmers (more than half in the study) also grew food crops such as maize (their staple food) and groundnuts. Maize and groundnuts were

[8] Interview with the village head of Mali village in Ward 7, on 13 July 2015, Mr. Mugaza, on 13 July 2015, and Mr. Mashangwe, on 2 August 2015. See also Sadomba (2008) for the initial stage of land occupations in the late 1990s.

[9] Interviewed on 10 May 2015.

[10] Interview with a TIMB official on 10 May 2015.

[11] The wife of the Mali village head showed 'her garden' where she grows spinach, pumpkins, groundnuts, and round-nuts. She expressed that 'this is my garden, I have 100 per cent control. Tobacco is grown and supervised by men, as my husband does, and these 'small crops' are supervised by us, women' (Interviewed on 13 July, 2015).

grown mainly for family consumption. For the majority of the households, tobacco sales are their main cash income. In this sense, and as observed by Mazwi et al. (2020), tobacco farmers do not typically abandon food crop production because of their venture into export crops like tobacco.

In terms of land use, the average land sizes committed to tobacco production between 2010 and 2015 was 1.28 hectares for independent (non-contracted) farmers and 1.29 hectares for contracted farmers, an insignificant difference. However, the average size of land committed to tobacco for independent producers was shifting upwards when compared to that of contracted tobacco farmers. From 2013/2014 to the 2014/2015 agricultural season, the average land size committed to tobacco by independent growers increased from 0.92 to 1.8 hectares, while the average land sizes for contracted farmers decreased by 0.1 hectare during the same period. The non-expansion of the area placed under tobacco for contract farmers is attributable to the fact that contract firms only provide inputs for a maximum of one hectare for smallholder farmers (Scoones et al. 2017; Sakata 2018). However, independent farmers are flexible in their cropping and are able to adjust the land sizes by choice. Independent farmers opted to increase the land sizes for the 2014/2015 season based on their positive expectations of an expanded harvest. Both independent and contracted farmers, however, show a marked increase in the average land sizes for tobacco production when compared to the 2010/2011 season. In the case of the contracted farmers at least, this upward shift reflects the positive effects of the reliberalisation of the tobacco sector, including higher levels of re-investments in agricultural production by farmers.

4.4 Smallholders and International Contracting Firms

The study also examined the recruitment process into contract farming. Results show that all the contracted farmers except five were approached by contracting firms in their local areas. Out of these five farmers, four stated that they had approached the contracting firms, while the remaining 1 farmer indicated that he had been introduced to a contracting firm by someone else. Overall, this shows how international contracting firms have decentralised their operations through extension workers (or field officers), to the extent that contracting firms communicated directly and proactively with nearly all contracted farmers. An analysis of the character of the contracts and the process leading towards contract signing shows that contracting firms do explain clearly the obligations of the farmers and those of the contractor before recruitment. All the interviewed contracted farmers stated that the contracting firm had, through their field officers, fully detailed the contract arrangement, both in the local language (Shona) and also in English. As well, these field officers monitored and provided advice to the contracted farmers. Some farmers, however, indicated that the extension officers do not regularly visit the farmers to provide agronomic advice but only see them once a year during the signing of annual contracts and the provision of inputs. This leads to poor agronomic practices by farmers, which ultimately affects the yields of farmers and their incomes when marketing tobacco.

The kinds of inputs provided by the different contracting firms to farmers, alongside the coverage of operating costs (for labour and transport), were similar but subject to variation. All four contracting firms provided fertiliser, chemicals, and tobacco baling materials. Contracting firm B, in addition, provided transportation money in advance to the tobacco farmers for post-production delivery, which was at about US$10 per bale. Contracting firms C and D provided labour costs valued at US $100 per hectare while contracting firm D also supplied cash for firewood—a development receiving criticism from policy makers and climate justice activists as they view it as environmentally unfriendly. Out of the total of 36 contracted farmers, 35 farmers expressed concern and disappointment over the inadequate inputs provided by contract firms. While the farmers indicated that the chemicals provided were adequate, they went on to state that the amount of fertilisers supplied amount to almost one-half the amount recommended for use per hectare of tobacco. As observed by a number of critics, besides reducing tobacco quality and incomes, the provision of inadequate inputs, by reducing contracting firms' costs, is one mechanism used by agrarian capital to exploit smallholder farmers (Mazwi 2020).

4.5 *Costs of Growing Tobacco: Contract vs. Independent Tobacco Producers*

Tobacco is a crop that demands high inputs. An extension officer within the tobacco department in the Ministry of Agriculture and Lands (Marondera) explained that the average input cost of growing tobacco (excluding operation costs, such as labour and transport costs) is US$600 per hectare.[12] The input costs for independent and non-contracted farmers per hectare were examined during the study. For contracted farmers, agricultural inputs are provided in advance, and the credit is deducted at the time when the tobacco leaf is marketed. Though the contracted farmers claimed that the tobacco contract had been fully explained to them, observations from the field indicate that some of the contracting firms do not clearly break down the cost of each input item on the invoices provided to the farmers. What is reflected on the invoices, rather, is the total cost of all inputs without providing specific details. This often results in misunderstandings with farmers at the time of tobacco sales and is another way by which contracting firms tend to exploit farmers.

A comparison between contract-based production and independent tobacco production was also made. Study results show that contract farmers incur more costs in production when compared to non-contract farming. The average input cost for independent producers was US$579 and US$1034 for contracted farmers. Although inputs provided by contracting firms are more expensive, contracted tobacco farmers

[12] Interviewed on 29 July 2015.

Table 2 Annual net income from Tobacco (median, US$)

	2010/2011	2011/2012	2012/2013	2013/2014	2014/2015
Independent (% change)	2050	2450 (20%)	4450 (82%)	3000 (−33%)	1788 (−40%)
Firm A (% change)	N/A	4000	4700 (18%)	4750 (1%)	500 (−89%)
Firm B (% change)	1057	1650 (56%)	3500 (112%)	5000 (43%)	0 (−100%)
Firm C (% change)	6000	3395 (−43%)	5000 (47%)	6290 (26%)	1579 (−75%)
Firm D (% change)	5700	4000 (−30%)	6000 (50%)	6000 (0%)	1000 (−83%)

Source: Survey data

also applied more inputs per hectare when compared to independent producers. Also, among the contracting firms, the cost of inputs varies. For example, contracting firm B charged US$1400 per hectare for each farmer, contracting firm C a total of US$738, and contracting firm D US$1066 for the inputs. Admittedly, the amount of chemicals and fertiliser provided by companies varied as well, but the input costs were remarkably higher for contracted tobacco farmers.

4.6 *Farmer Incomes for Tobacco Producers*

Table 2 shows the median net incomes of the tobacco farmers under each category, after deductions by contracting firms in the case of contracted farmers and input costs for independent farmers. It indicates that contracted farmers received more income compared to independent producers over a number of years, though this income varies widely across years. The variations in income can be attributed in large part to price fluctuations in international markets. The incomes of independent farmers were lower than for the contracted farmers for a number of years but, during the 2014/2015 agricultural season, the median incomes for tobacco producers were highest amongst the non-contracted farmers.

The study found that droughts and access to dams and irrigation facilities also impact the levels of income for farmers engaged in export crops such as tobacco. For example, during the 2014/2015 agricultural season, the incomes of farmers were comparatively low, mainly due to the delays in rainfall as well as the long dry spell during the season. A number of farmers who had planted their tobacco at the beginning of the rainy season in November 2014 suffered losses as their crop was destroyed due to the long dry spell between mid-November 2014 and the beginning of January 2015. In this respect, the Tobacco Research Board (TRB) indicates that the 2013/2014 season received normal to above normal rainfall while the 2014/2015 season experienced large rainfall deficits, with the start of the rainy season delayed 5 weeks compared to the average year.[13] Accordingly, the tobacco production volume decreased as a result of this dry spell.[14] The late onset of the rainy season, as well as lack of rainfall, leads to the challenge of severe leaching of nutrients for tobacco plants (TRB 2014). To overcome such challenges, tobacco requires 'elevated fertilizer use, premature ripening of the leaf and a substantially higher labour requirement' (TRB 2014: 7). The Tobacco Research Board (TRB) further notes that these challenges bring 'a reduction in the quality of most of the crops, particularly in the case of small-scale tobacco growers', and eventually a reduction in their prices (TRB 2014: 7). Hence, severe weather changes impacted negatively on the incomes of farmers during the 2014/2015 agricultural season in the studied site.

As shown earlier, although the average size of land committed to tobacco between independent and contracted farmers was almost similar, independent farmers increased their average size of tobacco crop from 0.92 to 1.8 hectares between the 2013/2014 and 2014/2015 agricultural seasons. Independent producers did not suffer the level of income loss as contracted growers did, because input costs for the latter were higher when compared to those for the former. Since the input cost of contracted farmers is almost double that of the independent farmers, their net income turned out to be severely affected when the credit is deducted at the time of tobacco sales. For instance, the farmers contracted with Firm B were left with no income after the firm deducted their credit. Independent producers were able to keep their income as they had already self-supplied their inputs at the beginning of the season.

Additionally, the research found that a substantial number of farmers dropped out of contracting arrangements. This was partly because of their lack of capacity to repay input credit advanced by contracting firms at the end of each agricultural season. Due to indebtedness, some farmers also lost their assets to the contracting firms which had been advanced as collateral. Such assets include cattle and scotch carts.

The overall results from the survey indicate that smallholders under contract arrangements generate more income than independent (non-contracted) farmers, although input costs from contracting companies are much higher than inputs purchased by independent farmers. From a study conducted in Mashonaland Central province, Scoones et al. (2017: 9) show that contracted farmers who are 'able to afford inputs and grow sufficient maize to cover food needs can profit significantly from tobacco'. The contract arrangement does not guarantee success for the tobacco farmer. Since input costs are higher than those of independent farmers, the danger arises when weather is not suitable for farming, and also in agricultural seasons when

[13] Presentation made by Magama F, Shava J and S Dimbi (representing the Tobacco Research Board) at the Coresta Congress 2016, Berlin. The abstract and the presentation material are available at https://www.coresta.org/abstracts/t75-new-kutsaga-drought-tolerant-tobacco-variety-30126.html (accessed on 7 July 2021).

[14] Interviews with farmers in Ward 7.

the crop fetches low prices due to global price volatility. Their losses during such agricultural seasons tend to be more serious than for independent farmers. Only those who can afford to avert their risks can profit sustainably from tobacco contract farming.

5 Conclusion

This chapter discussed the reconfiguration of the tobacco industry in Zimbabwe and sketched the economic impact of contract farming on smallholders. It shows that the tri-modal agrarian structure formed through FTLRP has been reproduced in the tobacco industry. De-racialisation and the penetration of capital in tobacco have led to smallholders emerging as the dominant class in the sub-sector.

The reinsertion of capital ignited by the entrance of a Chinese firm, Tian-ze, with support from the Zimbabwean government, internationalised tobacco production in the country. There are more than 30 tobacco contracting firms in Zimbabwe with origins in China, Japan, the USA, the UK, a Gulf state, and Zimbabwe itself. Interestingly, although Africa is regarded as 'an undisputed sphere of Western influence' by some analysts (Melber and Southall 2010: xix), the case of Zimbabwe shows growing Asian influence in the production, marketing and export of a commodity like tobacco, a development that can be attributed to the 'Look East Policy'.

However, the new internationalisation can also be viewed as a 'new scramble for Africa' (Carmody 2011; Melber and Southall 2010; Moyo et al. 2012). There are many companies from different countries flocking into rural Zimbabwe, and this reflects the 'new scramble' seen in the field site. The 'new scramble' connects small-scale farmers to transnational capital and integrates them into the tobacco global value chain. Contracted small-scale tobacco farmers in Zimbabwe experience at times a sharp decline in their income since they need to pay expensive input costs back to the contracting companies even when the weather is not favourable to them. The government, meanwhile, is steadily benefitting from the contract farming arrangement through the increase in tobacco production volumes and export value. The 'new scramble' in the context of contract farming should therefore be perceived along three dimensions, that is, capitalist companies, governments, and peasants.

References

Arrighi G (2002) The African crisis- world systemic and regional aspects. New Left View 15 (May-June):1–32

Binswanger-Mkhize H, Moyo S (2012) Zimbabwe from economic rebound to sustained growth: note ii: recovery and growth of Zimbabwe agriculture. World Bank, Harare

Carmody P (2011) The new scramble for Africa. Polity, Cambridge

Chambati W (2013) The political economy of agrarian labour relations in Zimbabwe after redistributive land reform. Agrar South J Pol Econ 2(2):189–211
FAO (2006) Fertilizer use by crop in Zimbabwe. FAO, Rome
Hammar A (2001) 'The Day of Burning': eviction and reinvention in the margins of Zimbabwe. J Agrar Chang 1(4):550–574
IMF (2000) Press release: IMF declares Zimbabwe ineligible to use IMF resources. Press Release No.01/40. https://www.imf.org/en/News/Articles/2015/09/14/01/49/pr0140. Accessed 3 Jul 2021
Jackson J, Cheater A (1994) Contract farming in Zimbabwe: case studies of Sugar, Tea, and Cotton. In: Little P, Watts M (eds) Living under contract: contract farming and Agrarian transformation in Sub-Saharan Africa. University of Wisconsin Press, Madison, WI
Mamdani M (2008) Lessons of Zimbabwe. Lond Rev Books 30(23):3
Mazwi F (2020) Sugar production dynamics in Zimbabwe: an analysis of contract farming at Hippo Valley. Rev Afr Polit Econ 47(166):568–584
Mazwi F, Chemura A, Mudimu GT, Chambati W (2019) Political economy of command agriculture in Zimbabwe: a state-led contract farming model. Agrar South J Pol Econ 8(1–2):232–257
Mazwi F, Chambati W, Mudimu G (2020) Tobacco contract farming in Zimbabwe: power dynamics, accumulation trajectories, land use patterns and livelihoods. J Contemp Afr Stud 38(1):55–71
Mazwi F, Muchetu R, Mudimu G (2021) Revisiting the Trimodal Agrarian structure in Zimbabwe. Agrari South J Pol Econ. https://doi.org/10.1177/2277976020973837
Melber, H, and R. Southall (2010) A new scramble for Africa?, in Southall, R, H. Melber (eds), A new scramble for Africa?: imperialism, investment, and development. Scottsville: University of KwaZulu-Natal Press.
Moyo S (1992) Land tenure issues in Zimbabwe during the 1990s. Center for Applied Social Sciences, University of Zimbabwe, Harare
Moyo S (2000) Land reform under structural adjustment in Zimbabwe: land use change in the Mashonaland provinces. Nordiska Afrikainstitutet, Uppsala
Moyo S (2011a) Changing agrarian relations after redistributive land reform in Zimbabwe'. J Peasant Stud 38(5):939–966
Moyo S (2011b) Three decades of agrarian reform in Zimbabwe. J Peasant Stud 38(3):493–531
Moyo S (2013) Land reforms and redistribution in Zimbabwe Since 1980. In: Moyo S, Chambati W (eds) Land and agrarian reform in Zimbabwe: beyond white-settler capitalism. CODESRIA, Dakar
Moyo S, Chambati W (2013) Introduction: roots of the fast track land reform in Zimbabwe. In: Moyo S, Chambati W (eds) Land and agrarian reform in Zimbabwe: beyond white-settler capitalism. CODESRIA, Dakar
Moyo S, Nyoni N (2013) Changing agrarian relations after redistributive land reform in Zimbabwe. In: Moyo S, Chambati W (eds) Land and agrarian reform in Zimbabwe: beyond white-settler capitalism. Dakar, CODESRIA
Moyo S, Yeros P (2013) The Zimbabwe model: radicalisation, reform and resistance. In: Moyo S, Chambati W (eds) Land and agrarian reform in Zimbabwe: beyond white-settler capitalism. CODESRIA, Dakar
Moyo S, Chambati W, Murisa T, Siziba D, Dangwa C, Mujeyi K, Nyoni N (2009) Fast track land reform baseline survey in Zimbabwe: trends and tendencies, 2005/06. Harare, African Institute for Agrarian Studies (AIAS)
Moyo S, Yeros P, Jha P (2012) Imperialism and primitive accumulation: notes on the new scramble for Africa. Agrar South Pol Econ 1(2):181–203
Mukwereza L (2015) Situating Tian Ze's role in reviving Zimbabwe's flue-cured tobacco sector in the wider discourse on Zimbabwe-China cooperation: will the scorecard remain win-win? CBAA Working Paper, 115, February
Richardson C (2005) The loss of property rights and the collapse of Zimbabwe. Cato J 25(2): 541–565

Rubert S (1998) A most promising weed: a history of tobacco farming and labour in colonial Zimbabwe, 1890–1945, Monographs in International Studies, Africa Series: No.69. Centre for International Studies, Ohio University

Sachikonye L (1989) The state and agribusiness in Zimbabwe plantations and contract farming. Leeds Southern African Studies, No.13, September

Sachikonye L (2016) Old wine in new bottles? Revisiting contract farming after agrarian reform in Zimbabwe. Rev Afr Polit Econ 43(1):86–98

Sadomba WZ (2008) War veterans in Zimbabwe's land occupations: complexities of a liberation movement in an African post-colonial settler society. PhD dissertation, submitted to Wageningen University

Sakata Y (2018) Reactions of peasants to global capital in Zimbabwe: a case study of tobacco contract farming in Mashonaland East Province. Afr Stud Monogr 57:121–145

Scoones I, Marongwe N, Mavedzenge B, Murimbarimba F, Mahenehene J, Sukume C (2011) Zimbabwe's land reform: myths and realities. J Peasant Stud 38(5):967–993

Scoones I, Mavedzenga B, Murimbarimba F, Sukume C (2017) Tobacco, contract farming, and agrarian change in Zimbabwe. J Agrar Chang 2017:1–21

The Herald (1998a) Svosve villages remain defiant, the Herald, 24 June 1998

The Herald (1998b) Svosve villages agreed to return home, the Herald, 28 June 1998

TIMB (Tobacco Industry and Marketing Board) (2014) TIMB Annual Statistical Report. TIMB, Harare

TIMB (Tobacco Industry and Marketing Board) (2015) TIMB Annual Statistical Report. TIMB, Harare

TIMB (Tobacco Industry and Marketing Board) (2018) TIMB Annual Statistical Report. TIMB, Harare

TIMB (Tobacco Industry and Marketing Board) (2020) TIMB Annual Statistical Report. TIMB, Harare

TRB (Tobacco Research Board) (2014) Annual Report and Audit Accounts. Tobacco Research Board, Harare

UNCTAD (2009) World Investment Report 2011. UNCTAD, Geneva

Watts M (1994) Life under contract: contract farming, agrarian restructuring, and flexible accumulation. In: Little P, Watts M (eds) Living under contract: contract farming and Agrarian transformation in Sub-Saharan Africa. University of Wisconsin Press, Madison, WI

World Bank (2007) WDR2008—World Development Report 2008: Agriculture for Development. World Bank, Washington DC

Zamchiya P (2011) A synopsis of land and agrarian change in Chipinge district, Zimbabwe. J Peasant Stud 38(5):1093–1122

Zimstat (2012a) Census 2012: Mashonaland East. Zimstat, Harare

Zimstat (2012b) Compendium of statistics 2012. Zimstat, Harare

The manufacturer's authorised representative in the EU is Springer Nature Customer Service Centre GmbH, Europaplatz 3, 69115 Heidelberg, Germany. If you have any concerns regarding our products, please contact ProductSafety@springernature.com

Printed and bound by CPI Group (UK) Ltd, Croydon, CR0 4YY
22/09/2026
02220982-0008